US AND THEM

CANADA, CANADIANS AND THE BEATLES

JOHN ROBERT ARNONE

 FriesenPress

Suite 300 - 990 Fort St
Victoria, BC, V8V 3K2
Canada

www.friesenpress.com

ISBN
978-1-03-911571-2 (Hardcover)
978-1-03-911570-5 (Paperback)
978-1-03-911572- (eBook)

1. HISTORY, MODERN, 21ST CENTURY

Distributed to the trade by The Ingram Book Company

TABLE OF CONTENTS

Prologue: My First Beatles Breath vii

Introduction: The Beatles' Great Canadian Adventure xiii

Chapter One: 1953 to 1961

Harrison's Canadian Kin 1

Little Paul in Grey Shorts, Ringo's Last Roar and the Canadian
Army's Billy Butlin 4

Eric Clapton's Canadian Story 7

"She met this Canadian ... " 8

Yukon Deck Hand Turned Lennon Nemesis? 9

Canadian Beer Offensive: "Re-Run of World War II" 15

Beatle Boots on the Ground 17

Mississauga's Dorothy (Rhone) Becker 20

Canada's Connections to the term "Beatlemania" 23

Chapter Two: 1962 to 1967

The Beatles' Early Conquest of Canada 27

Canadian Fan Club Soared to Number One 32

Ottawa's Paul Anka Played Beatles Matchmaker 34

The Legend of Barefoot Bruce Decker's Daring Winnipeg Dash 36

The Beatles' Riotous Canadian Debut 44

Janette Bertrand and The Beatles' Québec Reality Check 52

The Beatles in Toronto 1965 and 1966 57

Sergeant (Randall) Pepper 62

The Night a Canadian Helped Coax The Beatles with LSD 68

Ghost Lake, Kitsilano and All You Need is Love 71

Chapter Three: The White Album's 2.5 Canadians and Rishikesh

While My Guitar Gently Weeps and Eric Clapton 75

Savoy Truffle and Moose Jaw's Son   78

Don't Pass Me By's Ontario Fiddler   82

Guelph, Ontario's Tommy Reilly, MBE   85

Toronto to Rishikesh: "We See Everything for Moments Like This"   86

Chapter Four: John Lennon's Canada in 1969

The Ballad of John and Yoko and Cynthia and Canada   97

The Three Lennon Visits That Changed Canada   101

1. "We all thought it was sort of like home … "   106

Give Peace A Chance   115

The Remarkable Story of Montréal's André Perry   119

Come Together's Montréal Origins   127

When Peace Was Denied a Chance   130

Bed-In Revisited   133

2. Vulnerabilities, Vagabonds and The Eaton Brothers   136

Toronto was Lennon's Last Paid Concert Gig   143

3. December: "Canada is Canada. Show us the way"   144

Whatcha Doin' Marshall McLuhan?   146

First Light   155

Chapter Five: The 1970s

Intermission   157

The Short Life of Curt Claudio   158

Winnipeg's Randy Bachman Asked Harrison for a Job   160

Live and Let Live: New Brunswicker Battles a Beatle   162

Spies Like Us   165

Up in Smoke   166

A Bluenose Salute: Nova Scotians Cover The Beatles   171

Victoria's David Foster   172

When Pattie Boyd Harrison Visited Prince Edward Island   174

Harrison and Starr's Canadian Waltz Partners   177

Calling Occupants: The Strange Tale of the "Canadian Beatles"   179

Chapter Six: The 1980s and 1990s

Ringo's All-Starr Canadian Line-Up   183

Jeff Healey's Harrison-Clapton Circle Route 186

In His Life: George Martin, Celine Dion and Jim Carrey 186

Lennon, McCartney, Harrison and Neil Young 188

Chapter Seven: 2000 to Today

George Harrison: Love and Barnacle Bill in Montréal 191

Canadian Actors Play Ringo Starr, Heather McCartney 196

How Toronto's Lorne Michaels Nearly Reunited John and Paul 197

Sealing the McCartney's Marital Fate in Charlottetown? 198

Gratis 202

Anglo-Saxon Idol Crashes Québec City's Birthday Party 204

Canada's Love Affair with Mull of Kintyre 205

The Tennant Family 216

Right Honourable Beatles Fan 219

Hey Grandude, My Illustrator is from Peterborough 224

Emma's Cape Breton (My Unama'ki) 226

Chapter Eight: Connecting The Beatles' Canadian Dots

Some final words on my heroes John, Paul, George and Ringo 246

Epilogue

Johnny's Top Ten Canadian Bands and Their Beatles Connections 257

Author Interviews 263

End Notes for Main Narrative 265

End Notes for Sidebar Stories 281

Author's Note by His Daughter Terra-Ann Arnone 283

Dedication by the Author 285

Acknowledgements 287

About the Author 289

PROLOGUE

My First Beatles Breath

Watching one, two or all three of *The Ed Sullivan Shows* featuring The Beatles' breakout performances in February 1964 is the response you'll most often get from Boomers when asked when and where they drew their first Beatles breath.

As a late blooming, second-generation Beatles fan, I inhaled that first breath six years later at age nine. I was hopping and skipping on a bakery errand for my grandmother when I stopped to investigate a commotion just inside the Dufferin Street doors of the music department at our local S.S. Kresge Co.

To my right, across a vast upper wall display, were rows and rows of just-arrived boxed *Let it Be* albums. On that iconic cover were four faces, serious and forlorn (except for a smiling George Harrison), linear and staring back at me. Below the display in the music department's pit, a turntable spun the album over the Kresge speakers. I listened while clutching that loaf of bread in my little arms; at that moment was ignited a longing for rock 'n' roll, an aural thirst I didn't even know existed but would last a lifetime.

That was 1970, the Age of Aquarius, long hair and beautiful people kicking down the doors of the establishment, waving peace signs and saying groovy, but for The Beatles it was *annus horribilis*. Their union ended that spring with no new material emerging from the boys until 1995. Like millions of others, my progression as a Beatles fan was actually an act of regression—Johnny Come Lately rolling backwards on a nostalgic Beatles journey, the highlights of which are carved like a road map of the last 50 years of my life, with Point A starting at Kresge's and winding to the present.

The arbiters of cool in my family were my older brother and first cousin, both named Pat. I would watch as they gently dropped the turntable needle and perfectly notch the edgy guitar intro and then the cowbell in "You Can't Do That" on *The Beatles Second Album*.

When I skated to "Get Back" blaring on the local arena's loud-speakers, it felt more like flying and the first time I heard the vastly underrated "Baby You're a Rich Man" I thought it was not of this world. I devoured their music, every album, and every nuance. Even as a pre-teen, I felt I was being shaped by The Beatles.

In the fifth grade my speech on The Beatles took runner-up in an all-school public speaking final. My dad and mom were there for the finals, helping to assuage my nerves when delivering my gushing opus in the school gymnasium.

In History class we learned that the Soviets had their Five-Year Plans, but as for me I had my Five-Year Spans of believing the world's greatest compositions were, in no particular order, the clarity, harmonies and gentle touch of the volume pedal in "I Need You", the rising and resolved narrative of hope in "Dear Prudence", the joy and smile inducing "Here Comes the Sun", the innocent and unrestrained pleas of "Please Please Me", the pounding bass and transcendent drum rhythm of "Rain" filling my ears, the smash-and-grab excitement of "I Saw Her Standing There", the insistent, can't-argue-with-me vocal of the greatest B-side ever "Don't Let Me Down" and, well, I can't forget how I lost myself in the mood altering solitude of "Strawberry Fields Forever" during Grade 11 CanLit (John Lennon's "living is easy with eyes closed, misunderstanding all you see" is my favourite Beatles lyric), followed thereafter by a note-for-note cranial synaptic journey devoted to the "long-one," the term Beatlemaniacs use to describe the eight-song spliced together perfection on *Abbey Road*'s second side.

And is there a more perfect Beatles song than "Lovely Rita"? If Paul McCartney's bouncy and seamlessly choreographed ditty is not in your top-five Beatles songs, give this critically overlooked beauty another listen.

On their three visits to Toronto, The Beatles would overnight at the downtown King Edward Hotel. Built in 1903 and named for the eldest son of Queen Victoria, King Edward VII, it was once home to Ernest Hemmingway and would be The Beatles only overnight accommodation in Canada as all other Canadian tour stops were day-tripping stop overs. Coincidentally, Lennon also stayed in the King Edward's Royal Suite when he returned to Toronto in 1969.

As it happened, the King Eddy loomed large in my family history and offered two memorable intersections in my Beatles roadmap. It's where my father got his first job as a barber after arriving from southern Italy (he was paid in groceries) and where, at a lavish auto industry banquet in 1987, I got my 15 minutes of fame after winning the Automobile Journalists Association of Canada Journalist of the Year national writing award.

I saw McCartney for the first time on December 7, 1989 at Toronto's SkyDome. He was on tour to support his critically-acclaimed *Flowers in the Dirt* which featured four songs he co-wrote and produced with Elvis Costello—including the concert opener "My Brave Face".

Another of my favourite Beatles-esque tracks from the album, "We Got Married", was co-produced by Victoria's David Foster. (Foster has worked with or appeared on the same album with all four Fabs as solo artists).

The road map got really personal, skin deep you might say, with my mid-life ensemble of Beatles tattoos, which began around 1998. There is Lennon's face in caricature on my upper arm with his aquiline nose and glasses askew; a spiritual Om symbol was my nod to Harrison's admirable commitment to a faith that fell well outside the parameters of his mother's Catholicism; an opposing pair of stars for the drummer Ringo Starr; and, for my fortieth birthday, a stretched interpretation of McCartney's classic Hofner bass guitar which, befitting its sensuous and symmetrical hollow violin design, curves slightly upward with the headstock resting on the edge of my shoulder cuff.

Many years later my wife, Tamara, surprised me with tickets to see Starr in the 5,000-seat concert venue in Rama, Ontario, very near to our summer home on Georgian Bay and where the drummer had years earlier recorded a concert DVD with an impressive line-up of touring studio musicians.

There he was, a Beatle in the midst, arms swaying, telling goofy stories, singing non-Beatle songs and drumming to the hits from his very talented All-Starr array. I was surprised that perhaps the most sentimental of the four didn't mention The Beatles, only teasing us with: "You may have heard that I was once part of a band … Rory Storm and the Hurricanes," referring to the Liverpool band from which John, Paul and especially George pried him away to join their outfit. It was a feel-good moment and magical just to be under the same roof as a living Beatle.

On a December business trip to London in 2010, I became a flash opportunist by inventing dubious reasons to sneak away to Liverpool for a few days. I spared my employer, Bombardier Aerospace, the expenses because it would have revealed the true nature of my side-show to places like The Cavern Club, The Beatles Story on Albert Dock, tickets aboard The Magical Mystery Tour bus, photo stops at Strawberry Fields, Beatle childhood homes at Forthlin Road, Mendips Lane, Arnold Grove and Madryn Street, and a well-tipped cabbie who agreed to circumnavigate the roundabout at Penny Lane over and over again evoking funny memories of Chevy Chase's dizzying, dusk-to-dawn roundabout ride near Big Ben in *National Lampoon's European Vacation*!

On the night before my final night in Liverpool I was left breath-less after attending a concert by some of The Quarry Men, including original banjo player Rod Davis, plus Beatle musician friend from Hamburg Tony Sheridan, Badfinger guitarist Joey Mulland, Lennon actor Mark McGann and original Plastic Ono Band drummer Alan White to a capacity crowd at Liverpool's Echo Arena.

We were there to remember Quarry Men and Beatles founder Lennon on the 30th anniversary of his death—they affectionately call him Johnny Lennon in Liverpool; one of their own, one of the greats and, as you'll soon discover, a man who held a very special relationship with Canada. They all did, and that's the story I'm going to tell you.

Eight years after that Liverpool concert and a profoundly important visit to The Beatles' birthplace that proved to be the earliest inspiration for this project, I quit my day job and eventually set out to write this book. I hope you like it.

The author near the Penny Lane roundabout during a life-changing visit to the cradle of The Beatles, Liverpool, in 2010. Photo by Adrienne McGill.

INTRODUCTION
The Beatles' Great Canadian Adventure

Around the time I was born, a struggling, little-known bar and dance-hall band made up of teenage boys and early twenty-somethings from Liverpool, England, were dodging flying bar stools and beer bottles while ducking under metal tables from the wailing fists of drunk and disorderly Canadian soldiers. The band was called The Beatles and they were playing away from home in the seediest city on earth.

That otherwise insignificant piece of bar brawling history involving the early Beatles and Canadian servicemen in Hamburg in 1961, was my jumping-off point for a book about The Beatles and Canada.

It's very Canadian of me to fixate on what others think of us, and when I read about the bar fight my thoughts turned to a barely 18-year-old Harrison: What must the junior Beatle have thought about Canada when, presumably, his first experience with anyone or anything Canadian involved a donnybrook at Hamburg's Top Ten Club that was so large and so ugly that it was quelled only by volleys of tear gas? We're not so polite and orderly after all, eh George?

You know what they say about presumptions.

As I set out to read, click and re-absorb myself in The Beatles' history, it was soon clear my presumption about Harrison was blown to bits: The youngest and most impressionable Beatle had a Canadian-born niece and nephew, along with a sister, uncle, brother-in-law and cousins living in Ontario and Québec. And the boots he was wearing to kick bottles and glass off the stage were purchased at an Ontario haberdasher as a trans-Atlantic gift.

That Harrison wore Canadian boots to repel and kick away the riotous materials fomented by the Canadian Infantry during that Beatles performance is not a serious historic parallel, let alone enough to begin writing a book about The Beatles and Canada, but here's what is ...

During the same year as that bar fight, his super-fan mother, Louise, was visiting relatives in Ontario. But here's the kicker, and the point where my jumping off spiraled luminously into a state of bliss: Julian Lennon's grandmother, Lillian Powell, was actually living in Toronto at the same time!

C'mon, really? Yes, Harrison's mother and Lennon's mother-in-law were both in Canada the year their boys were brawling with Canadian soldiers some 6,000 km away in West Germany.

So it goes. The Top Ten fracas wasn't Lennon's first encounter with Canadians either; The Beatles' founder nearly came to blows with a Vancouver talent scout in 1957.

At the time, 16-year-old Lennon was very much the *Nowhere Boy* in film—angry, tempestuous and seeking solace in rock 'n' roll, and girls; in my view, the mid-20th century's truest rebel with a cause. So when a talent scout's stage extravaganza deemed his pre-Beatles group, The Quarry Men, not good enough in a band competition in Liverpool he took the scout to task in a heated back-stage argument.

The object of Lennon's scorn was Carroll Levis, the Vancouver-raised one-time resident of Whitehorse, Yukon.

Just how big of a deal are we to make of this? The big picture shows that the United Kingdom was ground zero for The Beatles' time on earth as a band and as individuals with the United States not far behind particularly at the band's peak, but Canada held a solid, second-tier footing throughout their historic career arc—their beginning, rise and fall—like no other nation. The Maple Leaf can rightfully take its place alongside the Union Jack and the Stars and Stripes in The Beatles' history, as Canada and Canadians were front and centre in volumes of largely untold and unheralded stories that are rife with a narrative that helped to shape the band and their music.

For instance, popular history tells of Britain's Decca Records as making the music industry's most colossal blunder when it auditioned The Beatles and turned them down for a recording contract in 1962. But a granular fleck of research about The Beatles and Canada tells us a Vancouverite was at the centre of The Beatles' first major rejection. Not only did Carroll Levis miss the greatest star-making opportunity of his life, he pre-dated and exceeded Decca's more mainstream and well-known screw-up by several years.

It would happen again.

This time another Canadian, raised in New Brunswick, rose from virtually nothing to became a big-time film producer in the United Kingdom; in 1964 he was offered the movie script for *A Hard Day's Night* and took a pass, turning down not only a defining film for a generation, but also one of the most successful and lucrative films of the year.

So I kept at it, wondering what other historical arches placed Canada and Canadians in The Beatles' orbit. And sure enough, every upturned stone revealed more and more fascinating Canadian connections to The Beatles, whether tracing their activities while in Canada, or discovering which Canadians had an impact on—or in some cases nearly nullified—the music that has coursed through the veins of millions upon millions for well over 50 years.

But like all ideas swirling in my head, this project held a wee burden of self-doubt, or, more precisely, the question of relevance. Would anyone care that the teenage founder of The Beatles' Canadian fan club would allow that experience to inspire her pursuit of a doctorate and become a leader in the field of social gerontology? Or that the only journalist permitted to join The Beatles during their 1967 meditation in India would years later share grand children with a Canadian prime minister? Or that a Guelph, Ontario-born harmonica player would contribute to the first solo album by any Beatle (while still a Beatle), go on to be knighted by Queen Elizabeth II and have a granddaughter who starred on *Murdoch Mysteries?* Or how about the fact a young Canadian helped to send an unwitting Lennon and Harrison on their first acid trip? Or that a sax player from Moose Jaw not only played on the *White Album* but alleges having written an un-credited horn arrangement for The Beatles?

And profoundly, some of the key events in The Beatles' career that stand as bookends of their founding and break-up, were connected to or even occurred in Canada.

On one hand, a pre-teen McCartney sang publicly for the first time at a campground in Wales owned by a veteran of the Canadian Army and former Eaton's employee; it's the same campground chain where Starr bid adieu to his band in order to join The Beatles in 1962!

On the other, seven years later in September 1969 in Toronto, with Jim Morrison and The Doors not far from him, Lennon played a stadium concert for the first time without The Beatles and very soon thereafter upon returning to England secretly dissolved the band. And as if Canada fueled his courage further, Lennon returned to Toronto that December, and told a journalist The Beatles were over—some five months before McCartney broke the news of the band's demise to the world.

For Harrison, while still a Beatle, it was meeting and spending quality time with The Band's mostly Canadian musicians that inspired him to write the song that he would tuck away, only to record and release to huge acclaim very soon after The Beatles dissolved.

Is that the sort of thing that would adequately tap into the collective curiosity of the sons and daughters of Canada or should I spend my time writing questions and answers for a hoser version of Beatles Trivial Pursuit?

The final worry—more like intimidation—had to do with the sheer labyrinth of books written about the most thoroughly probed and investigated foursome of all time. The Beatles are familiar territory in the world of non-fiction publishing. *One Two Three Four: The Beatles in Time* recently won the prestigious Baillie-Gifford prize and there are Beatles cookbooks, titles that explore the homes in which they lived, and even books that lay out all the playing and recording equipment and instruments they used in exquisite detail.

University of Liverpool professor Dr. Mike Brocken, perhaps generously, puts the number of Beatles books at over 8,000[1]; would there be enough material to add the 8,001st to the Fab Four stockpile?

Discouraging words kept piling on. "It takes some formidable organizational chops to serve as a competent Beatles bibliographer,"[2] wrote *Rolling Stone* magazine, and in *The Guardian's* assessment, any new book on The Beatles "can provide only a précis of a phenomenon that fills whole libraries."[3]

Yikes!

Then it occurred to me that in order to write a meaningful book that was more than just a précis of The Beatles, I would need to revisit the original book premise of The Beatles and Canada, tap dance around its margins, stretch them out a little and ask this question: Did The Beatles have any meaningful impact on the political, cultural and musical fabric of Canada and Canadian society? Could I make this about us too?

I poked around a little until I nearly tripped over a scene in that film by American director Richard Linklater; you know, the one that took 12 years to make, *Boyhood*.

While driving in the family minivan, star Ethan Hawke looks over at his teenage son and gives him a very special gift: Dad has dubbed a homemade CD of something called *The Beatles Black Album*—a three-disc fantasy compilation of 51 concurrent songs from the individual Beatles, truly the best of John, Paul, George and Ringo's solo work. One disc, for instance, leads with "Band on the Run", then "My Sweet Lord", "Jealous Guy" and "Photograph".

Hawke's character puts in popular context how for years we moaned and groaned about The Beatles' break-up without adequately seeing the trees from the forest; that is, when you play their best solo work back-to-back it sounds very, well, Beatles!—assuming the right frame of mind, of course. Here's how he put it and, remember the context, it's a dad trying to find some common ground with his adolescent son while offering a ray of hope for the immediate future:

> I've put the band back together for you. You know
> when you listen to too much of the solo stuff it

becomes a drag, but when you put them next to each other ... they start to elevate each other, and then you hear it ... it's The Beatles. It's in the balance ... like the perfect segue, you got Paul takes you to the party, George talks to you about God, John says it's about love and pain and then Ringo just says 'hey, can't we enjoy what we have when we have it?'"[4]

Hawke, who in real life owns an island east of Antigonish, Nova Scotia, had me at "they elevate each other." Thanks Ethan. You were the voice inside my head confirming that there were no wrong paths for The Beatles after their break up—only more great music, events and a trove of opportunities to expand the original book premise to something grander; namely ...

The contribution of Canada and Canadians to the music, art, history and phenomenon of The Beatles as a band and solo artists (and what they gave Canada in return)

It may sound like a dissertation but this book would certainly be no précis! With a single rotation of the dial the camera lens that peered into The Beatles and Canadian history was stretched to its widest aperture and raised by over fifty the years my research horizon; a timeline that went from around 1960 to 1970, now extended to 1953 when the first Beatle families arrived in Canada to the present day and beyond, considering that the surviving Beatles, Starr, 81, and McCartney, 79, remain, blessedly, active.

Stripping away the complexity of individual market variations (Canada certainly had a few) re-releases, greatest hits and other compilations, The Beatles released 13 studio albums in just under eight years. As solo artists, longevity rules with McCartney's 26 albums and Starr's 19; Harrison released 11 albums and Lennon eight. That's a total of 77 albums (and growing) and the opportunity to mine for Canadian connections and contributions with unearthed musicians, arrangers, recordings, collaborators, producers, concert tours, films, videos, books, appearances and unique situations from across Canada supporting Beatles music.

Beyond the records, John, Paul, George and Ringo's solo activities in Canada and with Canadians really opened things up, like notching out a key that opened the door to a tidal wave of information. Consider, for instance:

1. Lennon testified to a Canadian royal commission, had tea with a prime minister, scolded a Québec separatist, compared notes with Marshall McLuhan, was driven around Ottawa by Canada's future UN Ambassador and was schooled by an Alberta woman on ancient Cree values.

2. McCartney brought international attention to the Mi'kmaq language and the Gulf of St. Lawrence seal hunt, shared his stage with Canadian musicians in six provinces and turned historic, pre-Confederation sites in Halifax and Québec City into massive outdoor concert venues.

3. Harrison's friendship with two Canadians had profound outcomes on his position with The Beatles; one inspired him to raise his game as a songwriter (if that was even possible!) and, years later, he and another spawned the massive *The Beatles LOVE* project to widespread acclaim.

4. Ontario was the setting for Starr's *Tour 2003* live recording where he performed "Don't Pass Me By", a song from the *White Album* that featured a Canadian fiddle violinist, the first of many Canadians with whom the drummer would later collaborate in nearly six decades as a solo artist.

And don't get me started on the great Eric Clapton. The half-Canadian guitar god is a colossally influential figure throughout The Beatles' timeline who, like Leonard Zelig in the movies, weaves in and out of their careers as a band and as individual artists.

That much of The Beatles' activities and influences happened in Ontario and Québec should come as no surprise given these provinces account for 60 per cent of Canada's population. But that didn't stop The Beatles from deploying their love and influence across the land. When it came to Canada, The Beatles knew no borders etching a vast number of dots with connections from British Columbia to Newfoundland and Labrador and all places in between. As far as Canada's north is concerned, The Fabs did not shine a light in Nunavut or the Northwest Territories but there is an early Beatles connection with the Yukon Territory.

Canadians even got a head-start on Beatlemania, absorbing The Beatles on our airwaves and record shelves at a time when the lads were virtually unknown elsewhere in the Western Hemisphere thanks to our pre-wiring of things British. Key to the early success in Canada was a Capitol Records of Canada executive and a 14-year-old high schooler.

So away I went, joyfully pulling together the stories that link my two great passions: The Beatles, the most influential musical power-house of the past 100 years, and Canada, the beloved country of my birth. Them and us, *Us and Them*!

Without The Beatles, rock 'n' roll as we know it would not exist, the world would be a different place and my life's sound track would be missing not only their songs but the way their music made me feel—a sweet entanglement of redemption, introspection, joy and sorrow. As poet Maya Angelou once said, while people might forget what you said or did, they will never forget how you made them feel.

1953 TO 1961

Harrison's Canadian Kin

If ever there was a beginning to the *Us and Them* story, it happened in 1953 with the arrival of George Harrison's uncle Edmund French in Ontario.

An authority on The Beatles in Canada, Piers Hemmingsen, confirms the first of Harrison's family to move to Canada was his mother's brother, Harrison's uncle Edmond French. Of Irish-Catholic stock, French, his wife Mimi and two young sons, George and Gregory, left Liverpool in 1953 and settled in the Toronto-area towns of Richmond Hill and later Don Mills. A former police officer in England, French worked in the trucking industry in southern Ontario.

Three years later, prompted in part by her uncle but more so by her new husband, the next Harrison, George's older sister Louise arrived in Canada and lived in northern Ontario and Québec before eventually setting roots in the United States. Through his sister Louise, Harrison's bloodline includes at least two Canadian-born relatives, establishing George as the Beatle with the most familial links to Canada.

Before they were Beatles none of the four set foot in Canada—not surprising as post-war England was beset by economic hardship and

1

rationing, putting something as discretionary as overseas leisure travel low on the priorities list. But later, with The Beatles' fortunes rising significantly in England but not yet outside of Europe, a scruffy and mop-topped Harrison became the first Beatle to travel overseas. It was September 1963 and with his older brother Peter, Harrison travelled to Illinois. It would very likely become the last time any Beatle could travel anonymously to North America without being recognized, or mobbed.

The Canadian slice of Louise Harrison's journey in the Americas lasted seven years. It began in 1956 when she married a Scottish mining engineer, Gordon Caldwell, and the newlyweds set sail for Ontario; or more specifically North Virginiatown, a small mining outpost 600 km due north of Toronto near the Québec border where, according to Hemmingsen, they lived until 1960. The Caldwells produced Harrison's nephew Gordon Jr. (April, 1957) and niece Leslie (September, 1959) in Canada.

Louise (Harrison) Caldwell's life in Canada's cold, open, frontier spaces differed vastly from that of her Uncle Edmund, who would have had greater comforts (and longer summers) living along the warmer edges of Toronto. But that didn't deter George's mom, the elder Louise Harrison, to make the voyage across the Atlantic to visit her daughter, brother and grandchildren in 1960—a visit that lasted for five months into 1961.

With all this family activity in Canada, it's not at all surprising that pre-eminent Beatles historian Mark Lewisohn referenced Harrison's curiosity about The Great White North. In 1959, with fame but a distant fantasy and good-paying gigs hard to come by, the 16-year-old, newly-minted Beatle was looking to escape several uninspiring school or work options in England and "tried to persuade his parents to consider a family move to Australia, which they rejected. Then he thought of emigrating alone, a 16-year-old planning to live in Malta … or Canada. He went as far as requesting the application forms but lost heart when he saw parental authority was needed."[5]

That Harrison never acted on his wanderlust is a blessing of untold proportions because he opted instead to remain with his band as they gained experience and respect in Liverpool and Hamburg. As for his sister, brother-in-law, niece and nephew, the Caldwells continued pursuing Gordon's career with a move to the just-established mining town of Gagnon, Québec, where they lived until 1963. Located less than 200 km from Labrador City near the provincial border with Newfoundland and Labrador, Ville de Gagnon had 4,000 residents at its peak, a church and an airport. (Today it technically no longer exists, its post mining-boom remnants declared a ghost town.)

While in Québec and later in the United States, the younger Louise would correspond regularly with her mom in Liverpool. Louise the elder had become an enthusiastic letter writer to fans and family alike and, with her daughter, became early facilitators of unofficial Beatles or Harrison fan clubs. The two Louises would provide family updates but, in particular, the elder Louise would give her daughter detailed updates of their George and The Beatles. It was a fascinating turn of events that a Beatle sister living in Québec would learn of her younger brother's growing fame in the United Kingdom via Canada Post or, in this case, *Postes Canada*.

Twelve letters penned in 1963 between mother and daughter are tenderly voiced by the younger Louise on the website *lettersfrommum. com*; says Louise, "when I moved overseas from Britain in the late 1950s, I became my mom's newest pen pal. Receiving her letters and packages week after week, it was soon clear to me why so many people from all walks of life and from all over the world enjoyed her warm chatty letters."

The collection includes this letter sent from mother to daughter in Québec on February 8, 1963:

> Dear Lou and Gordon … George is away at present on a Yorkshire tour with Helen Shapiro. By press reports, they're bringing the house down everywhere. Mrs. Williams sent me a big clipping from the *London Evening Standard*, "Why The Beatles Create all That Frenzy?" were the headlines. Every paper carries The Beatles in large print. One report on the Bradford show with Helen Shapiro and other big names said "The Beatles Stole The Show" as the audience repeat-edly called for them whilst the other artists were

performing. The record "Please Please Me" is now number three in the top 50, "Love Me Do" is still at number 43 after being on the charts for 17 weeks. Tell me if you got the copy I sent and if you got the plum pudding I sent at Christmas … "[6]

Affectionately referred to as "Lou" and dropping Caldwell from her name after a 1970 divorce, Louise Harrison returned to Canada in 2009 as a guest of Upper Canada College in Toronto. On a speaking tour, she gave a lecture on the planet's environmental crisis and also took questions about her one-time residency in Canada. At the time of publication, the 89-year-old Beatle sister continues to live in the United States. Her son Gordon Robert Caldwell eventually resettled in Florida where he died at age 52 on January 17, 2010, of cancer, leaving a wife and son. Her daughter is now Leslie Rodgers, and she resides in Florida with her husband and son.

Little Paul in Grey Shorts, Ringo's Last Roar and the Canadian Army's Billy Butlin

A year after the first member of Harrison's family arrived in Canada, across the Atlantic in Wales a 12-year-old Paul McCartney auditioned at a talent competition with his brother Michael. The audition was held at a summer camp that bore the name of its founder, Butlin's, a one-time soldier in the Canadian Armed Forces.

Born in South Africa to British parents, Sir William Heygate Butlin was an entrepreneur who pioneered the concept of British holiday family camps, opening his first facility in 1936 near the North Sea coastal town of Skegness, inviting famed aviator Amy Johnson to cut the ribbon. His Canadian connection began in 1911 when his mother immigrated to Canada, leaving her son in the care of his grandparents in England. By 1913 she settled in Toronto's Cabbagetown district and arranged for 13-year-old Billy, as he was called, to join her.

Butlin attended local school and worked in the advertising department at Eaton's department stores. On December 29, 1915, he signed the necessary Attestation Paper with the Canadian Army declaring himself to be "faithful and bear true Allegiance to His Majesty King George V" although at 15 he lied about his age stating he was 16, fit and ready to fight for Canada and its king. Initially he signed up as a "dispatch rider"—essentially a motorcycle courier in the theatre of battle, but was eventually assigned to the Canadian Expeditionary Force consisting of four divisions earmarked for the western front of France and Belgium. He then joined the 170th (Mississauga Horse) Battalion, followed by the 216th (Bantams) Battalion in England. Butlin ultimately saw battle in France in his role as a stretcher-bearer with the 3rd Canadian Division in some of most heroic fighting in Canadian military history, including at Vimy Ridge, Passchendaele and Arras. Impossible to quantify, Butlin would take on the grim but noble task of helping to lay countless Canadian and Allied soldiers in their final place of rest in the killing fields of France and Belgium.

He never returned to Canada as, after the war ended in 1919, Butlin re-settled in England. His start in business was to run ring-toss stalls at fairs and circuses where he earned enough to repatriate his mother back home from Canada. In time his business acumen grew and he would launch a string of popular family campgrounds throughout the United Kingdom and the Caribbean.

Butlin repurposed his main campground in Wales as an army training facility during World War II. After the war it was re-converted and became a popular campground by the sea. It was there, in summer 1954 on a McCartney family outing, where Butlin hosted a talent competition in which 12-year-old Paul McCartney and his younger brother Michael, wearing short grey trousers and school caps, sang a song by early Beatles influencers, the Everly Brothers.

"We got up on stage and sang 'Bye Bye Love' and didn't win. We never won talent contests; The Beatles never won anything. We once famously got beaten by an old woman playing spoons. She was good, mind you, she had talent,"[7] McCartney recalled to David Frost in a 2012 interview.

Eight years later, Butlin—who was married three times, knighted in 1964 and died in 1980 at age 80—would also host another future Beatle, Ringo Starr, in the same resort.

Starr's pre-Beatles band, Rory Storm and the Hurricanes, became an entertainment staple at Butlin's. A lucrative arrangement, their first engagement in Wales lasted 13 weeks, from June to September in 1960, and they were paid 80 pounds a week for three-hour sessions, six nights a week with accommodations.[8] Located in Pwllheli on the northern coast of Wales, the sprawling facility attracted thousands of visitors every summer, and many guests grew fond of the flamboyant drummer. The popular Starr (born Richard Starkey) is said to have signed autographs prefacing his name with "The Sensational"[9] and Butlin's is also where he dropped "Richard" to become "Ringo."

The Hurricanes returned for another round in 1961 and were hired by Butlin's for a final run in 1962 at the Skegness location's Rock and Calypso Ballroom in England. It would be Starr's last engagement with Rory Storm and The Hurricanes. As a professional drummer, Starr was extremely well regarded and kept beat like a metronome. Always wanting to improve his situation, he was looking for a better band while back in Liverpool. The stars were aligning as Lennon, McCartney and Harrison decided to oust drummer Pete Best. Harrison was perhaps the band's top proponent to add Starr to their ranks, although the others were very familiar with the left-handed drummer who occasionally filled-in for Best and others when The Beatles found themselves drummer-less. Harrison was tasked with learning Starr's whereabouts and called Starr's mom Elsie only to learn he was playing at Butlin's; that information was passed onto their manager Brian Epstein.

In 2017, Starr told radio host Howard Stern about the call he received at Butlin's that would change his life: "I was with Rory and we went away to play another holiday camp and I get a phone call (asking if I) would join The Beatles. This was Wednesday, and I said when? And Brian Epstein said today! I said I can't go today I've got a band here we got to sort this out, I'll be there Saturday … and (the Hurricanes) got another drummer by then."[10]

On August 17, 1962, Starr left the employ of the former Canadian resident and army veteran, leaving Rory Storm with one less Hurricane three days before the end of their three-week run at the summer camp. The next morning, Starr got into his car and journeyed back to Liverpool to debut with his new band, making history as the final piece of the puzzle to form The Beatles. The late Neil Aspinall, who went from The Beatles' road manager to head of Apple Records, explained it succinctly: "They'd had a succession of drummers through the years and finally now they found one who integrated, someone who fitted. Until this point it was always 'John, Paul, George and a drummer'— now it was John, Paul, George and Ringo."[11]

Eric Clapton's Canadian Story

Throughout their careers both in the band and out, The Beatles would have deep links to guitarist Eric Clapton, particularly Harrison who made a profound, bittersweet and life-long connection with the guitar great. The connection between Clapton and the band began in late 1964 when Clapton's band, the Yardbirds, were invited to participate in *Another Beatles Christmas Show* at London's Hammersmith Odeon Theatre. It's there where Clapton met Harrison.

Of course, Clapton was not in The Beatles, but the task at hand is to find contributions of Canadians to "the music, art, history and phenomenon of The Beatles."

Clapton is half Canadian on account of his Montréal-born father, Edward Fryer. Patricia Clapton, Eric's English mother, never married Fryer but did marry another man from Canada. Between them, Clapton and Harrison had so many Canadian-born or Canadian-raised parents, stepparents, cousins, nieces, nephews, half-brothers, half-sisters and expats that the two rockers had much more in common than Pattie Boyd, the beautiful woman they each married. Let it be said that Harrison was fond of calling Clapton his husband-in-law.

The point is Harrison and Clapton were best friends in life and in music. Their collaborations were legendary and Clapton was bestowed the rarest of opportunities to play guitar on a Beatles song in studio, something not done before or after, when he played on the band's *White Album*.

The two also collaborated on the minimalist rocker "Badge" which appeared on Cream's final album *Goodbye*. You've heard it, "She cried away her life since she fell off the cradle ... " As a co-writer, Clapton becomes the only person with any Canadian blood to share a songwriting credit with a member of The Beatles and more remarkably it happened while Harrison was still very much a Beatle—the two also played guitar on the track which was released in February 1969.

Clapton's Beatles pedigree went further, much further, and in a span of 50 years he often played, recorded and even performed live not only with Harrison but with all four of The Beatles as individual artists, including on a Toronto stage with Lennon.

"She met this Canadian ... "

Clapton's biological father, Edward Fryer, was born in Montréal on March 21, 1920—something Clapton had no knowledge of until a Canadian investigative reporter revealed to him the truth about his father in 1998. Sources vary on some details but there is little doubt Fryer was a free-spirited, piano-playing soldier with the Royal Canadian Air Force who was shipped overseas to England during the latter part of World War II, and it was there that he met another free spirit, Patricia Clapton, in a Surrey pub in 1943.

In the *BBC* documentary, *Eric Clapton: A Life in 12 Bars*, aunt Sylvia Clapton described what happened next with Fryer and her niece, Clapton's mother Patricia: "She met this Canadian, (he was) over here ... and it was a one-night stand. In those days to be pregnant and young and you're not married was awful."[12]

Clapton was one of an estimated 1.74 million illegitimate children born in Britain during World War II.[13] His father, Fryer, eventually shuffled off to Canada and didn't remain in England long enough for his son's birth. For her part, Patricia suffered acts of shaming in her village of

Ripley, and was treated so badly that soon after giving birth, on March 30, 1945, she fled to Canada, leaving her newborn son in England.

It's unclear if Patricia headed to Canada to seek out Fryer—for if she found him, it would have been a rude surprise to learn he returned to Montréal to be reunited with his wife and family. What's more likely is that she fled with another Canadian soldier, Frank MacDonald. They married and would produce three Canadian half-siblings to Clapton who, back in England, was raised by his maternal grandmother.

Clapton wasn't told about his mother's abandonment, nor his Canadian father, but rather made to believe Patricia was his older sister when she would sporadically re-enter his life, with her Canadian children.

It was during one of those visits when Clapton was nine that he was finally told the truth about his mother. In a heart-breaking retelling of his childhood, Clapton revealed that he asked Patricia, "You're my mom, are you going to be my mom?" to which she replied "No," denying the future guitarist a life with either of his biological parents.[14]

Fryer died of leukemia at Toronto's Sunnybrook Hospital Veteran's Centre in 1985 at age 65; Patricia Clapton and Frank MacDonald remained married for over three decades until their late 1970s divorce; she died in 1999 at age 70.

Yukon Deck Hand Turned Lennon Nemesis?

The "Maker of Stars" Carroll Levis entered The Beatles' orbit very early in their careers.

Born in Toronto on March 15, 1910, Carroll Richard Levis was an infant when his family re-settled to Vancouver. An ambitious lad filled with boundless energy, Levis managed a movie theatre when he was only 17, moved to Whitehorse, Yukon, to work as a deck hand on a steamer, painted houses and had a stint as a lumberjack.

A man of many talents, the extroverted Levis returned to his Vancouver home to ply his newfound trade as, yes, a hypnotist until the growing popularity of radio and his knack for showmanship led him to *CKWX* radio to run a talent show with a live studio audience.

By age 25, Levis was a popular talent scout in British Columbia but it wasn't long before his wanderlust returned and he set sail for England. Quick to make contacts, adept at pitching ideas and gifted, as hypnotists tend to be, with the power of persuasion, he convinced the *BBC* that the United Kingdom was ready for a radio talent show and the *Carroll Levis Discovery Show* was born.

The Discovery Show grew to become a national phenomenon, travelling to towns and cities as a countrywide radio pastime, prompting *Maclean's* magazine to publish a feature story on the portly, 240-pound Levis in February 1946. Headlined "The Maker of Stars" reporter Lester Matthews noted, "half a million hopefuls, young and old, have passed through his talent mill. It's meant stardom for many." In no time Levis became one of the best-known, best-loved Canadians in the UK and, in the course of his career, would twice encounter members of the future Beatles.

In 1953 Levis' radio show morphed into a television program on *ATV* (*Associated TeleVision*—an *ITV* network broadcasting in London and the Midlands) known variously as *Carroll Levis Junior Discoveries* and *The Carroll Levis Discovery Show*. On June 9, 1957, the travelling show landed in Liverpool, hometown of sixteen-year-old Lennon and his pre-Beatles band, The Quarry Men, formed a year earlier.

The Quarry Men were a skiffle band in which Lennon played guitar and sang. It was made up of the kids he hung out with in school including Eric Griffiths, guitar, Pete Shotton, washboard, Ivan Vaughan, bass, and Colin Hanton on drums. The short-lived skiffle craze swept the UK in the 1950s—blending blues, folk and jazz music from the American south and using both conventional (guitar, banjo) and homemade (washboard, jugs, kazoo) instruments.

It's difficult to gauge just how good The Quarry Men actually were but what was certain was Lennon's confidence, it thrilled him to sing and play to audiences. Says author Bob Spitz: "John was determined to test this new power under more challenging circumstances."[15]

And along comes the Canadian and his date with The Beatles' history.

Lewisohn picks up the story when Lennon and The Quarry Men lined up to register (a preamble to actually appearing at a later date) as "one of scores of Liverpool skiffle bands" for the talent competition:

> On the morning of Sunday, June 9 (The Quarry Men) were in the queue that snaked around the Liverpool Empire (Theatre), a ragged line of guitars, washboards and tea chests … John Lennon … was now pinning his hopes on Carroll Levis.
>
> Levis was a particular player in British show business for a quarter century, an overweight, silver-haired Canadian in a tailored Savile Row suit who'd abandoned his own career as a variety entertainer (his act was hypnotism and necromancy) … to start a touring talent show. Winners of his stage show were offered a spot in his fortnightly *ATV* series … In these early days of television, if you appeared 'on the box' in any capacity you were instantly a star.
>
> When The Quarry Men got into the Empire … Levis sat at a table stage left, John said, 'We're The Quarry Men' and a couple of minutes later the great man said, 'That's fine' and booked them for the show.[16]

About 10 days later The Quarry Men returned to the Empire as one of eight acts to perform in three-minute allotments for Levis and a live audience in the first elimination round, choosing to play Woody Guthrie's 1940 simple guitar beauty "Worried Man Blues"—"it takes a worried man, to sing a worried song, I'm worried now but I won't be worried long." The song was well received but The Quarry Men were in tough as a band from Wales called the Sunnyside Skiffle Group jumped all over the stage in a manic performance and drew more applause.

Levis declared a playoff round between The Quarry Men and the Sunnysides. To adjudicate the final decision he rolled out a primitive and entirely unreliable device to measure audience noise and reaction and it gave the edge to the band from Wales.

"Drummer Colin (Hanton) recalls they had quite a few support-ers in the audience, though not as many as another group who not only got more applause but were also, he says, mysteriously given the chance to play a second number. The Quarry Men drew less applause … and weren't chosen to proceed to Saturday's final. It was over."[17]

Spitz writes that things didn't end so smoothly. Lennon, he said, took exception to losing the competition to a Welsh band that, in his view, stacked the audience with supporters to fix the outcome.

As the Sunnysides were given the go-ahead to perform a second song, Spitz quotes drummer Hanton retelling the story slightly dif-ferently: "John began arguing with Levis: 'That's not right. You're giving them the upper hand.' We were all mad as hell." Spitz con-tinues: "But it was too late. Levis offered a halfhearted apology but stood adamantly aside while the Welsh group put their luck to good use, turning up the heat" on their second number.

"'We were robbed,' Hanson says … and Carroll Levis knew it, too. While he was lining up for the grand finale, he apologized, saying, 'I might have been a bit unfair there, lads, but it's too late now. Don't despair—you were quite good. Just keep at it'"[18]

To Lennon, the "if at first you don't succeed … " motto rang true as 16 months later on October 18, 1958, at 18, he took another run at gaining entry into the now renamed *Carroll Levis Star Search* qualifying round. Now known as Johnny and the Moondogs and featuring new guitar-playing recruits, George Harrison, 15, and Paul McCartney, 16, the drummer-less band would return to Levis' circuit, this time successfully passing the audition at the Liverpool Empire Theatre on Lime Street for a berth in the finals in Manchester.

McCartney was star struck and saw something worldly about the Canadian who by now was viewed as a slick foreign talent in the UK. It seemed the young McCartney had met few if any Americans and thought that Canada—where they also spoke a different brand of English—was the next best thing as a path to pop music's Promised Land: America.

"We thought Canadians were like Americans, so they were very special to us. They could easily get into entertainment … just because of their accent."[19]

The threesome rehearsed on the train from Liverpool, brought several friends with them, perhaps taking a page from the earlier Welsh band's boisterous entourage. So there they were, three future Beatles with two guitars playing and singing a Buddy Holly tune at the Manchester Hippodrome on November 15, 1958.

Harrison draws a delightful image of himself and McCartney flanking "Johnny" on stage in Manchester: "We performed 'Think if Over' with John standing in the middle with no guitar, just singing with a hand on each of our shoulders. Paul and I were on guitars—one pointing this way, one that way—doing the back-up voices. We thought we were really good."[20]

But this time it ended without argument and neither a Canadian nor the Welsh could be blamed. Although by every account John's lead vocals blending with Harrison and McCartney's harmonies sounded great, there was the nagging issue of getting home to Liverpool before the last train departed, so the Moondogs essentially exited the competition and, with their supporters, shuffled off to Manchester Station before a winner was declared—the alternative being stuck in Manchester with no money to afford a hotel room.

"We Thought We Were Really Good", said George when, six years before this photo was taken, his pre-Beatles band Johnny and The Moondogs featuring him, Paul and John competed in a talent competition run by Canadian Carroll Levis. Photo by Eric Koch / Anefo (licensed under CC0 1.0).

Historical events have a funny way of re-tracing paths, crossing over others and creating connections from seemingly disparate events. For instance, five years after the unknown Johnny and the Moondogs played for Levis in Manchester, the trio added a drummer and called themselves The Beatles. They would explode onto the world scene like a meteor hurling from space, kicking-off the Canadian leg of their first North America tour in Levis' hometown of Vancouver in front of a near record-breaking 20,000-plus delirious fans.

Far from a villain in the early careers of Lennon, Harrison and McCartney, Vancouver's "Maker of Stars" Levis—who retired in 1961, took ill and died at 58 in London on October 17, 1968—did advise the boys to keep at it, and they did including the now infamously failed audition with Decca Records on New Year's Day in 1962.

As the band's leader, Lennon was The Beatles' voice of confidence despite their early setbacks. In fact when things were looking down, and at times futile—just look at Harrison's contemplation of leaving England for greener pastures—the others would ask their leader, "Where we going, Johnny?" And he would reply "to the top ... the toppermost of the poppermost."

Canadian Beer Offensive: "Re-Run of World War II"

As a five-piece band, The Beatles worked very hard to grow as musicians and, later, songwriters, and that work ethic led them to Hamburg where they took up two separate residencies as a bar band, in 1960 and 1961. They played clubs along the Reeperbahn and Grosse Freiheit— party streets in the West German port city's St. Pauli red-light district that was infamous for its debauchery, gangsters, drink, sex and drugs. On their first night performing at the Indra Cabaret, for instance, The Beatles played to a handful of spectators, mostly prostitutes and their clients.

In 1961, The Beatles played 92 nights with backing singer Tony Sheridan at Hamburg's Top Ten Club. Drunk and disorderly was the standard for most Top Ten patrons described by Lewisohn as "St. Pauli's gangsters" who, typically between one and three in the morning, "would walk into the Top Ten (as) swaggering, loudmouthed, big-shot bastards, drunk and belligerent, with floozies on their arms."[21]

On one particular night, or morning, the usual riff-raff and gangsterism stepped aside for hundreds of Canadian servicemen who stormed the club, drank excessively and mounted a barrage of fist fights with waiters and staff the likes of which the Top Ten, even by Reeperbahn standards, had not seen before.

The Canadian Beer Offensive, as the incident has become known, was eventually quelled as allied employees from neighboring bars converged on the Top Ten and, together, they managed to push and pull the Canadian instigators out of the bar.

The Beatles and Sheridan continued to play, barely missing a beat while wounds were treated and waiters took to sweeping glass and all manner of mayhem scattered throughout.

But on that particular night The Beatles were denied a lasting peace as the uninvited Canadians returned with reinforcements. The Beatles' original drummer Pete Best recalls, "The Canadian trouble-makers … hurriedly rustled up a few hundred more of their compatriots and within a short time marched on the Top Ten, bent on retribution."[22]

The sequel would be prolonged and nasty, much worse than the original hostilities and a clear demonstration of drunken Canadian behavior at its worst.

Best devotes two pages of vivid memories to the lurid incident in his heartfelt autobiography *Beatle*, including this recollection of the chaos triggered by the Canadian troops' return visit:

> We manfully soldiered on (playing) as waiters, tough-ies and soldiers pitched into each other in a 1961 re-run of World War II … The Canadians tore the glass-fronted showcases from the passage walls, where our pictures were displayed. Bottles were being hurled like hand-grenades in every direction and tables clawed from the barricade were hurtling into the defenders. 'They're bloody mad!' Paul yelled when the Canadians managed somehow to start a fire at the makeshift barrier.[23]

The out-of-control scene lasted two hours and was finally quelled when Top Ten waiters elevated their rank to riot control officers and fired rudimentary canisters of tear gas into the fighting mobs to disable the respiratory systems of the Canadians, and all others, who retreated, half-blinded, into the early morning darkness of Hamburg for fresh air. As flames were being doused, local police arrived and arrested 30 or so soldiers. It's unclear if the Canadians ever paid for their drink as that was likely the cause of the brouhaha in the first place.

And here's the best part. Befitting their true Canadian nature, two well-mannered soldiers (perhaps fearing if word of the incident got to Ottawa their masters would be unimpressed) were ordered to re-appear and make amends the following night offering apologies on behalf of the Canadian Armed Forces.

Who were these troops that turned the Top Ten into a battlefield and why were they in West Germany? After the fall of Germany ended the war in Europe, some 25,000 war-weary Canadian soldiers did not repatriate back to their homes and families in Canada but were instead assigned to the Royal Canadian Army Occupational Force in the so-called British Zone—a large, northwestern carving of Germany that included Hamburg.

The men who roughed up The Beatles while on stage were likely part of the 4 Canadian Infantry Brigade Group that was stationed across four bases throughout North Rhine-Westphalia. Troops were rotated every three years and a typical brigade consisted of up to 5,500 sol-diers, making the ill-fated drummer's report of "hundreds" of Canadian soldiers pushing their way into the Top Ten far from an exaggeration. Probably on furlough, the Canadian infantrymen travelled several hundred kilometres from their base of operations to let loose.

Imagine the scene for a moment, the pent up energy, testosterone-fueled bravado of the young soldiers leaping off their trucks, cars and buses to maraud the lurid Reeperbahn—far from the judgment of loved ones at home and their base commanders, and smack-dab in full view of The Beatles. In less than two years, The Beatles would graduate from gritty cellar bars to packed stadiums and fandom fueled by mass hysteria and riotous teenagers like the world had never seen, making the night the Canadians set fire to and tore-up a Hamburg music club seem like a schoolyard quarrel in comparison.

Beatle Boots on the Ground

While on stage at the Top Ten and other venues in which The Beatles played during their final Hamburg residency, Harrison was wearing Canadian cowboy boots, and the story of how he got them, and the trend his boots may have inspired, offers a unique connection to Canada.

With an established fan base and growing confidence, the early Beatles once meager financial situation improved and that helped them launch their own brand of style, turning heads in both Liverpool and Hamburg because often the clothing they wore on stage was also what they sported on the streets and in the bars as civilians. Apropos of their youngest member, it was Harrison who adopted a fashion sense before the others—especially when it came to footwear. In Hamburg in 1960, for instance, to complement his black leather jacket and ubiquitous skinny jeans, Harrison purchased a pair of wood-heeled cowboy boots, or "Texan Boots" as they were called. It wasn't long before the others, John, Paul, Pete and, to a lesser extent, bassist Stuart Sutcliffe (who, as the edgiest Beatle, would swap dark, fringe clothing with his German fiancée) followed suit.

Word got to Harrison's family back home of his penchant for struttin' cowboy chic and it motivated his dear mom to launch a trans-Atlantic search for her son's teenage style fetish.

While Harrison was in Hamburg in the fall of 1960, his mother Louise, who supported and encouraged her youngest son to learn the guitar, set off to Canada on an extended trip to visit her brother and daughter, both of whom moved to Ontario separately in the 1950s. It was while in a northern community near Kirkland Lake, Ontario, visiting with her daughter Louise, son-in-law Gordon Caldwell and her grandchildren (George Harrison's Canadian-born niece and nephew), that Hemmingsen asserts the elder Louise purchased local boots for her son George.

There is no preponderance of evidence to confirm where exactly the senior Louise bought the boots for her Beatle son. One source suggests Harrison's boots were bought at Bill's Men's Wear of Kirkland Lake but in checking with the now Timmins, Ontario-based family of the late proprietor William Zapotochny, his haberdashery did not open until 1969 and that leads to a conclusion that Louise Sr. bought them elsewhere while visiting Ontario—either at another store in Kirkland Lake (the nearest city to her daughter's home in North Virginiatown) or while visiting her brother and his family in the Toronto area.

Meanwhile during all the goings-on in Ontario with the Harrison family, back in Hamburg in late 1960 The Beatles were declared undesirable aliens and landed in a world of trouble with all but George briefly put in jail for a variety of youthful misdemeanors and contractual disputes.

With his mates sorting out their messes with West German authorities, a broke and solitary Harrison lugged his worldly possessions and sailed the North Sea by way of Holland to the English coast before at long last arriving in Liverpool, only to learn his mother was still in Canada.

By December his band mates reunited in Liverpool and The Beatles returned to local stages with a vengeance having used their intense playing schedule in Hamburg to showcase their improved sound and image. Upon her return from Canada in spring of 1961, Louise Harrison presented her son a pair of Canadian-made, kick-ass, pointy-toed, half-calf length black leather boots with overlaid white flaming brushstrokes running vertical from top to ankle.

By April 1961, on the promise of good behavior and following a flurry of bi-lateral wheeling and dealing for renewed travel documents, The Beatles returned to Hamburg with Harrison sporting the gift from Canada on each foot. Hemmingsen tells us the Canadian boots impressed Lennon and McCartney enough that they sought a Hamburg boot maker to create a copycat pair for each of them.[24]

In a photo of Harrison, McCartney and Lennon on the roof of the Top Ten, Harrison's boots bare a distinctive, possibly made-in-Canada style compared to the locally-made facsimiles worn by the others.

The decision to source quasi-matching boots might not have been theirs alone since, before Brian Epstein entered their lives, the boys were also getting their styling clues from their German muse, Astrid Kirchherr. The Hamburg artist and photographer was a Beatles friend and engaged to Scottish-born Sutcliffe, who left the band in July 1961 to pursue painting, but died in 1962; Kirchherr died in 2020.

If the shock-and-awe of Harrison's flashy Canadian boots gave Lennon and McCartney a touch of boot envy, they certainly took it to the next level later that same year as while en route back to Liverpool after a vacation in Paris, they held over in London on a shopping trip.

It was there, perhaps while ogling guitars at music shops along Charing Cross Road, that they visited a shoe store called Anello & Davide and spotted what were known as Chelsea boots—snug fitting, above-ankle Spanish-style boots with smooth leather uppers, and sharp pointed toe with either elastic or zipped side gussets. Aha! Now was their opportunity to best Harrison's monopoly on cool boots. They ordered four pairs—one each for themselves, Harrison and Best—with low Cuban heels "to complement their new suit image upon their return to Hamburg."[25]

The band's boot obsession seems to owe at least some of its inspiration to the flashy Canadian pair Harrison donned in Hamburg in 1961 that were so admired by the other Beatles.

The whole boot episode and timeline is enough to consider that maybe, just maybe, the genesis of what was to become a global style trend in the 1960s called the Beatle Boot occurred in the northern or southern Ontario places where Harrison's mother lived for five months.

Whatever the origins, the Beatle Boot has been famously worn by The Rolling Stones (although they opted for taller heels), The Monkees, Elvis Presley, James Brown, Roy Orbison, Jimi Hendrix, The Doors, Bob Dylan and Andy Warhol to name a few.

Mississauga's Dorothy (Rhone) Becker

If ever a near miss that could have changed the course of The Beatles' (and world) history, it involved Liverpool-born bank clerk Dorothy Rhone, who has lived in Canada for the past 57 years. She was McCartney's serious girlfriend during his Quarry Men and Beatles days. They met in 1959 when Dot, as she was known, was 16 and McCartney was playing at the Casbah Coffee Club, a bar and performance venue in the remodeled basement of Pete Best's mother's home. By February 1961, two years into their romance, Dot became pregnant and, with the support and blessing of McCartney's widower father, she and Paul became engaged and they decided to get married.

But wedding bells were soon silenced as Dot miscarried. And while they continued their relationship for a short while—she even visited her fiancé during The Beatles' run in Hamburg, things eventually fizzled, and with some biographers suggesting McCartney's sexual escapades in West Germany being the catalyst for the break-up. "I could see that Paul was growing away from me. I knew what was coming. All these years he had been having his bits on the side and it was getting so easy for him. He was young and he couldn't resist," she once said.[26]

Disillusioned and seeking a fresh start—and now rid of the gold engagement ring McCartney had purchased in Hamburg—Dot moved to Canada in 1964 where she found emotional sanctuary, married, and became Dorothy Becker and has lived happily ever after in Mississauga, Ontario.

Many have speculated on whether The Beatles would have gone on to fame and fortune had she become the first Mrs. McCartney and the couple would go about their new and unchartered roles as teenage parents. Could half of the Lennon-McCartney songwriting team have continued had 17-year-old Paul become a husband and father? One could argue it would, given John's leap to parenthood when Julian was born to him and Cynthia Powell in 1963, but McCartney and Rhone's relationship was earlier, and certainly before Beatlemania had really gathered steam.

Do the math. Had the two followed their intended marital trajectory and raised a family, some of McCartney's greatest compositions for later-in-life muses like Jane Asher (fiancée), and wives Linda Eastman, Heather Mills and Nancy Shevell might have never been written, including "And I Love Her", "You Won't See Me", "Every Little Thing", "I'm Looking Through You", "We Can Work it Out", "Here, There and Everywhere", "For No One", "Two of Us", "Maybe I'm Amazed", "The Lovely Linda", "My Love", "Heather" and the more recent "My Valentine" for Nancy, to name a few.

A few years after Rhone's arrival in Canada, a Beatle would be barreling through a Canadian winter in a snowmobile not far from where she lived. You'll learn later of Lennon's time on a 20-acre farm in Mississauga, Ontario. He and Rhone were friends; in fact Rhone and John's first wife Cynthia (remember her mom Lillian Powell lived in Toronto) were inseparable during their Liverpool youth and even lived together for a while.

There are at least two reports swirling that Cynthia Lennon may have reunited with Dorothy Rhone Becker in Toronto in June 1994. Lennon was in the city—coincidentally with original Beatle drummer Pete Best—to participate in a celebration of the popular *1050 CHUM* radio show *Breakfast with The Beatles*. In the days before satellite radio and podcasts, morning segments featuring exclusively Beatles music were fixtures on many FM and AM radio stations across North America.

While in town, Lennon took the opportunity to meet-up with Rhone Becker—a Canadian reunion of Liverpool friends that was decades in the making. More than a social call, Lennon was somehow in possession of the engagement ring McCartney had bought his first true love back in Hamburg, likely in 1960. Rhone Becker graciously received the golden symbol of McCartney's long-ago commitment to her from Lennon's first wife after some 30 years.

By all accounts Rhone Becker has lived a quiet, anonymous life in Canada. It appears the man she met and married in Canada was from the motor trade. During his career, Werner Becker supplied bearings for the auto industry in southwestern Ontario; the two have raised three Canadian daughters and are now grandparents. For a while there was intense curiosity about Rhone Becker's life in Canada with several unsuccessful attempts by reporters and biographers to locate her.

Apparently she and McCartney did remain in contact. During a Wings stopover in Toronto in May 1976 for a concert at Maple Leaf Gardens, McCartney tactfully arranged limo service for her and her family to attend his show.

Beatles historians often point to an endless array of events and timing situations that, if even slightly altered or missed, could have denied the world The Beatles. Rhone Becker is just one example. As for Canada, the band's early success could have been significantly delayed if not for the fine orchestration of things by a pair of Pauls and a Trudy.

Canada's Connections to the term "Beatlemania"

Ringo, John and Paul at Toronto Airport, 1964. The first album issued by The Beatles in North America occurred a year earlier in Canada: *Beatlemania! With The Beatles*. Archives of Ontario (licensed under CC BY-NC 2.0).

There exist several claims on the first use of the term "Beatlemania" although among the more widely accepted versions occurred in Dundee, Scotland on October 7, 1963. It was there that booking agent and dance-hall promoter Andi Lothian hosted The Beatles. Lothian partnered with promoter Albert Bonici of Inverness to bring The Beatles to Caird Hall in Dundee, north of Edinburgh.

During one of the Dundee concerts, the hysterical, mostly female audience rushed the stage. A reporter with *Radio Scotland* turned to Lothian and asked, "for goodness sake Andi, what's happening?" to which he famously said, "Don't worry, it's only Beatlemania."[1]

Now to our Canuck connection: To secure The Beatles in Scotland, Bonici negotiated with booking agency Cana Variety, established in 1952 by London, Ontario-born jazz musician Jack Fallon. Fallon, who was with the Royal Canadian Air Force and remained in England after World War II, cleared the way for The Beatles to play in Dundee where Lothian is said to have first used the term. Fallon would remarkably become the rarest of Canadians by notching a second, entirely unrelated link to The Beatles five years later when he played on the *White Album*.

Like a westward ocean current, the term "Beatlemania" would make its way to Canada where Capitol Records of Canada, an enlightened and daring organization with remarkable autonomy despite its foreign ownership, would name the first album issued by The Beatles in North America, *Beatlemania! With The Beatles.* The Beatles' debut album cover featured the four iconic photos of their faces in shadow along with excerpts from two Canadian media sources, *Canadian Press* (correspondent Alan Harvey) and the *Ottawa Journal*, as well as *Newsweek* and *Time*.

The *Ottawa Journal* excerpt originated from a November 9, 1963 article by music reporter Sandy Gardiner wherein he used wildly sensational language to inform an unsuspecting readership of a new contagion sweeping the world called "Beatlemania", colouring the piece with a selection of medical metaphors and naming a pair of characters from American TV medical dramas to make his point.

Ottawa's John Whelan posted the article on the website *beatles. ncf.ca*. Here's a taste of the Gardiner story under the headline "Heavy Disc Dose Spreads Disease in England":

A new disease is sweeping through Britain, Europe and the Far East ... and doctors are powerless to stop it. The name of this new addition to the world of the Ben Casey's and Doc Kildare's is— BEATLEMANIA. Most of the victims have fallen prey to Beatlemania by desire ... and the majority of them are teenagers. What is it then that a jag from a hypodermic needle or a long hospital confinement can't stop? Beatlemania first started to spread 10 months ago in Liverpool, England, when a new group, The Beatles, hit the public with their first disc dose. At first it dazed the public, then with their second waxing The Beatles knocked them out. The disc—'Please Please Me'—written by two of the Liverpoplians zoomed to the top of the charts in Britain as fast as an injection takes effect.[2]

Capitol Canada plucked these words from Gardiner's full article for the cover of the Canada-only pressing of The Beatles' first North American album *Beatlemania! With The Beatles*:

"The newspapers say ... A new disease is sweeping through Britain ... and doctors are powerless to stop it ... it's Beatlemania! This Liverpool group play to packed houses wherever they go ... Sandy Gardiner."[2]

2

1962 TO 1967

The Beatles' Early Conquest of Canada

Fueling Fan Hysteria: One day before the debut show of their 1964 North American
Tour, The Beatles got their first true taste of fan and media hysteria in Manitoba
during a Winnipeg fuel stop. Photo by David Bonner, Winnipeg Free Press.

In the early 1960s the business and marketing behavior of Capitol Records, a subsidiary of Electric and Musical Industries, or EMI, of the UK, differed vastly between its Canadian and American offices; some might say the division north of the border was more daring and imaginative.

Capitol Records of Canada had significant autonomy and made its own decisions about The Beatles' records. And while not immediately apparent, through its tactics Capitol Canada gave the nation of (then) only 18 million people an early foothold on Beatlemania.

Around the 50th anniversary of The Beatles' arrival in the United States, *Forbes.com* contributor John Covach played myth buster in a February 7, 2014, article entitled "Five Common Myths About The Beatles U.S. Invasion." First among these is the perception that "I Want to Hold Your Hand" was the first Beatles single released by Los Angeles-based Capitol Records in North America.

"It is true that this song was the first released by Capitol *in the US*. (Chicago-based record label) Vee Jay released 'Please Please Me' and 'From Me To You' and (Philadelphia label) Swan in the US released 'She Loves You' when Capitol rejected them. But Capitol Canada released all three of these songs plus 'Love Me Do.' These first three Canadian singles did very poorly, seemingly confirming the Capitol US decision; 'She Loves You,' on the other hand, did very well up north, prompting sales of the previous releases in its wake. "She Loves You" was a hit in Canada … before 'I Want To Hold Your Hand' was released in the US."[27]

The point is Capitol US wouldn't touch Beatles songs during the band's breakthrough in the UK, raising the temperature on what was already a tense relationship since the American company was bought by EMI in 1956. The Beatles were essentially caught in the crosshairs of trans-Atlantic corporate infighting. However, Capitol's Canadian arm (also owned by EMI) was more receptive and pursued, at least in the short team, a different strategy.

The scenario laid down Beatles roots in Canada much earlier, producing at first a modest and later a groundswell of support for Beatles music—something not lost on the boys and their management team that would manifest itself in a special relationship with Canada.

So what was going on at Capitol Canada that it provided a steady flow of Beatles releases in Canada while its US sister company looked the other way, offering distribution and sales rights of early Beatles singles to lesser labels?

Was Canada's earlier adoption of The Beatles simply an exercise in trial and error on the part of Capitol or were there underlying conditions such as Canada's membership in the British Commonwealth— the so-called imperial family of nations that still exists but whose relevance has dwindled? Perhaps a bit of both, but what's clear is that the Canadian company didn't simply sit on the sidelines while the big boys argued.

Beatles historians point to Paul White, the artist and repertoire (A&R) executive at Capitol Canada for being "the man who first brought The Beatles' music to Canada—a year before America embraced Beatlemania," wrote the *Globe and Mail's* Nicholas Jennings in White's obituary when he passed away on March 13, 2018.[28]

After seeing a promotional film about life in Canada, White left his native England in 1957 to continue his career as a journalist in Canada. But the journalism dream was quashed by an immediate need to earn a living so he found himself working in shipping and receiving doors at Capitol Records in Toronto.

White's responsibilities soon moved from the warehouse to Capitol's front office and, in late 1962, he was made aware that a very new and marketable sound was emanating from Liverpool when he heard "Love Me Do" (B-side "P.S. I Love You") for the first time. It was The Beatles first UK hit when it was released there in October of that year. White's new job was to find international songs that had potential in Canada and, as a result, Capitol Records released "Love Me Do" in Canada on February 18, 1963. The 45 rpm singles bore the familiar yellow and orange swirl design and, in small white typeface curving upward along the bottom of the label ran: "Mfd. in Canada by Capitol Records of Canada, Ltd."

To say the Great White North's response to White's discovery was lukewarm would be kind as "Love Me Do" sold a total of 170 copies! But he persevered, convincing Capitol Canada to later release "Please Please Me/Ask Me Why" (April 1, 1963) and "From Me to You/ Thank You Girl" (June 17, 1963); again, both received very limited radio airplay and didn't exactly shake the foundations of pop music or AM radio in Canada.

Despite swinging and missing on three-straight pitches, White didn't concede and remained steadfast in the batter's box. He swung on a fourth pitch called "She Loves You/I'll Get You" on September 16, 1963, and launched a direct hit.

"It went berserk," White told *Postmedia* in 2014.[29] "She Loves You" raced to the top of the Canadian charts, occupying the number one spot for nine weeks and all this five months before The Beatles' break-through appearance on *The Ed Sullivan Show*. The song was originally played on *CKWS* radio in Kingston, Ontario, a top-40 station that derived its call letters from the city's local daily, the *Kingston Whig-Standard*, and eventually got mass-market air play in Toronto on *1050 CHUM*, landing squarely on its influential music chart.

Reaching number one with "She Loves You" was a coup for White and Capitol Canada as a single, but what of The Beatles' albums? And there lay another plan that initially distinguished the company from its American counterpart: White compiled and packaged several Canada-only albums by the Fab Four. In doing so, White mimicked the playbook of Capitol in the UK whereby he would assemble Beatles 45 rpm singles and strategically package them as albums. In those days, albums weren't conceptual narratives or themes or held together by any particular event; as The Beatles' producer George Martin acknowledged, "we weren't thinking in terms of albums back then ... we would record singles."[30]

In Canada, White's efforts at bundling singles produced three superb album releases over a span of some five months:

1. *Beatlemania! With The Beatles* was a 14-song album including "All My Loving", "Please Mr. Postman" and "Money", released

on November 25, 1963, and it became the first Beatles album issued in North America.

2. *Twist and Shout* had 15 songs, including chart-toppers "Please Please Me", "Love Me Do", "From Me To You", "PS I Love You", "Twist And Shout" and "She Loves You", and was released February 3, 1964.

3. *Long Tall Sally* came out on April 27, 1964, with 12 songs including "I Want To Hold Your Hand", "I Saw Her Standing There" and "This Boy".

White's visionary approach, and the Canadian label's confidence in his abilities, gave Canadian fans a head start with broader distribution of Beatles songs on radio and on store shelves and are the reasons Beatles albums took on a unique look and made-in-Canada song list from 1963 until *Revolver* was released in the summer of 1966.

His efforts to give The Beatles a market profile in Canada were aided and abetted on the outside by a Toronto high school student named Trudy Medcalf who founded what would briefly become the largest Beatles Fan Club in the world.

Film and music editor Bill Wyman (no, not *that* Bill Wyman!) is downright critical in his assessment of Capitol Records in the United States, suggesting the risk averse, giant record label was late to the party and tossed Beatles songs over the fence for others to release: "A determinedly buffoonish series of steps by EMI's US arm, Capitol Records, led to The Beatles' work being released on a variety of labels Stateside, all of them licensed, you might say, for a song. "She Loves You," for example, came out here on an unknown label called Swan. And when, in April 1964, The Beatles achieved the unthinkable— holding down the top five spots on the U.S pop charts—no fewer than four different labels had a piece of the pie."[31]

In 2011, Mary-Lu Zahalan became the first to graduate from the world's only degree program based on the study of The Beatles at Liverpool Hope University. Zahalan, who was originally from Renfrew, Ontario, and grew up in the Lake Ontario city of Oakville, completed an 18-month Master's degree program called *The Beatles, Popular Music and Society.*

The thesis of the Canadian professor, singer and actor explored the question of why and how The Beatles took off in Canada before they did in the United States. Part of Zahalan's general assertion included this: "Because of the British roots in Canada, we were kind of pre-programmed to accept The Beatles, and we did so a full year earlier than our US neighbours," she said. "I looked at British immigration statistics, and just the fact that we still had the Queen on our currency, and our mailboxes looked like British mailboxes. There's just a British sensibility woven into our society that I think made us really receptive."[32]

Zahalan is now among Canada's truest Beatles scholars and was one of only 12 full-time students in the initial graduating year for the course when it debuted in 2009. While the Liverpool Hope program has since been removed from the university's curriculum, another Master's degree initiative, *The Beatles: Music Industry and Heritage,* has sprung up at the University of Liverpool. Leading the new Master's program in Liverpool is Dr. Holly Tessler, an American academic with Canadian roots: Her family emigrated to Canada in the early 20th century and her grandfather was raised in Winnipeg.

Canadian Fan Club Soared to Number One

Early Beatles fans in Toronto and throughout Canada were likely familiar with the aforementioned Trudy Medcalf. Born in England in 1949, the Scarborough, Ontario, teenager showed remarkable and savvy organization and promotion skills to establish the first Beatles Fan Club in North America in September 1963—the Ontario Chapter—and was duly rewarded for her efforts and those of her fan club colleagues with several face-to-face meetings with The Beatles, including spending time with them on the eve of their second 1964 *Ed Sullivan Show* appearance in New York.

Medcalf's Beatles fandom began at age 14, when her cousin took her to a Beatles show in the seaside town of Margate in July 1963 while she was visiting family in the southeast of England. Smitten by the Fab Four, upon returning to Canada the Midland Avenue High School student contacted Beatles Fan Club central in London and was given the green light to begin a fan base in Canada, likely by Freda Kelly, the 18-year-old secretary to Brian Epstein and president of The Beatles Fan Club in the UK.

Fan response to her efforts was swift and sustained and soon Medcalf recognized she could not keep up with the volumes of membership requests from the confines of her suburban bedroom and kitchen. So she decided to seek out a media sponsor and approached *1050 CHUM*, one of Toronto's fledgling pop radio stations. *CHUM* embraced the young fan's initiative by providing office space to run the fan club and also gave Medcalf a Beatles radio program that she would tape at the station every Friday after school. Her radio outreach helped grow the band's popularity and soon thousands of fan letters began arriving at the radio station.

She handled her celebrity well, making appearances in parades, television programs, posing for photos with the band, media interviews and even signed autographs at *CHUM* events. By the time The Beatles arrived in Canada in August 1964, her club membership was over 50,000 from across the country, briefly eclipsing even the original fan club in the United Kingdom to become the largest in the world.

Medcalf remained the head of the fan club for about 18 months and was credited with signing-up 90,000 members across Canada before retiring at the ripe age of 16.

A life-long educator, Medcalf taught school, was a grief counselor and, later, earned a PhD in gerontology, the seed for which she admits was sown during her time at The Beatles Fan Club—basically following the mental and physical progress of those young fans as they became older adults. A leading social gerontologist, Dr. Medcalf lives in Ottawa.

Razzle Dazzle: Michelle Finney, host of the *CBC* kid's program *Razzle Dazzle*, meets The Beatles in Toronto, 1964. Photo by *Toronto Telegram* (York University Libraries, Clara Thomas Archives & Special Collections, fonds ASC02024).

Ottawa's Paul Anka Played Beatles Matchmaker

Long before Avril Lavigne, Justin Bieber and Shawn Mendes, Canada's original teen idol was Paul Anka. Born in Ottawa in 1941, the singing and songwriting Anka was a global sensation with hits like "Diana" which he wrote about his first crush at age 15 and recorded in 1957. It reached number one on the music charts in Canada, Australia, Belgium, the Netherlands, the United Kingdom and the United States.

"Diana" was followed by "Lonely Boy", "Teddy", "Put Your Head on My Shoulder" and by the early 1960s with hit singles and starring roles in films, Anka became Canada's greatest musical export just barely out of his teens. If he were playing hockey instead, and The Beatles' game-winning goal was their breakthrough in the United

States, then the young Canadian singer earned a primary assist important enough to take a place in The Beatles' history.

A gig at the historic Olympia Hall in Paris in early 1964 put young Anka at destiny's door with The Beatles. Anka, who had been performing at the Olympia since he was 17, recalled seeing The Beatles for the first time. Apart from four shows in Sweden, The Beatles had not played outside the United Kingdom until their successful three-week run in France's capital. Anka was mightily impressed and got to know the band, spending time with them backstage in Paris, and also in London.

For Anka, The Beatles' path to international success would be a no brainer: "One evening I walked into the Olympia … and I saw a shocking sight I'll never forget. A British rock and roll group was on stage, they were the opening act but they were phenomenal. They had a whole look: the guitars, the songs, the hair. I was stunned … just to hear this new sound, you sat there and went 'Holy shit! What is this?'"[33]

Anka said he got to know The Beatles and enjoyed his time with McCartney best because the bassist was talkative, forthcoming and very curious, wanting to learn more about the music scene in Canada and The United States. In the early 1960s media coverage and communications between the continents was slower and less reliable. But more to the point, Americans may have considered their music to be inherently superior:

> I had discovered them just as they were discovering us, but the thing is, Americans hadn't really caught up. We weren't living in the glare of the media, like we do today. I'd come home with these (Beatles) records and they'd say … 'Who were they guys? Whaddaya, crazy? … Nobody's interested!'… But that was just part and parcel of American insularity.[34]

Anka became an advocate for The Beatles—a Canadian in the role of Mop Top Emissary—and claims he went to work promoting the band with his management company, General Artists Corp. (GAC).

Anka asserts he tipped off his agent, the influential Norman Weiss, and events began to unfold quickly. Weiss flew to England to meet with Brian Epstein while GAC's Sid Bernstein, who would go on to become a legendary music promoter, pursued a deal for The Beatles to play at New York's Carnegie Hall. While there were many more pieces and persons in the puzzle that secured The Beatles' break-out performances on the *Ed Sullivan Show*, including Sullivan's European talent scout Peter Prichard, Anka's agency played a key role in landing The Beatles' historic debut in the United States in February 1964.

Remarkably, the tenacity of a young Canadian singer helped in no small way to launch The Beatles outside of Europe and, by a long extension, the heralded British Invasion of North America that followed. Cutting through American obstinacy proved for Anka to be a selfless act as that same invasion took away record sales from established recording artists like he and other fledgling 1960s Canadian acts such as Gordon Lightfoot. Anka would eventually recover, relaunching his career by penning the lyrics to "My Way" for Frank Sinatra in 1969 and making huge recording comebacks in the 1970s and 1990s.

The Legend of Barefoot Bruce Decker's Daring Winnipeg Dash

All the local hype, airplay, fan club support and Paul Anka notwithstanding, the first two visits to Canada by The Beatles or individual band members were nothing more than fuel stops. In May 1964, John and George set off on an ambitious vacation with partners Cynthia and Pattie. The flight itinerary for their Tahiti destination included London to Amsterdam to Vancouver to Honolulu before reaching their South Pacific island vacation spot. Nearing the final leg of their long journey, the couples deplaned in Vancouver for twenty minutes as the aircraft refueled. If there were any Beatle sightings in Vancouver that day, it certainly didn't receive nearly the publicity as another fuel stop three months later.

On August 18, 1964, it would be a massively different outcome at Winnipeg International Airport. Throngs of fans made it to the airport in Manitoba's capital after an Air Canada public relations director tipped off local *Channel 7 TV* personality Bob Burns of the Pan American Lockheed Elektra's imminent stop over, and soon local radio stations blasted the news that The Beatles were coming to town.

That afternoon, the aircraft was inbound from London en route to San Francisco where The Beatles would play the first show of their summer tour of North America the following evening.

On that warm, summer day in Winnipeg The Beatles were stormed by media and some fans at the base of the stairs while the aircraft was being fueled; Burns muscled his way through the bedlam to the Lockheed's air stairs and thrust a microphone in McCartney's face becoming the first journalist to put the band on camera on Canadian soil: "Hello Winnipeg … it's a luverly welcome," the Beatle told him. A few more interviews, including with an acerbic Lennon, took place while perhaps hundreds of screaming fans lined the airport's upper observation deck. What a surreal backdrop it must have seemed to The Beatles when they touched down, but also to the airline crew, airport fuel handlers and a curious nation watching on television later that evening.

The impromptu scrum contained all the choreographic cues of a Brian Epstein initiated publicity opportunity. After perhaps 10 or so uneasy hours in the air, the boys emerged nattily dressed in ties, shirts and blazers stepping off the aircraft together. Epstein could be seen behind them, visibly pleased that something as mundane as a fuel stop in the middle of Canada could garner headlines.

All that frenzy ended in the blink of an eye and after about 35 minutes it was over; that is, except for something that happened moments before the Lockheed's door closed and the aircraft departed for San Francisco.

In the hours leading up to the aircraft's arrival, a 17-year-old guitar-playing Grade 12 student from Silver Heights Collegiate named Bruce Decker was with friends en route to the beach when word arrived on the car radio of The Beatles' impending arrival. In no time, Decker and his friends diverted to Winnipeg International.

Resourceful and determined, Decker made his way past the airport terminal to the apron—the section near the taxiway where passengers walk off the aircraft toward the air bridge when deplaning outdoors.

Watching events unfold during The Beatles' stop-over, Decker was only a couple of dozen metres away and, with airport security considerably less present than today, Decker saw the aircraft door (was still) open and made the quickest decision and perhaps the boldest move of his young life. In bare feet and cut-off jean shorts, he sprinted across the pavement to the Lockheed for a glimpse of The Beatles. Scaling the air stairs just as the aircraft door was closing, Decker was cheered on by the mob and, peering for a moment through the open door, made eye contact with The Beatles until three burly Mounties raced up from behind and grabbed him. They restrained Decker, clutching his flailing limbs, and escorted him down the stairs just as the aircraft door closed behind them.

With all the stories of frenzied Beatle fanaticism around the world, Decker's run would rise to the top. "Decker's Dash" made headlines, including being immortalized with photos in the pages of the *Winnipeg Free Press* newspaper, and is beautifully captured in his own breathless and delirious words on the Manitoba Music Museum website:

> Seizing the moment, he dashed across the runway, some twenty-five yards, to the stairs of the plane. 'Quick thinking, that's all it was,' reflected Decker. 'I just figured I could make it up those (aircraft) steps and I no sooner thought of it and I was gone. The crowd roared when they saw me go. I got right up the stairs before the Mounties grabbed me.'
>
> His impulsive move amused The Beatles. 'Just as they were wrestling with me I caught a glimpse of The Beatles through the door and they were chuckling.' Released by authorities, Decker became the object of instant adulation. 'Kids crowded around me, touching me and screaming. Tears were streaming down their

faces as they asked me: What do they look like? Did they say anything? The girls thought there was some kind of magic about me just because I'd got so close to them.'

Dozens of dazed teens remained behind after the plane was long gone. 'It was a little embarrassing having to tell kids to stop kissing the runway,' commented RCMP Sgt. E. G. Varndell. Others sat on the grass weeping. 'We've never seen anything like this before and I hope we won't see it again.'[35]

And thus was born the legend of barefoot Bruce Decker's daring Winnipeg dash.

Decker's Dash would be legendary enough if it ended on that airport apron, but it didn't. Earlier that same year the young man joined The Deverons, a north Winnipeg rock 'n' roll band that included none other than one of Manitoba's greatest musical sons, Burton Cummings.

In 1964, Winnipeg was both geographically and literally at the centre of Canadian folk rock and in many ways helped to define that sound for a generation. Decker, who was born in Winnipeg in 1946, played rhythm guitar and would perform with Cummings; the two also composed a song together called "Lost Love". By 1965, Cummings left The Deverons to grace The Guess Who with his exquisite vocal and keyboard skills. Decker would rejoin Cummings when he was asked to play with The Guess Who during a tour of Saskatchewan and Alberta, although his time with the soon-to-be-world-famous band lasted only three months.

Decker's older brother, Robert, is a long-time resident of Oakville, Ontario, but with roots firmly planted in Western Canada. He recalls their father, Samuel Morley Decker, played in a band in the small Prairie town of Balcarres in southern Saskatchewan. While raising their children in Winnipeg, Samuel and his wife encouraged them to take piano lessons and, at age 11, Bruce was given an acoustic guitar for Christmas.

"Bruce played in bands in Winnipeg before The Beatles came to prominence so I don't think that The Beatles were the reason Bruce got into playing in bands. The Deverons were, however, really into Gerry and The Pacemakers, and The Who. They opened for several name acts, notably Roy Orbison," Robert Decker recalls.

(As a historical parallel, at the height of their fame The Deverons opened for Roy Orbison at the Winnipeg Auditorium. Like The Deverons, The Beatles also opened for Orbison when they played in England, Wales and Scotland during a 1963 tour).

Robert Decker was studying Chemical Engineering at the University of Alberta in Edmonton during his brother's musical career and at the time of Bruce's dash in Winnipeg.

Decker's Legendary Dash: Making the boldest move of his life, 17-year-old Bruce Decker raced up the air stairs and caught a glimpse of The Beatles in the aircraft before being carted away by RCMP officers at Winnipeg Airport.

"Regrettably I can't recall any in-depth conversations with Bruce about 'Decker's Dash' but I have, over the years, made sure that all his cousins were aware of it. All my relatives across Canada saw the newspapers and photos."

As a young adult, Bruce Decker continued to play the guitar but his life took a meaningful turn when he chose to contribute to two key Canadian historical projects.

Beginning in 1977 and for several years he helped manage the rebuilding of Fort Gibraltar, an early 19th century, pre-Confederation outpost comprised of 12 log buildings where the Red and Assiniboine Rivers meet in what is today known as The Forks of Winnipeg. The outpost served as headquarters for the North West Company—active

"The girls thought there was some kind of magic about me just because I'd got so close to them", he said. Photos by David Bonner, *Winnipeg Free Press*.

in the trading of pemmican, the dried bison meat and lard product that served as sustenance for voyageurs, the boatmen who transported goods and passengers to and from trading posts.

The reconstructed Fort Gibraltar is today at the centre of the largest annual winter festival in Western Canada and includes historical interpretations of Canadian history involving voyageurs, Métis and First Nations people.

Bruce Decker left another important mark on the history of Canada involving the collection and preservation of collodion negatives—derived from an early photographic process invented in 1851 whereby a chemical brew is applied to glass plates to create light-sensitive material that capture images from a camera lens—which he was given in lieu of pay for helping the family living in the former home of late Winnipeg photographer and draftsman Charles Ellis around 1979. The historic trove was discovered in the attic of the home. Ellis was born in England in 1844, came to Canada in 1868 and lived in Ontario and Manitoba until his death in Winnipeg in 1921.

Decker had over 300 collodion "wet plate" negatives and prints depicting some of the earliest images ever recorded of pre-Confederation Canada including early rural settlements, activities and people in Winnipeg and in several central Ontario towns such as Barrie, Bracebridge and Orillia and surrounding areas. For several years his research project took him to places throughout Ontario; he became an expert in the collodion process, printed and sold some of the historic images and, quite directly, added to a nation's history. Among the benefactors of Decker's historic imagery was Winnipeg businessman Maitland Steinkopf who "persuaded banks in Manitoba to display Bruce's photos."

The original wet plates and negatives are now in the possession of official archival departments of the provinces of Ontario and Manitoba—donations by the Decker family. His passions around the preservation of Canadian history are noted by the Archives of Ontario, part of the Ministry of Government and Consumer Services: "Decker spent several years trying to determine who the creator of the negatives was and precisely where the Ontario photographs had been taken; he also researched the collodion wet glass plate process."[36]

Shortly after Decker embarked on his historic quest, The Deverons reunited for a *CBC* television special in 1980. Hosted by Burton Cummings and co-written by Rick Moranis, the part comedy, part biopic hour-long show was named after Canada's most famous street corner, *Portage and Main*. At about mid-point in the special, The Deverons were on stage at St. John's High School in Winnipeg and Cummings took the microphone telling the live crowd "This is an amazing day … we have not played together for almost fifteen years … " and introduced the band: Derek Blake, Ron Savoie, Edd Smith and "on electric guitar and vocals Mr. Bruce Decker."

In August 1986, Decker was visiting a friend in the southeast Winnipeg community of St. Boniface where he was proudly showing-off his new Gibson guitar. His departure home was unexpectedly interrupted when bus service was unavailable for the last leg of the trip so he decided to hitchhike. Decker was unaware the Chrysler that picked him up was driven by an Alberta man who, with his passengers, had been drinking that day. The driver was speeding. A police chase ensued, the car crashed and rolled killing Decker and two other occupants, a young male and female, while the drunk driver at the centre of the tragedy survived.

Bruce Decker was a day shy of his 40th birthday.

"Bruce was a fun-loving, sensitive and easy-going guy. He became a talented musician, had a passion for music and life, and achieved some success in what many consider were two of the best rock 'n' roll bands in Winnipeg at the time—The Deverons and The Guess Who. Later in his professional life as a researcher and craftsman, he left an important legacy to Canada's musical and cultural history; we miss him dearly," said Robert Decker whose son Gregory carries on the family's musical tradition as a jazz Hammond B3 organ player.

The Beatles' Riotous Canadian Debut

Squeeze Play: Little dude peers through a police gauntlet at Maple Leaf Gardens, 1964. The Beatles were virtually unscathed during their two-day stay in Toronto and considered local security arrangements—that at times resembled a military operation—to be top notch. Photo by Joe Black, Graphic Artists.

Four days after their dramatic stop in Winnipeg, The Beatles returned to make their Canadian concert debut in Vancouver at the open-air Empire Stadium on the Pacific National Exhibition grounds. It would be the only venue the band ever played in Canada that wasn't a hockey arena.

Crying and screaming fans, confusing logistics and strained security arrangements were commonplace at Beatles performances during their 1964 tour, but for the band's first Canadian gig on August 22 it was particularly insane. They had played in Seattle the night before and, after nearly arriving in Vancouver, had to turn back to Seattle in mid-air to clear up some border-crossing paper work.

When they finally landed at RCAF Station Sea Island airport in Richmond (today part of Vancouver International Airport), the boys had worked-up an appetite and, during a police escorted tour of Vancouver, they feasted on local 19-cent hamburgers from King's Burgers, before arriving at the concert venue for a news conference.

Reporters gathered in Meeting Room 19 of Empire Stadium and when The Beatles finally arrived they were asked to explain their tardiness to which Lennon quipped Canadian officials would not allow his band in the country until they were deloused!

At nearly 9:30 p.m. with the crowd's anticipation for The Beatles at a blistering pitch (and the main stadium lights were inexplicably turned off), it was up to Vancouver radio personality Red Robinson of *CFUN 1410* to stand under the stage lights and introduce The Beatles for the first time in Canada, even though competing station *CKNW* had negotiated to run the entire 11-song concert live on the radio.

The screaming 20,621 fans made it virtually impossible to hear the opening song "Twist and Shout". And those fans at field level wanted to get closer, unabashedly advancing toward the barricades and tempting police with their intentions. Then the dam burst and fans began storming the stage. It was precarious enough that, for the first time during the tour, the concert was stopped. Robinson returned to the stage just as Harrison's finished singing Chuck Berry's "Roll Over Beethoven" and McCartney had just begun to introduce the next number, "Can't Buy Me Love".

Robinson recalls the mayhem and his attempt at invoking some crowd control at midpoint during the concert: "I walked out on the stage at the end of a number, and said, 'We have to back some people up, there's been two kids crushed already, they'll have to cancel the show, hold it, everybody down, or no show. The Beatles want to perform for you but they can't do it if you don't sit down, so sit down.'"[37]

During his remarks Robinson was approached by an angry Lennon who protested by saying, "Get the fuck off our stage, nobody interrupts The Beatles!"

Robinson maintained his composure knowing his attempt to restore some order had been sanctioned by The Beatles' manager; he turned to Lennon and said "'John, Brian Epstein sent me up here.' And he looked down, and Brian's giving him the 'Hi' sign, meaning let him do it, and he goes, 'Okay, carry on mate.'"

(Lennon's comments were retold by Robinson and not captured on any microphone but, at their next stop at Los Angeles' Hollywood Bowl, he could be heard asserting his leadership on stage telling a spotlight operator to "go away with that light will ya" and then "thank you" when his wish came true.)

But things only worsened. As The Beatles played on, the stadium lights were turned on revealing with clarity the mayhem under way, including many dozens of injuries and St. John Ambulance crews moving about dealing with hysterical and fainting fans.

Embedded with The Beatles during the North American tour was Larry Kane, news director at Miami's *WFUN* radio station. In the 2016 Grammy-winning Ron Howard documentary *Eight Days a Week*, Kane saw firsthand the inherent risks when out-of-control fans collide with overwhelmed security arrangements. Witness to the mania in the preceding three cities of San Francisco, Las Vegas and Seattle, he had this to say after the band's first Canadian concert: "Four cities later in Vancouver, British Columbia seven thousand kids rushed the stage … none of the police in any of these cities was prepared for this … no one was prepared for this."[38]

The Vancouver chaos also got the attention of the entertainment newspaper *Variety* which reported 160 concertgoers were treated for injury and distress.

The Beatles performed five of the six remaining songs on their set list as the escalating breach in on-field security put a premature end to their first show in Canada. Like something akin to a rescue mission, four Cadillac limousines and 15 police motorcycles roared onto the field, scurrying The Beatles out of the Pacific National Exhibition grounds for a slick and abrupt exit straight to the airport for a flight to Los Angeles.

The band's earsplitting, at times frightening, and unforgettable debut in Canada would nearly establish an attendance record for any concert in The Beatles' 32-shows-in-33-days 1964 invasion of 24 cities in North America: Vancouver's 20,621 attendance was second only to the estimated 23,000 fans who attended the desegregated show at Jacksonville's Gator Bowl Stadium on September 11, 1964.

The near-record ticket sales in Vancouver should not have come as a surprise to The Beatles and its management as they were keenly aware of Canada's disproportionate (to population) fan base. For a time, the Canadian chapter of The Beatles Fan Club had the world's largest membership at 50,000, some 500 more members than the next largest chapter, that being the United Kingdom.[39]

It's unlikely though that William Littler counted himself among the 50,000. The *Vancouver Sun*'s classical music reviewer was given the assignment to cover the show—either a bold move by the *Sun*'s assignment desk or, more likely, the fact that in those days there really weren't rock or pop music reviewers on staff at daily newspapers so the job fell on Littler. With the Vancouver concert lasting less than their fuel stop in Winnipeg (inclusive of Decker's Dash) four days earlier, it set Littler off on a tangent and his piece included this memorable summary: "Seldom in Vancouver's entertainment history have so many paid so much for so little";[40] apparently the comment so enraged local fans that the *Sun* was overwhelmed with letters of complaint.

Two weeks later, after playing 10 shows in the United States, The Beatles re-crossed the border for two shows each in Toronto on September 7, and September 8 in Montréal. Before each afternoon and evening show, four opening acts warmed up the crowd, including the soulful Righteous Brothers.

In Toronto, the police security plan for The Beatles was significant and comparatively effective; apart from McCartney's shirt being torn by an overzealous fan and reports of dozens of young girls treated for fainting and hysteria, the Toronto shows perhaps demonstrated the best security arrangement experienced by The Beatles in Canada.

For instance, the task of getting The Beatles 1.6 km from the back door of their King Edward Hotel to Maple Leaf Gardens, the storied, 33-year-old hockey rink that was home to the Toronto Maple Leafs, included a structured plan where most of the driving route was cordoned off in advance and a massive police presence kept the band's commute to and from the concert venue relatively open and safe.

At the venue, an estimated 4,000 police officers and Mounties were on duty, and a five-block surrounding area was sectioned off for 12 hours before the group's arrival. That equates to about one police officer for every nine Beatles fans given that a total of 35,522 screamers attended both Toronto shows.

The Toronto security planning stood out as top-notch. In the melee of The Beatles' pre-show news conference, an unidentified reporter's on-camera interview included a question about their safety while in the city:

> **Reporter:** Ringo, how was that drive in from the airport?

> **Starr:** Very good, one of the best actually … It was well organized by the police, you know.

Nine days earlier in New York City a fan lunged toward Starr and ripped the lucky St. Christopher gold necklace from his neck sending him into a funk of unhappiness. It's no wonder that he seemed keen to answer questions about security at the many venues the band played and offer due credit when warranted.

In the same interview Harrison was asked about Canada and, typical of the understated Beatle, didn't mention his uncle and cousins living a short distance away nor his family's roots in the country or even his teenage flirtation with someday living there:

> **Reporter**: What is your impression of Canada?

> **Harrison**: It's very nice. Yeah. I like it.

> **Reporter**: When you are finished touring around the country as a Beatle (have) you given any thoughts to

perhaps using a few of those shekels you've earned to come back and perhaps see the cities you've been in?

Harrison: Yeah probably, but we haven't made any plans so far. We'll wait until that happens and then we'll start arranging what we're going to do.

Lennon took a more direct approach on a similar question: "We've come here to do a tour and work. We're not here to sight see or see buildings … "[41]

If by now you get the impression the news media had little idea what to make of Beatlemania apart from supporting the hype, you would be correct. Where was the journalism? Why wasn't Starr asked a follow-up question, as in, "What made the Toronto police security plan better than in other cities?" Or, "Do you feel your security needs are not met elsewhere?"

During that tour, it was rare for The Beatles to be asked thought-provoking questions about anything, such as their creative process, inspirations, musicality or the years of training that got them to stardom. At times it seemed their hair was being interviewed, not the talented musicians and songwriters attached to it. A close second to questions about their hair was the ubiquitous media fascination of their longevity as a band. Imagine for a moment being in your early 20s and finally tasting fame after a long slog of playing dirty cellars, dance halls and seedy bars only to be incessantly asked when the bubble would burst! It probably came down to the fact that Canadian newspapers and radio stations saw The Beatles as a novelty act; a shallow, flash-in-the-pan fad that soon would pass, and therefore assigned the wrong kind of reporter to cover their media briefings.

Which brings us to Ivor Davis, a former journalist with London's *Daily Express*. While promoting his 2014 book *The Beatles and Me on Tour*, he was offered an opinion about the woeful and clumsy job reporters were doing covering The Beatles while, by contrast, there seemed a much better alignment when the band traded banter and questions with, say, non-reporters like disc jockeys: "I think one reason The Beatles preferred talking to DJs was because the newspaper journalists were so square. The music writers were jazz guys who hated rock 'n' roll or news guys who didn't have a clue. So you got some strange press conferences."

Davis was asked to describe some:

> Every city we went to, within an hour, there was a press conference. Most of these people didn't know rock 'n' roll. They were thrown into it. You show up in Toronto and you've been there for one minute and a guy says, 'Well, John, how do you like the women in Toronto?' And John says, 'How could I know the women in Toronto?' They managed to get through those press conferences because they were very funny. If you remember the movie, *A Hard Day's Night*, I think somebody says to George, 'How did you find America?' and he says, 'We turned left at Greenland.' The press conferences were ludicrous. Not only did they have writers who knew nothing about rock 'n' roll, but they brought in prizewinners from fan mags and they were sometimes allowed to ask a question. So it was a total unprofessional masquerade.[42]

In Toronto, local disc jockey Jay Nelson, whose real name was Frank Coxe, introduced The Beatles at the Gardens, likely impersonating Ed Sullivan's roar of "Ladies and Gentlemen, The Beatles!" Nelson, who at the end of his career would be recognized by the Rock and Roll Hall of Fame, gave the familiar introduction at all future appearances by The Beatles in Toronto.

Terry Ott, a freelance journalist from Hamilton, Ontario, was nine when he attended The Beatles' first Toronto appearance, the 5:30 p.m. matinee show on September 7. The tickets for the sold-out show were courtesy of his grandmother who had secured three tickets for her grandson at $3.50 each, a bargain compared to the $5.25 general admission cost to see the band in Vancouver earlier in the tour. He wrote of it on his blog:

Calm and Cool: A rare camera position captures Paul and George, at ages 22 and 21, taking the extreme heat and concert madness in stride during one of The Beatles' two August 1964 shows at Maple Leaf Gardens. Photo by *Toronto Telegram* (York University Libraries, Clara Thomas Archives & Special Collections, fonds ASC29608).

It was Labour Day Monday … at least 85 degrees and muggy in Toronto. Maple Leaf Gardens (had) no air conditioning. It was really just a sweatbox that day, but I think we barely noticed. Our seats were a long way from the stage, and only bits and pieces of the 22-minute concert (where they played a standard 12 songs) were audible … The screaming was so loud my ears rang for at least two days, and the thousands of flashbulbs going off all concert long were hard on even young eyes.[43]

And as if to continue William Littler's theme of morning-after wry headline humour, the *Toronto Star* saw The Beatles' Labour Day concerts this way: "34,000 Beatles fans pay $100,000 to hear themselves."[44]

Janette Bertrand and The Beatles' Québec Reality Check

One and Done: The Beatles' first and only appearance in Montréal consisted of two shows in 1964. Neither show was a sell out, although the boys—especially John—learned a thing or two about Québec's unique place in Canada. Image from Bradford's Timeline Photos.

The next stop was Montréal where The Beatles would play two shows at the city's main hockey venue and home of the legendary Montréal Canadiens, The Forum. As was typical, between shows The Beatles and manager Epstein hosted a media conference. While most of the questions were the predictable fan fodder about girlfriends and love interests, favourite this and favourite that, a local reporter rose above the din.

Journalist Janette Bertrand raised her hand, was acknowledged by Epstein, and asked, "Were The Beatles aware the majority of their Montréal fans (this) evening would be French speaking?"

Lennon was known for providing honest (infused with frequent doses of sarcastic) responses to the media but before he or any of The Beatles could respond, an overly sensitive Epstein—perhaps sensing some fear of a political fracas—quickly dismissed the reporter's query and said, "next question"; as interview responses go, a rude second cousin to "no comment."

Bertrand re-told the Epstein snub to *Le Journal de Montréal* and her interview included a rarely discussed vignette of a personal moment she had with Lennon. Here's how Bertrand described what happened when the media conference ended: "I felt a hand on my shoulder. I turned around and it was John Lennon. He asked me what was going on and I explained to him that he was in Québec," she says believing The Beatles had no idea where they were at this point on their tour. "It pissed me off that everything was done in English, like we didn't exist."[45]

Lennon responded in his broken French and that small gesture seemed to amuse Bertrand who saw it as an opportunity to give the Beatle a brief review of the complex history of her province. The encounter seemed to have an effect on Lennon and the band for when they got up on stage for their second (and final) Montréal show evening they said "*bonsoir*" to the crowd.

Bertrand took credit for The Beatles' simple but courteous nod to the Francophone audience that evening at The Forum. Bertrand, who was born in 1925, began her career on radio and in the early days of television. Her popular advice column for *Le Petit Journal* newspaper from 1950 to 1967 would be a stepping-stone to a decorated career as a journalist, feminist, author, and television drama writer, producer, and human rights advocate.

In 1992, Bertrand was made a Knight of the Ordre national du Québec followed by Governor General's Performing Arts Award in 2000 and an Officer of the Order of Canada in 2002.

At the same media event, another strong question asked by an unknown reporter queried why other Canadian cities weren't considered for Beatles concerts:

> **Reporter:** Would The Beatles like to appear in other cities here in Canada ... not only Montréal, Vancouver and Toronto ...
>
> **Lennon:** We'll appear anywhere where there's enough people and enough money, you know.

And on whether a return visit to Montréal was planned, this response:

> **Lennon:** We don't plan, but we'd like to.
>
> **McCartney:** We'd like to.
>
> **Lennon:** (giggling) There's a lot of money over here.[46]

Money or not, it didn't come to pass. When The Beatles toured a year later on a 10-city North American run, both Vancouver and Montréal were dropped from their schedule leaving Toronto as the band's only Canadian destination for the balance of their touring career.

In and of itself, the near riot at Empire Stadium or even the immigration border snafu may have been enough to turn the boys away from a return to Vancouver. But Lennon's comment that "there's a lot of money over here" surely applied to the near record gate receipts in Vancouver; in short, the city certainly proved its revenue potential.

If indeed logistical issues and crazed fans were reasons to stay away, The Beatles would probably have permanently stopped touring after the 100+ mad-capped shows they performed across three continents by the end of 1964. Was it really about money, as in making more of it? Epstein underestimated The Beatles' drawing power in 1964 and tried to fix the error the following year by moving them to larger outdoor stadiums. Larger venues, it was also reasoned, offered improved security, as fewer people would be shutout of seeing The Beatles, ergo less build-up of crazed fandom on the sidelines.

In 1965, six of the nine venues played in the United States were indeed much larger, revenue-rich baseball fields except, ironically, for the one nearest to Vancouver! An hour's flight away in Portland, Oregon was the 12,000-seat Memorial Coliseum hockey arena where The Beatles played two shows and realized half of the potential ticket sales awaiting them had they performed twice in Vancouver. We may never know what really motivated the band and their management to abandon future shows in Vancouver, but the facts probably suggest the worry outweighed the money.

Dropping Montréal from future visits is more explainable. In this case the concern for The Beatles was the combined double whammy of safety—as in direct threats to their well being—and a reduced revenue stream.

Back to 1964, The Beatles arrived in a rainy Montréal on September 8 and were greeted by 5,000 soaked fans at Dorval Airport and 117 RCMP officers to control the crowd.

While both Montréal concerts yielded all the frenzy and excitement that had become commonplace during their North American invasion, the Forum didn't sell out. At the time the arena had a 13,551 seating capacity yet The Beatles' afternoon show garnered only 9,500 fans, and 11,500 made it to the evening performance.

But it was also a dangerous experience in the city (in addition to the empty seats) that kept The Beatles away from Montréal during subsequent tours.

In 1964, a death threat was leveled at Starr by a Québec separatist group, resulting in increased police presence that included assigning Starr a full-time plainclothes police officer for his entire time he was in Montréal.

As a final note, in both Vancouver and Montréal, The Beatles hurried their exits—the footage of them scurrying on foot across the field to get to their limos after cutting short their Vancouver show (they didn't play their finale "I Wanna Hold Your Hand" as in other cities) is dramatic and, in Montréal, they scrubbed a planned overnight at The Queen Elizabeth Hotel with Harrison recalling "fuck this, let's get out of town."[47] Their unplanned and sudden departures got them to their next concert stops at the exhausting hour of 3:30 a.m.—Los Angeles from Vancouver and Jacksonville from Montréal, respectively.

It's not hard to conclude that neither experience was conducive to a return trip. Instead The Beatles fixed their gaze on Toronto where they returned in each of the next two years, 1965 and 1966, both appearances on August 17.

Customs Clearance: Long before celebrities got special airport treatment including pre-clearing customs, they lined up like everyone else. Here The Beatles, and their manager Brian Epstein, proceed to Canada Customs in Toronto after arriving from Philadelphia on August 17, 1966. Photo by *Toronto Telegram* (York University Libraries, Clara Thomas Archives & Special Collections, fonds ASC29638).

The Beatles in Toronto 1965 and 1966

Connected: George was the only Beatle with Canadian relatives and he even once considered moving to Canada, or Malta or Australia. He is seen here during his final performance in Canada as a member of The Beatles in 1966. He would return in 1974 on a solo tour. Photo by *Toronto Telegram* (York University Libraries, Clara Thomas Archives & Special Collections, fonds ASC29637)

Terry Ott's description of the scorching heat from the 1964 concert at Toronto's Maple Leaf Gardens returned to greet the band and the sold-out crowd in 1965 with reports suggesting the arena's lack of air conditioning brought August temperatures of 100 degrees Fahrenheit, or 38 degrees Celsius.

When The Beatles arrived for their only Canadian gig of 1965, they were fresh off two record-breaking mid-August performances at New York's Shea Stadium—perhaps the beginning of the "stadium rock" performing trend that remains with us to this very day. With those concerts attracting a total of 110,000 fans and filmed by 12 cameras for a future documentary, "Toronto the Good" might have seemed a tad underwhelming or, on the flipside, perhaps a welcome respite for their post-Shea buzzing ears.

Tickets were $5.50 and it was reported the band was paid $100,000 for both sold-out Toronto shows which consisted of twelve numbers including "Twist and Shout", "She's A Woman", "I Feel Fine", "Dizzy Miss Lizzy", "Ticket To Ride", "Everybody's Trying to be my Baby", "Can't Buy Me Love", "Baby's in Black", "Act Naturally", "A Hard Day's Night", "Help" and "I'm Down".

One of the standout reminiscences from the 1965 show included the crisp photography of the boys during their performance, but also at the media briefing and behind-the-scenes candid shots. Better, more modern cameras and lighting had something to do with it but it was also the keen eyes of local photographers—perhaps none better than the late Joe Black.

The word photography stems from its Greek roots of "writing with light" and Toronto-born Black possessed a remarkable ability of doing just that. His mother introduced him to photography at age nine in 1935 which led to a self-taught trade or, more accurately, art form, and a successful and versatile seven-decade career of hockey (he would lay on the ice to capture player's movements), football, automotive, wrestling, news, feature and aerial photography. A photo of Starr in silhouette behind his drum kit, framed by parted stage curtains, was one of the finest photos to emerge from Black's coverage of The Beatles' three visits to Maple Leaf Gardens. It stands as one of the better composed and lit photos taken of Starr on stage while with The Beatles.

Black-Lit Beauty: Joe Black's exquisite and unconventional composition of Ringo in Toronto is considered among the finest images of the drummer playing live with The Beatles. Photo by Joe Black, Graphic Artists.

Another talented photographer, John Rowlands of Oshawa, Ontario, spent considerable time with The Beatles and even developed a friendship with Harrison, which included getting a brief guitar lesson from the Beatle.

He also bore witness to their evolution as a touring band and made these observations of their two 1965 concerts at Maple Leaf Gardens which attracted crowds of 36,000 people combined:

> Their wardrobe was better ... The musical instruments
> had changed a bit ... Their equipment was better too:
> They were using (specially designed 100-amp) Vox
> amplifiers, but still going through the house sound
> system. It was a much slicker show, with smoother

segues. They would mention Canada in general, which was probably the safe thing to do, because in the turmoil of the day they might not remember what city they were in. They knew they were riding a wave. The attitude was 'get it while you can grab it,' because it might not be there to get next year.[48]

The Beatles as a mop-top boy band ceased to exist by the time they set out for their final concert tour in 1966. Influenced by Bob Dylan, beatnik poetry, art nouveau, anti-war resentment, and the mind-bending effects of illicit narcotics, their music took a significant turn upward to more complex compositions, experimental structures and, generally, a more mature and interesting sound; in many ways, the world had never heard anything like it before as their new way forward replaced yeah, yeah, yeahs with more relevant, lyrical verse and musicality as evidenced on *Rubber Soul* and particularly the *Revolver* albums.

So when they set out for what would become their 29-show, 19-city, five-country final tour on June 24, 1966, The Beatles predictably would repeat their Toronto formula with two same-day shows at Maple Leaf Gardens, sandwiched between one-nighters in Philadelphia and Boston except that the improbable happened: Toronto didn't sell out. In fact local promoters scurried to do something so fundamental—although it had never before been required, aggressively promote The Beatles! Looking back on that final Canadian appearance by The Beatles of August 17, 1966, *Toronto Life* magazine offered some context:

> Sixty-six was a hard year for The Beatles. John Lennon made the comment that The Beatles were bigger than Jesus, and their records were being burned by Christians. Fans and critics had a hard time coming to terms with the new sounds on *Revolver*. They had a disastrous tour of Asia. Their shows weren't selling out anywhere in North America, including Toronto (or even their return to Shea Stadium in New York, for

that matter). As a result, Maple Leaf Gardens Limited actually had to produce posters to advertise the concerts, something they didn't have to do in '64 and '65. In the end, they didn't even sell out their final shows.[49]

Marking The Beatles' three consecutive annual performances in Toronto is a plaque on the wall of a downtown Loblaws grocery store, where Maple Leaf Gardens once stood (MLG is now a multi-use facility repurposed for the 21st century). Written by sports columnist and broadcaster Stephen Brunt, the plaque reads, in part:

> Beatlemania wasn't quite dead, but it was clearly on the wane ... Maple Leaf Gardens was the only building The Beatles visited on all three of their North American tours, and after that show in 1966 they would play only eight more concerts, and then never do an official live show again. But of course that was hardly the end of the story.[50]

It is Canada's only historical marker for The Beatles, whereas in England, the ubiquitous Blue Plaques exist all over the place. Beatles Blue Plaques include one where Brian Epstein kept his mid-1960s London office, another at Lennon's residence at 34 Montagu Square, and even one to celebrate their rooftop live performance in Savile Row. A town in the county of Kent even boasts a Blue Plaque to mark a location used in the filming of *Magical Mystery Tour*.

The Beatles Québec-Style

If ever you thought McCartney's "Michelle" was the only time French lyrics made their way into Beatles songs, think again. A popular song-and-dance trio, Les Baronets, became Québec teen idols in the 1960s primarily on their strength in interpreting Beatle songs in French and recording them.

"Si Je Te Donne Mon Coeur" for instance, was Les Baronets' "If I Fell" although their title was more about "If I give you my heart"—a partial lyric in the English version. There was also "Laisse-Moi Me Reposer" or "Let me rest" for "A Hard Day's Night", which playfully evokes the essence of the song, doesn't it? And this one's a dead giveaway: "Un P'tit Sous-Marin Jaune", none other than "Yellow Submarine".

The band, which played in Montréal clubs and toured the province, was composed of Pierre Labelle, Jean Beaulne and René Angélil—he being the future manager and husband of Celine Dion. The Montréal-born Angélil died in Las Vegas in 2016 at age 73.

Sergeant (Randall) Pepper

History is more or less bunk, said Henry Ford over a hundred years ago, making a point that the world puts too much value on historical study. It's in this vein that trying to determine if a veteran Ontario Provincial Police sergeant is, possibly, the namesake for The Beatles' landmark 1967 album, *Sgt. Pepper's Lonely Hearts Club Band* is a delightfully difficult task.

Could it be that Sgt. Randall Pepper is the one? He led The Beatles' security detail during their final 1966 visit to Toronto, the band in his care for 24 hours.

McCartney has always claimed that it was airline salt and pepper shakers aboard a flight that inspired the naming of The Beatles' alter ego pseudonym, its song, its refrain, the album title and a full-on musical revolution spurred by a palette of sound the world had never heard.

The Patch: Beatles folklore is filled with stories about the Ontario Provincial Police patch worn by Paul in the band's *Sgt. Pepper's Lonely Hearts Club Band* album gatefold photo. It spawned rumours of his death (untrue!) and led some to believe the album was named after an OPP sergeant with the real-life surname Pepper whom Paul and his band mates befriended in 1966 (perhaps true!). Photo courtesy of The Beatles Story, Liverpool.

Let's delve beyond the obvious as this tale is about more, much more than the sergeant's surname. At the centre of the Randall Pepper-Sgt. Pepper connection is that recognizable, black and gold "OPP" patch that McCartney wore on his left arm for the album's inner sleeve photo. Dressed in their colourful Sgt. Pepper uniforms, the mustached Beatles were seated in a pose looking straight at the photographer. Just below McCartney's shoulder epaulet and partially obscured by his bended knee was the OPP patch.

(As a side note, the patch is slightly folded due to McCartney's cross-legged seating position, cutting off part of the final "P" in OPP. That crease in McCartney's shoulder—along with a bare-footed McCartney and an ominous licence plate number on the cover of *Abbey Road*—led "Paul is dead" conspiracy theorists, who obviously didn't do their homework, to conclude the letters OPD stood for a death certificate's status of "Officially Pronounced Dead" and the silly but persistent rumours the bassist died in a car crash.)

Familiar to Ontarians, the patch represents the emblem of its provincial police force, which was founded in 1909, and today is Canada's second largest police service with 6,200 uniformed and civilian officers. The logo features a crown above the letters O.P.P. and a crest version of Ontario's flag but without the Union Jack, instead it integrates a red St. George's Cross above three gold-stemmed maple leaves.

So we have McCartney wearing an OPP patch on the same album that bears the same name and rank of an OPP officer who not only was familiar to the band, but established a close working relationship with them nearing the end of their touring days after which they hunkered in a studio to create said album. This is where the delightfully difficult task comes into play because Canadians want to believe the massively successful and landmark *Sgt. Pepper's Lonely Hearts Club Band* breakthrough album had its naming inspiration in Canada, and it would appear there is a body of evidence to support this:

There are at least two accounts circulating on how this patch ended up with The Beatles—that the boys received it on their first visit to Toronto in 1964 and kept it around for three years, or the likelier theory that Sgt. Randall Pepper himself, or a member of his detail, presented it as a gift while driving The Beatles to the airport for their flight to Boston on August 18, 1966, the day after their Toronto shows. One of these accounts is correct; the other is obfuscation.

The two shows in Toronto, the only Canadian city on the 1966 North American tour, occurred only 12 days before The Beatles played their last ever full concert in San Francisco on August 29, 1966, after which they took a long, three-month hiatus and returned to the studio to begin work on the seminal *Sgt. Pepper* album.

Because Sgt. Randall Pepper's granddaughter Cheryl Finn thinks so!

The story of Cheryl Finn whose maiden name is Riddle, and her mother's father, Randall Pepper, came to light on the 50th anniversary of the release of *Sgt. Pepper's Lonely Hearts Club Band* in 2017 and has become one of Canada's biggest, but not entirely proven, contributions to the volumes of Beatles folklore.

Finn is originally from Elliott Lake, Ontario, and is currently the head of tourism for the city of London, Ontario. In an email exchange, she offers an endearing and consistent account of her discovery of the family connection to The Beatles:

> I only found out about this in Grade 9 as I sat in my English class for the first time at Elliott Lake Secondary School. My English teacher, John Young, was a huge Beatles fan and started the class by indicating we had a 'celebrity' in our midst. Everyone started looking around the class (including myself as we were from a small town and already knew everyone). Mr. Young introduced me as the granddaughter of Sergeant Pepper.
>
> I ran home for lunch and berated my mother for not sharing this news with me! She didn't think I would think this was any big deal! Also, there was an underlying concern that we were young children and the 'drug culture' associated with the lads was not something my parents, uncle or grandmother wanted

to draw attention to as we were at an impressionable age and they wanted to play this down.

Finn said she never had the chance to discuss the Sgt. Pepper connection with her granddad, who passed away in 1970. The story of his Beatles connection lives on and has been part of the Pepper family legend for the last 54 years.

"This is certainly a large part of our family history. It was something that was always played down and looked at as 'not a big deal.' My Grandmother always dismissed this conversation with me when I tried to broach it with her as she thought it was 'silly' and could never really understand the 'big fuss' regarding those 'long haired ruffians'. It wasn't until her grandchildren showed some interest in this that we began to talk about this a little more! Mostly I believe because my grandfather had an incredible professional reputation and this was just a very small part of his legacy."

She believes what helps the story rise above coincidence is that OPP patch, and the laundry list of theories it conjures: "It may be interesting to note that to this day, as the story goes, no one really knows how McCartney received the OPP patch. My grandfather got some flak from his higher ups that thought he had given it to the band. This is a bit of family lore as to where the badge actually came from. Also, I may or may not have used this story to negotiate a couple of speeding tickets."

For the record, Lennon didn't necessarily buy McCartney's "salt and pepper" story. He said the name came to McCartney "after a trip to America ... when people were no longer The Beatles or The Crickets—they were suddenly Fred and His Incredible Shrinking Grateful Airplanes. I think he got influenced by that."[51]

Moreover, McCartney's recollection of things is sometimes disputed among Beatles aficionados. It would be grossly unfair to suggest he purposely revises the band's history given his central part of the entire phenomena—after all, he stands as one of only four humans ever to walk Planet Earth who truly know what it was like to be a Beatle. Despite this, the possibility of revision, or perhaps fog of memory, does emerge from time to time. The title of his remarkable song, "Eleanor Rigby" is one such example. He has said "Eleanor" came from his *Help* film co-star, the English actor Eleanor Bron, and that "Rigby" was part of the name of a shop in Bristol. Yet there exists a cemetery a short bicycle ride from his childhood home, in the Liverpool suburb of Allerton, with a family gravestone that prominently bears the name of a deceased "Eleanor Rigby".

American comedian and Beatles nerd Conan O'Brien puts a finer point on it, suggesting the surviving Beatles suffer from a form of brain burden, "(they have) become the worst authorities on things Beatles ... because they have talked about it so much ... they've worn (out) their neural grooves!"[52]

In an endearing self-assessment of things, McCartney admits he cannot bring to the surface ideas and concepts that are developed deep in his subconscious mind, including perhaps the name of an Ontario police sergeant with whom he bonded on his final visit to Canada with The Beatles: "I suppose it was more likely in my subconscious ... but this is bigger than me ... Coincidence is just a word that says two things coincided. We rely on it as an explanation, but it actually just names it—it goes further than that. But as to why they happen together, there are probably far deeper reasons than our little brains can grasp."[53]

To offer balance to the debate, the possibility that the police sergeant was the namesake of the famous album is held mostly by Canadian media, websites and chats, with little fanfare made of the theory in international Beatle forums. But it remains a delicious slice of Canadiana fueled by a few respected music authorities including Manitoba-born Alan Cross, a well-regarded radio personality, writer and musicologist.

Cross offers the last word on the mythology surrounding Randall Pepper:

> The OPP officer and The Beatles got along extremely well. Despite their haircuts and their distasteful music, the cop was charmed by the band's humour and attitude. The Beatles seemed to be amused by him, too. A weird mutual respect developed. By the time

they parted on the morning of August 18, they were almost friends. The Beatles also thought this officer had a rather cool name: Sgt. Randall Pepper.[54]

A second, often overlooked piece of Canadiana emerged from the famous album. The iconic cover photo, which features an eclectic montage of writers, artists, entertainers, religious and political leaders, philosophers and others surrounding The Beatles, included a Canadian.

Designers Peter Blake and his wife Jann Haworth inserted a smallish head—just to Harrison's right and surrounded by artist H.C. Westermann, footballer Albert Stubbins and film legend Marlene Dietrich—belonging to Montréal-born Isadore Borsuk, better known as 1930s child singer Bobby Breen.

Among the many superb tracks on the deep, psychedelically immersed *Sgt. Pepper* album was a collaborative effort by Lennon and McCartney called "Getting Better". It demonstrated the ying and yang of their songwriting ethos at the time with McCartney's sunnier positive attitude ("it's getting better all the time") and Lennon's drearily pessimistic response ("it couldn't get much worse").

The Night a Canadian Helped Coax The Beatles with LSD

Few doubt that drug use had a little to do with *Sgt. Pepper's Lonely Hearts Club Band*. An oft-told story was, late at night during the March 1967 recording session for "Getting Better", Lennon mistakenly swallowed an LSD tablet from his pillbox thinking it was an amphetamine or stimulant to help keep him awake.

That Lennon had LSD on his person at all has a bizarrely Canadian connection.

It was April 1965 and Harrison, Lennon and their partners were having dinner at the London home of George's dentist Dr. John Riley and his 22-year-old Canadian girlfriend and future wife Cindy Bury. She was from Hamilton, Ontario and there are varying accounts of her occupation but Tony Aspler, the respected Order of Canada recipient, novelist and wine writer, describes Bury as a photographer and, later, "The Bunny Mother at the Playboy Club in London"—a sort of human resources role, *Playboy* style.[55]

Aspler, who was born in England but has mostly lived in Canada, and Riley were friends and shared a passion for wine collecting.

After dinner, the three couples shuffled off to the living room for coffee and tea and that's when things soon spiraled out of control. What The Beatles' couples didn't know was that Riley had earlier secured a quantity of LSD from Wales and, before their guests arrived, he dosed their sugar cubes with a liquid form of the hallucinogenic.

Published in *The Guardian*, an account by Cynthia Lennon confirms the Canadian had a pivotal role in the sordid affair. Cynthia said George and Pattie decided to take a pass on the coffee and leave but were coaxed by Bury to stay: "Cindy then said, 'You haven't had any coffee yet. I've made it—and it's delicious.' So they sat down and drank their coffee. (Before the effects of the drug could take hold) John made another move to leave ... 'You can't leave,' said Riley. 'You've just had LSD.'"

Riley's admission of the bizarre act took the guests by surprise as they considered their options. Confusion soon turned to anger as both Beatles and their partners bolted out the door vowing to never again associate with Riley and his companion from Ontario. They piled into Harrison's brown Austin Mini and carried out their intended goal of clubbing in the London night. An account of the rest of the evening: "The LSD took eight hours to wear off. Cynthia remembered the four of them sitting up for the rest of the night 'as the walls moved, the plants talked, other people looked like ghouls and time stood still'. For her, it was 'horrific, I hated the lack of control and not knowing what was going on or what would happen next.'"[56]

The incident involving Riley and the Canadian ranks profoundly in The Beatles' mid-career history with some biographers suggesting what the dentist and Bury did was nothing less than contribute to a newfound and intensely creative songwriting and music-making path for The Beatles.

Of the occurrence in Riley's Bayswater Place flat in London, music writer Steve Turner offers this depth of analysis in his book *The Gospel According to The Beatles*: "For George and John it was a perception-changing experience. LSD dissolves the normal sense of ego that allows one to distinguish between self, others and inanimate objects. The tripper feels united with all things: 'I am he as you are he as you are me and we are all together' as John put it in 'I am the Walrus'. On returning to normal waking consciousness, the tripper sees ordinary life with its distinctions and divisions as a charade."[57]

Turner continues with key songwriting, themes and music examples as the outputs of The Beatles' first, and subsequent, experiences with Lysergic Acid Diethylamide. It's generally accepted that both the *Revolver* and *Sgt. Pepper* albums seem to give a nod to the hallucinogenic the boys were ingesting. George Martin himself acknowledged the deeper and more colourful songwriting, and creative recording and editing ideas for the *Sgt. Pepper* album of 1967, was significantly aided and abetted by drugs: "Looking back on it, Pepper would never have been formed in exactly that way if the boys hadn't gotten into the drug scene."[58]

Not one to mince words, Lennon put a finer point on it, "*Rubber Soul* was the pot album, and *Revolver* was the acid."[59]

Starr once explained the process like this: "We found out very early that if you play it stoned or derelict in any way, it was really shitty music, so we would have the experiences and then bring that into the music later."[60]

Riley and Bury were married in 1966 and had two children; they divorced in 1970. Bury left England in 1981 and Riley died in a car crash in Ireland in 1986. Riley is named among some four or five real-life persons who were said to have inspired the mostly Lennon-written song "Dr. Robert", recorded exactly one year after he and Bury hosted the infamous dinner party.

When reached by Turner in 2005, Bury was living in Gibraltar near Spain. The Canadian said she had no idea the experience she and Riley shared with two Beatles would alter the course of their art.

"We never considered the significance. It was just something we had done at the time for fun. We never thought about tomorrow."[61]

It would be the last time both Lennon and Harrison ever had anything to do with the Canadian and her dentist partner although they did drop acid again that summer in California, this time knowingly and with their drummer Starr. McCartney would join the lysergic club in 1966.

And speaking of LSD, beloved Canadian actor William Shatner once recorded a very forgettable version of "Lucy in the Sky With Diamonds" with a goal of conveying the lyrics in a spoken word manner consistent with being under the influence of that drug.

It didn't work, not on any level! *The Transformed Man* album of 1968 was not only unconventional, it was dreadful; for one, Captain Kirk couldn't sing a note so the Montréal-born Shatner's attempt to "act" his way through the era's psychedelic classics like Dylan's "Mr. Tambourine Man" and the aforementioned "Lucy in the Sky With Diamonds" was so bad that hilariously, years later, American actor George Clooney said *The Transformed Man* is what he would bring along if ever marooned on an deserted island because "if you listen to (this song), you will hollow out your own leg and make a canoe out of it to get off the island."[62]

Turn off your mind George, relax and float downstream!

Ghost Lake, Kitsilano and All You Need is Love

The Beatles followed *Sgt. Pepper's Lonely Hearts Club Band* with *Magical Mystery Tour* in 1967, which included several songs from the film of the same name and also "All You Need is Love" a song in which Eric Clapton was among a bevy of celebrity background vocalists. The Lennon-written song reached number one in Canada during the Summer of Love in 1967, debuting on June 25 with a live Beatles performance during the first-ever global satellite television special called *Our World*.

Canada joined The Beatles' party as one of 19 nations on the satellite broadcast. For its part, the *CBC* contributed three arts and culture segments to the broadcast, watched by an estimated 400-700 million people, including an interview with philosopher Marshall McLuhan (who would sit down with John and Yoko in Toronto two years later), a rancher from the tiny village Ghost Lake, on Alberta's Bow River just west of Cochrane, and a final segment from Kitsilano Beach near Vancouver.

The band's next album, the 1968 double disc formally called *The Beatles* but more commonly referred to as the *White Album*, would feature key contributions by Canadians, a young Torontonian's witness to the early construction of several songs on the album, historic anecdotes and the mysterious claim of an un-credited arrangement by a Saskatchewan musician.

How Lennon (and a Canadian) Won The War

A Canadian actor appeared in Lennon's first film outside The Beatles, the absurd comedy *How I Won The War*. Strathroy, Ontario-born Alexander Knox played General Omar Bradley in the film directed by *A Hard Day's Night's* Richard Lester. Shot in Germany and Spain in 1966 and released the following year, Lennon shared top billing as the hapless Musketeer Gripweed, a role that seemed well suited for his sardonic wit and Python-esque sense of humour. Fifty-nine-year-old Knox, on the other hand, was already a veteran of stage and screen having long established himself a thespian by equally playing Americans and Britons, especially leaders and military men, in film. In 1944, for instance, the University of Western Ontario graduate played President Woodrow Wilson in *Wilson* earning a Golden Globe Award and also an Oscar nomination. In the Lennon film Knox played Bradley, the decorated American general from Missouri "as a senile old fool recounting history as if appearing in a documentary."[3]

The film also marked the first time Lennon donned the now famous "granny" glasses that would become his trademark eyewear for much of his adult life.

Working both in the United States and England, Knox appeared in 66 feature films including one Canadian film later in his career, *Joshua Then and Now*, the 1985 Ted Kotcheff-directed film based on Mordecai Richler's 1980 semi-autobiographical novel. Despite being Canadian, Knox was blacklisted during the peak of the 1950s *House Un-American Activities Committee* witch-hunt for alleged socialist or communist associations; the allegation by American politicians did not deter Knox, he simply resumed his career in England. Knox, who was also a novelist, died in 1995 at age 88 in the north of England.

THE WHITE ALBUM'S 2.5 CANADIANS AND RISHIKESH

While My Guitar Gently Weeps and Eric Clapton

On September 5, 1968, and after multiple takes in No. 2 Studio at EMI—better known as Abbey Road—Eric Clapton made history. It was there that he laid-down a memorable lead electric guitar part to The Beatles' "While My Guitar Gently Weeps". Other than the unknown flamenco guitarist on the Mellotron sample used on "The Continuing Story of Bungalow Bill", Clapton became the only non-Beatle guitarist to play on a Beatles studio recording.

Slow Hand: Eric Clapton was not a Beatle but the half-Canadian guitar great was an enormously influential outsider who played on the *White Album* and in countless collaborations with all four Beatles as solo acts, especially George. Photo by Ultomatt (licensed under CC BY 2.0).

"While My Guitar Gently Weeps" was a Harrison composition and it was he who insisted his friend Clapton contribute to its recording and, in so doing, gave Canada one of its most significant and treasured musical connections to The Beatles as a band and as individual artists. And that's because, as mentioned, Eric Clapton's father was born in Montréal and while the guitarist was absent of any relationship with Fryer, Clapton is biologically and undeniably the .5 Canadian in the title of this chapter.

Clapton's guitar work on "While My Guitar Gently Weeps" was played on Harrison's red 1957 Gibson Les Paul through a Fender

Deluxe amp. His note perfect play resides throughout the song, but the blistering lead part, alternating between the G and D strings, before descending sensually to the B string and then back up again, lasts about a minute and forty seconds as a powerful crescendo of bending strings and pure stabbing passion which continues right to the end of the track.

Guitar World offers this background:

> Harrison's master stroke was inviting his friend Eric Clapton to overdub lead guitar, which was recorded on a single track with Harrison's organ accompaniment … Clapton initially refused to participate, saying, 'Nobody ever plays on The Beatles' records.' 'So what?' Harrison countered. 'It's my song.'
>
> Clapton finally agreed to play, but he wanted his part to sound 'Beatle-y.' Harrison's solution was to process the track containing Clapton's guitar and the organ with Artificial Double Tracking, varying the speed to create a pitch-wobbling effect.[63]

With "Something", "Here Comes the Sun" (written in Clapton's home), "Taxman" and a Beatles-intended "Isn't it a Pity", "While My Guitar Gently Weeps" established Harrison as a songwriting force that, for the latter part of The Beatles' career, met and sometimes exceeded the standard set by Lennon and McCartney.

Just for fun, let's turn to music editor Bill Wyman to assess the quality of the first Beatles song to feature half-Canadian Clapton. Wyman dissected and ranked all 213 songs in The Beatles' catalogue in a 2017 groundbreaking, analytical critique for *vulture.com*.

Where does he place "While My Guitar Gently Weeps"? Wyman put the Harrison song at an impressive number 32 and includes Clapton's guitar part in this commentary:

> The lyrics are mushy; it's a George Harrison song, after all. But the song's drama is apparent in the first measures; the clarity of the arrangement and the

ornamentation hit highly emotional notes out of organic textures, not technological ones. Harrison's keening organ provides a shuddery backdrop for the guitar solo, by one Eric Clapton, recorded with a naked immediacy, and one of Clapton's best.[64]

Equally impressed is Canadian guitar virtuoso Randy Bachman who in 2018 told the *Waterloo Region Record* that "While My Guitar Gently Weeps" is "the standard guitar go-to song for where your guitar actually does what it says: it weeps. George and Clapton's playing is just amazing. It's like the guitar is crying and that's very hard to do with an instrument."[65]

Savoy Truffle and Moose Jaw's Son

Clapton makes a second "appearance" on the *White Album* but this time only as inspiration thanks to his legendary love of candy and chocolate. It was Clapton's sweet tooth that inspired Harrison to write "Savoy Truffle", one of his four compositions on the *White Album*. The upbeat "Savoy Truffle" features lyrics lifted from the names on the lid of a Good News box of chocolates and includes several distinctive stabs of saxophone, one of which—tenor sax to be precise—was played by the pride of Moose Jaw, Saskatchewan, Arthur Albert Ellefson. Recorded in a three-hour session on October 11, 1968, Ellefson was one of six sax players (four baritone and two tenor) to contribute the brass overdub.

In Lewisohn's *The Beatles Recording Sessions* technical engineer Brian Gibson recalled the saxophone session included an apology to Ellefson and the five other sax players:

> The session men were playing really well—there's nothing like a good brass section letting rip—and it sounded fantastic. But having got this really nice sound George (Martin) turned to (engineer) Ken Scott and said, 'Right, I want to distort it.' So I had to

plug-up two high-gain amplifiers, which overloaded and deliberately introduced a lot of distortion, completely tearing up the sound to pieces and making it dirty. The musicians came up to the control room to listen to a playback and George said to them 'Before you listen I've got to apologize for what I've done to your beautiful sound. Please forgive me but it's the way I want it.'[66]

Born in Moose Jaw on April 17, 1932, Ellefson played trumpet as a boy before launching a career as a saxophonist at age 16 playing with orchestra leader Bobby Gimby who was also from Saskatchewan and is famous for writing Canada's 1967 centennial theme song, "CA-NA-DA". Ellefson moved to England at age 20, where he flourished playing soprano, alto, tenor, and baritone saxophones and clarinet with several touring jazz, swing and dance bands and as a studio session player before returning to Ontario in 1974 (by way of Bermuda), then moved to British Columbia in 1988 to continue a remarkable, seven-decade musical career.

Ellefson died in 2018. His son Lee is a jazz guitarist in British Columbia. I was puzzled by Lee's indifference to my calls and notes until I spoke with Buff Allen, a jazz drummer who collaborated with and befriended the senior Ellefson. It seems, suggests Allen, that Ellefson didn't think much of The Beatles.

Said Allen in an email, "(When) I asked him many years ago about that he didn't remember, nor wanted to remember."

Ellefson's clear lack of enthusiasm wasn't necessarily sour grapes over having his sax part purposely distorted by Martin. Allen states Ellefson, a musical purist, was unimpressed that none of the Fab Four could read music, but it's perhaps an alleged unpaid, un-credited job by the late sax player that stuck furthest in his craw, said Allen. "He also complained (George) Martin was so busy with everything going on, that he got Art to write a horn (saxophone, trumpet or trombone) arrangement for one the tunes for the album, but never got paid extra for writing the arrangement."

Could it be, revealed here for the first time, that Moose Jaw's Ellefson wrote (either with or without George Martin, who is credited for it) a musical arrangement for a song on The Beatles' *White Album*? It would be quite a historic achievement as, to date, only one Canadian, David Campbell of Toronto, has ever been involved in arranging a song by any member of The Beatles. Campbell is a conductor and composer who provided string arrangements on the hypnotizing "Riding to Vanity Fair" off McCartney's 2005 *Chaos and Creation in the Backyard* album.

When pressed, Allen admitted Ellefson didn't specify the song for which he says he wrote the arrangement, preferring to forget it all, so let's narrow down the possibilities. Apart from "Savoy Truffle" and putting larger-scale orchestral settings aside for a moment, the 30-song, double *White Album* includes these four other tracks with a horn section:[67]

"Revolution 1" featured two trumpets and four trombones, an arrangement that was recorded early in the sessions on June 21, 1968 at Abbey Road's famed No. 2 Studio.

"Mother Nature's Son" included two trumpets and two trombones and was recorded on August 20, also in No. 2 Studio.

"Martha My Dear" was recorded on October 4, with three trumpets and a French horn at Trident Studios in London's Soho district.

"Honey Pie" was also recorded at Trident on October 5 with five saxophones.

Given that The Beatles recorded both the saxophone-laden, nostalgic "Honey Pie" and "Savoy Truffle" on October 5 at Trident in Soho it narrows the field considerably. The only hic-up in declaring "Honey Pie" the hands-down candidate is that Ellefson and several other sax players laid down their section for "Savoy Truffle" at The Beatles' mainstay EMI/Abbey Road studio, six days later.

But according to *Instagram's todayinbeatleshistory*, the Trident recording session "filled two tape reels with rehearsals and takes, the best of which was numbered 'take one.' At the end of the session a rough mono mix was created, presumably to enable George Martin to prepare a score for saxophone and clarinet."[68]

This suggests Martin brought the tape reels to Abbey Road and gave Ellefson a listen to the "Honey Pie" mono mix with the aim of asking the Canadian to suggest the sax and clarinet arrangement that plays so wonderfully in the song's background. While probable, it's still inconclusive for sure, but not at all an unusual situation. During the era, earning songwriting or arrangement credits, and being part of the royalty revenue stream, was a controversial and often uncertain subject.

Even among The Beatles, the Lennon-McCartney composition standard was barely relevant in the band's latter years with so many songs written (and even recorded) in isolation that the weight of contributions from one or the other have blurred with the passage of time. That Harrison didn't receive a writing credit for his dominant and defining guitar work on, for instance, "And I Love Her"— where he essentially provided the creative hook at the heart of the song—typifies the debate, making any brass arrangement Ellefson did or didn't offer Martin for the *White Album* among countless Beatles songwriting or instrument arrangements that will likely never be fully understood, or resolved.

And still with Allen, he mentioned trying, on another occasion, to resurrect the subject of The Beatles in conversation with Ellefson by asserting, "(Art, you were) involved with making modern musical history." The response by Ellefson says Allen was nothing if not consistent, he "didn't seem to agree."

Art Ellefson's long and distinguished career as a musician included three albums, a featured artist on five records and countless performances; author and journalist Jack Battan once described his playing as a "direct extension of the old masters ... "

Where do "Savoy Truffle" and "Honey Pie" rank among Beatles songs? Let's turn again to Bill Wyman's assessment. Wyman places "Honey Pie" and "Savoy Truffle" side by each at 155 and 156 and is particularly harsh when he asserts "Savoy Truffle" is indicative of the "lack of quality control" on the *White Album* and "Honey Pie" another example of what "Lennon called McCartney's worst instincts (toward) granny music."[69]

Don't Pass Me By's Ontario Fiddler

Ringo Starr sings about listening for footsteps and awaiting the rap-a-tap of knuckles on the door in his first solo composition with The Beatles, "Don't Pass Me By". During its recording he probably had ample opportunity to hear both since it was only he, McCartney and a Canadian violinist involved in the recording of this country ditty.

That sprite, inescapable and catchy fiddle-style violin heard throughout most of the 3:51 of Starr's first solo writing contribution with The Beatles was played by Jack Fallon on July 12, 1968. A jazz musician and promoter (including booking gigs for the early Beatles throughout the UK), Fallon was lured out of semi-retirement by The Beatles to play on their *White Album* at age 53.

Born in London, Ontario, on October 13, 1915, Fallon joined the Royal Highland Fusiliers of Canada light infantry regiment in 1941 and served with the Royal Canadian Air Force overseas during World War II. It was during basic training in St. Thomas, Ontario that the idea of forming a military band made up of soldier musicians came to light. After the war, Fallon and others remained in England playing in dance, brass and concert bands.

Fallon was a versatile musician, playing double bass but also violin, and would work with such greats as Duke Ellington, Django Reinhardt, plus Hoagy Carmichael and Big Bill Broonzy (coincidentally two of Harrison's earliest influences), to name some.

In England, Fallon would leverage his music industry knowledge and entrepreneurship to form Cana Variety, a booking agency for jazz and rock bands in 1952. He would later count The Beatles and The Rolling Stones among his clients and it was his relationship to the Fab Four that likely got him in into Abbey Road to play on the *White Album*.

Of the recording of his composition "Don't Pass Me By" Starr remembered: "It was a very exciting time for me and everyone was really helpful, and recording that crazy violinist was a thrilling moment."[70] Fallon visited No. 3 Studio at Abbey Road on July 12, 1968 to lay down the violin on track two of the recording.

On *vulture.com* Wyman ranked "Don't Pass Me By" at 192, with these comments inclusive of a note, perhaps harshly, on the Canadian violinist's role: "The odd piano sound and aimless violin don't do anything for it. And that repetitious backing track goes on for nearly four minutes."[71]

Aimless? Chill Bill. Fallon's fiddling is integral to the song, much like the harmonica on "Rocky Raccoon", offering a light-hearted tonality as was intended for the rare Starr composition, beginning about 40 seconds into the song and providing a leisurely fill to the simple (yes, repetitive) lyrics and instrumentation.

Although Fallon himself wasn't keen on his "aimless" 11-second extro either, noting: "George Martin had jotted down a 12-bar blues for me. A lot of country fiddle playing is double-stopped but Paul (McCartney) and George Martin suggested I play it single note. So it wasn't really the country sound they originally wanted. But they seemed pleased. Ringo was around too, keeping an eye on his song. When I heard it played back at the end of the session I was hoping they'd scrub that bit out but they didn't, so there I am on record, scraping away! I was very surprised they kept it in, it was pretty dreadful."[72]

For another perspective let's turn to one of the world's foremost Beatles tribute bands, the Analogues. The Dutch ensemble are among few Beatle cover bands that have performed "Don't Pass Me By" on stage, utilizing the skills of guest master violinist Camilla van der Kooij to play the Canadian's solo contribution to the track.

She studied the Fallon part note-for-note for some time, unaware he was born in Canada. What van der Kooij discovered was both charming and, in typical Beatles fashion, unorthodox.

"The strange thing in 'Don't Pass Me By' was that I could hear the open string sound, but it was not in the violin's standard notes of G D A or E. Instead, they were one whole tone lower, especially G and D both of which were used quite often, sounding as the higher open strings. From this I concluded Jack Fallon tuned the entire instrument one whole tone lower (to F C G and D) which is very peculiar in the violin world," she explained in an email. "This raised my curiosity. Why would Fallon do this? Maybe it was easier to play in this key or maybe it was carefully chosen because of the sound? Or was it just a fun thing they came up with, to add something crazy for insiders like me to ponder and try to solve?"

Fallon's unconventional approach in "Don't Pass Me By" gave van der Kooij, a classically trained violinist, her first opportunity to play a detuned violin. With the Analogues reputation of note-to-note perfection clearly weighing on her, she took no chances:

> So what I did was write down the notes one tone higher, so I could easily read them with normal fingering, but play them on the detuned violin. So in my head I was playing E but on the violin it would sound as D. It twists your mind, but in the end, it worked for me, the band and, most importantly, the audience that is usually filled with Beatlemaniacs, young and old!
>
> I think The Beatles in general were so creative and innovative, featuring so many (uncommon) instruments and crossing borders between all kinds of musical styles. These days being a versatile violin player offers people like me the most chance (and freedom) to make a living out of it. It's cool to see that The Beatles already were going this way, using the violin in a non-classical way in their music, making a statement to the world that violins in pop music are great!

Fallon died in London, England on May 22, 2006, at age 90 and was posthumously inducted into the London Music Hall of Fame. His obituary in *The Guardian* included this reference to his roots: "Fallon, a sturdy Canadian who settled in London after the Second World War ... was from Irish farming stock. His grandfather had sailed to Canada to escape the 1840s potato famine, settling in a remote part of Ontario. Fallon was born there in a log cabin and might have pursued life as a farmer but for his parents' musical inclinations."[73]

While London, Ontario, can claim one of its own in Beatles recording history, "Don't Pass Me By" was not the first time McCartney, Starr and a guest musician were the sole participants in a Beatles recording. In 1966, the beautifully melodic two-minute long "For

No One" was recorded without Lennon or Harrison, featuring only McCartney, Starr and Alan Civil on French horn. During his career, the English-born Civil played in a chamber orchestra run by Boyd Neel, a musician who lived in Canada and became the Dean of the Royal Conservatory of Music in Toronto and also Artistic Director of the Sarnia (Ontario) Festival Opera House.

Guelph, Ontario's Tommy Reilly, MBE

Thomas (Tommy) Rundle Reilly was born in Guelph, Ontario, in 1919, raised in St. Thomas, Ontario, and by age eight began playing the violin. His father, Captain James Reilly, was a bandleader, conductor and professional jazz musician who played accordion and harmonica and wrote instructional books for how to play the latter. The Reilly family moved to England when Tommy was 16 and the young musician began playing the harmonica professionally.

Reilly had the misfortune of studying music in Leipzig, Germany, at the start of World War II. He was arrested by the Gestapo and spent the duration of the war in prison camps throughout central Europe; he survived, returned to England at the end of the war and went on to perform on radio and television, in concerts and music festivals and with some of Europe's most prestigious orchestras. In the 1950s the Parlophone label signed Reilly and George Martin produced his 78-rpm recordings.

Martin himself recommended Reilly join the recording of George Harrison's 1968 album *Wonderwall Music* when the Beatle asked him if he knew any good harmonica players. The album would be the first foray for any Beatle on a major solo project, and included among the first recording collaborations between Harrison and Eric Clapton. Harrison took on and largely funded the sessions that would produce the soundtrack for the hippie psychedelic film *Wonderwall* directed by Joe Massot and co-starring Canadian-born actor Iain Quarrier

In 1992 Reilly was awarded the Member of the Order of the British Empire by Queen Elizabeth II for "services to music." It would prove to be the first time that a harmonica player had ever received an MBE, elevating the mouth organ to a classical standard:

"Tommy Reilly´s contribution to the development of the harmonica as a legitimate musical instrument was crucial".[4]

Reilly passed away in 2000. His granddaughter, Georgina Reilly is an actor who appeared in the Gemini Award-winning *CBC TV* series *Murdoch Mysteries* for three seasons. The popular period drama has featured several unexpected cases of cross hybridization among other Canadian thespians in The Beatles' orbit:

- Gemini-nominated Mike McMurtry, who was featured in *The Linda McCartney Story* to become one of only six actors ever to portray Ringo Starr in a film or docudrama—was cast as local artist Arthur Webster in a 2009 episode of *Murdoch Mysteries*.
- Montréal's impressively mustached William Shatner played Mark Twain in a 2015 episode—based on one of the American writer's four visits to Canada in the 1880s; Shatner infamously recorded a peculiar version of "Lucy in the Sky With Diamonds" in 1968.
- Niagara Falls, Ontario actor Ric Reid appeared as a chief constable on the show and was also part of the cast in the praised Lennon-McCartney dramatization *Two of Us* shot in Ontario in 2000.

Toronto to Rishikesh: "We See Everything for Moments Like This"

Many of the songs on the *White Album* were conceived and written in India, and naturally, there are plenty of Canadian threads to pull while exploring The Beatles' time there.

By February 1968, Harrison had finished recording the soundtrack for the film *Wonderwall*. The four-month, 19-song project was recorded in London and Bombay and became the first full-fledged solo project by a Beatle.

With contributions from both Indian and Western musicians, the album *Wonderwall Music* included Clapton on guitar and Guelph, Ontario-born Tommy Reilly on harmonica. Reilly, who passed away in 2000, is grandfather to Georgina Reilly, a television and film actress who has appeared in beloved Canadian dramedies like *Murdoch Mysteries* and the *Republic of Doyle*. Reilly would be the first of several Canadians to enter The Beatles' world during their Harrison-led interest in meditation and the mystical, uplifting spiritual traditions of India.

Harrison had already written and recorded several superb, Indian-style songs with The Beatles such as the acclaimed and thought-provoking "Within You, Without You" and now applied his interest in Indian instrumentalism to a film that "touched on themes that would come to preoccupy George Harrison critically, the objectification of celebrities and the shallowness of fame."[74]

It seemed his escalating interest in Indian music and his intensive study of Hinduism rubbed off on the others when, that month, the four Beatles agreed to assemble in northern India to learn about transcendental meditation. They arrived separately with wives, girlfriends, friends and others after long flights to New Delhi and the arduous, 230-km road journey to Rishikesh that followed.

Three unique Canadian stories emerged from The Beatles' spiritually and musically rewarding trip to India, one had an immediate consequence, and the others would take shape decades later.

The Beatles and others stayed for varying amounts of time in Rishikesh—10 days for Starr but much longer five- to seven-week spans for the others. They took up residence in the foothills of the Himalayas at the Maharishi Mahesh Yogi's 15-acre ashram.

Aware something special was going down on his estate, Maharishi was obliged to protect the privacy of his guests and thus didn't allow reporters inside the compound, but on most days he would come outside to brief waiting journalists on The Beatles.

There was one journalist, though, who received the Maharishi's blessing to visit his ashram. That journalist was Lewis H. Lapham.

A contributor to *The Saturday Evening Post*, Lapham had been assigned a feature story on the famous Yogi before The Beatles arrived in India. He was there to see the surrealistic scene where the world's most famous band, their wives or girlfriends, and an eclectic gathering of friends arrived. There was the band's long-time roadie Mal Evans, electronic whiz kid and Apple employee Magic Alex Mardas, Scottish singer-songwriter Donovan, and socialite Nancy Cooke de Herrera, who was assigned to handle The Beatles' requirements. Then there were a string of Americans including Mike Love of The Beach Boys, cowboy actor Tim Simcox, plus jazz musician and eventual British Columbia resident Paul Horn. Mia Farrow, along with her siblings John and Prudence, were already at the ashram—yes, that's the very same Prudence who is the subject of Lennon's masterpiece "Dear Prudence".

Lapham would write a 14-page, two-part feature article *The Saturday Evening Post*, running May 4 and 18, 1968, under the clever headline: *There Once Was a Guru From Rishikesh*. The subhead was clever too: "In which our reporter learns about Transcendental Meditation, makes a voyage to India and meets the Maharishi, The Beatles, a Beach Boy and other notables in search of something."

Insightful and well researched, his article stays clear of Beatles adoration and actually spends time describing how their VIP presence at the ashram ran afoul of the devout regulars who were studying at the Maharishi's retreat to become instructors of transcendental meditation. "The Beatles and their wives occupied places in the front row of wood and wicker chairs; the rest of us scattered through the rows in the back. Candles on the armrests of the chairs offered a dim and flickering light; the heavy scent of incense and coal smoke drifted on the night air."

Lapham's Canadian connection would come decades later. He and his wife, Joan, would have four children. Their son, Andrew, married Caroline Mulroney, yes *that* Caroline Mulroney, the Ontario cabinet minister and political scion, in 2000.

Lapham and Joan, along with former Prime Minister Brian Mulroney and his wife Mila, have a combined marital lifecycle of nearly 100 years.

Today they not only share the rarity of matrimonial longevity, but also grand-parenting duties to Andrew and Caroline's one American-born and three Canadian-born children. In 2005 Lapham, wrote *With The Beatles*, a 168-page book chronicling his time in Rishikesh.

Now for the Toronto to Rishikesh connection.

A young Canadian named Paul Saltzman was also in Rishikesh and, as fate or stroke of luck would have it, for seven days gained unfettered access to The Beatles. He took their photos, had a private audience with Harrison, who played the sitar for him and, just hung out, ate and joked with the lads from Liverpool with a dawn-to-dusk intimacy like no Canadian had ever achieved.

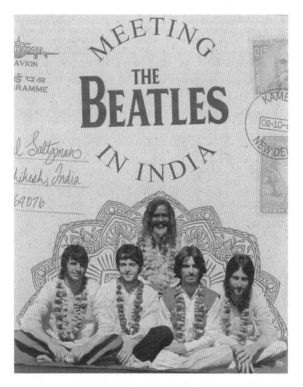

On the Road to Rishikesh: Filmmaker Paul Saltzman ranks among the most remarkable Canadians connected to The Beatles. From his intimate, embedded time with The Beatles and their partners while learning to meditate in India, he has written books about the experience and, in 2020, released the *Meeting The Beatles in India* documentary film, narrated by Morgan Freeman. Photo courtesy of Paul Saltzman.

Saltzman had just turned 24 and was in India with the National Film Board of Canada shooting a documentary. At the end of his six-week assignment, Saltzman headed to New Delhi where several events paved his date with destiny.

While there he witnessed a group of journalists harassing Mia Farrow and, in an act designed to put a smile on her face, tried to give her a flower but was met instead by Mia's sister Prudence who accepted his kind gesture. The good vibes were soon extinguished when he received a letter from his girlfriend in Canada informing him their relationship was over. In a distraught state, he happened upon a lecture on transcendental meditation while in New Delhi and thought it a useful path to follow. At that point, with nothing to lose and much to gain, he decided meditation could help mend his broken heart so he loaded his backpack and headed to Maharishi's ashram in Rishikesh, unaware the decision would reconnect him with the Farrow sisters and befriend the world's greatest band at the peak of their careers.

Saltzman had the wherewithal and good fortune to pack his Pentax 35mm camera, rolls of Kodak Ektachrome 64 slide film and, after spending eight days sleeping in a tent outside the ashram, which was enclosed by a barbed-wire fence and surrounded by jungle, was finally welcomed into the sprawling complex.

In his beautifully illustrated 2006 book *The Beatles in India*, containing 32 extraordinary, large-format photos of The Beatles, Saltzman describes his first contact with the famous foursome in a calm, quiet environment: "I was walking through the ashram when I saw John, Paul, George and Ringo sitting with their partners ... at a long table by the edge of the cliff that overlooked the Ganges and Rishikesh. Somewhat nervously I walked over."

As icebreakers go, Saltzman nailed it. Fresh off his first lesson on meditation and spiritually transported to a new found state of consciousness, he chanced upon The Beatles and their partners sitting at a long table, each of them in an equally wondrous state of relaxation and humour:

Saltzman: May I join you?

Lennon: Sure, mate … Pull up a chair.

McCartney: Come sit here.

Lennon: So, you're from the States, then?

Saltzman: No, Canada.

Lennon: (playfully turned to the others): Ah! He's from the colonies … So you're still worshipping Her Highness, then?

Saltzman: No. Not personally … but we still have her on our money.

Starr: Lucky you.

Saltzman: We may have her on our money but she lives with you!

Cynthia Lennon: Leave the poor chap alone. After all, he's just arrived.

Saltzman: No problem.

Lennon: Ah, you see mates, they still have a sense of humour in the colonies.[75]

Perhaps because he and the Canadian both found their shared exploration of an inner journey to their liking, or perhaps because they both celebrated their birthdays while in India, Harrison took a particular shine to Saltzman. One day, the two found themselves chatting about the sitar which led Harrison to invite Saltzman to come hear him practice, a one-on-one intimate sitar session with the Beatle that would bring them both a measure of solace and calm.

We walked over to his bungalow and into a small meditation room … George sat cross-legged near

91

the centre of the room and I sat facing him a few feet away … Everything was glowing. I could smell the faint aroma of sandalwood incense from somewhere outside as George closed his eyes and began to play. I felt a soft, delicious feeling of peace. When I opened my eyes, he was gently laying his sitar back down. The sunlight had shifted across the futons and there was a vibrant, soothing aura in the room.[76]

Saltzman would reunite with the Farrow sisters at the ashram, and Prudence in particular remembered him as the young man who brought her sister a flower in New Delhi.

In the decades that followed Saltzman's time with The Beatles, 54 of the 76 colour photos (transparencies, actually) he shot of their time together went largely unnoticed except for a few prints he gave Jane Asher in London, and several that appeared in a 1968 *Maclean's* magazine article. Clear, colourful images nicknamed the Class Photos of a very relaxed group, sitting cross-legged in their gypsy-like, cotton white kurta pajamas, saris, bright robes, local jewelry and leis of orange marigolds around their necks, and a second series of photos of the sandaled, white Sherwanis-wearing Lennon and McCartney playing guitars while Starr looks on are considered among the most intimate photos ever taken of The Beatles. The latter series captured the earliest attempt at The Beatles playing "Ob-La-Di, Ob-La-Da" with not much more than the chorus already written.

At the urging of his daughter (who recalled being told as a child her dad had met The Beatles), he decided to show them to a curator at Sotheby's in London in 2000.

I spread out the 54 slides … and he took a loop, leaned over the light box and started looking at them. When he saw the first one he said: 'Huh!' and on the second one he said 'Wow!' and he sat up and looked at me. 'You sure you're not a professional photographer?' he asked. 'No, I was just a kid with a camera in my back-pack,' I remember saying. He then looked at the rest, one by one, taking his time. When he was done he sat up, looked at me and said: 'We see everything for moments like this. Some of these are the best intimate shots we've ever seen of them.'[77]

To mark the 50th anniversary of his remarkable time in Rishikesh, Saltzman went on to produce a third iteration of his book in 2018, again showcasing the colours and the fellowship of the remarkable time he spent with The Beatles.

Saltzman has been back to India nearly 60 times since and, from 1973-1990, was married to Indo-Canadian filmmaker Deepa Mehta—the two are parents to Canadian-born author and journalist Devyani Saltzman. His father Percy was a Winnipeg-born television meteorologist and reporter and nephew Aaron is currently a *CBC* senior reporter; Saltzman lives in Toronto and is an accomplished, and award-winning prolific filmmaker.

I read about his remarkable time with The Beatles in India at The Beatles Story—the world's foremost museum and exhibit of The Beatles' history located in Liverpool. The Beatles Story has a superb website, *beatlesstory.com*, which includes a section on the love-lost Canadian who stumbled upon The Beatles and his rare and gentle insights of the Fab Four.

A third Canadian connection to The Beatles in India involves Paul Horn, the New York City-born musician who played flute, clarinet and saxophone for jazz greats Duke Ellington, Nat King Cole, Tony Bennett and also The Beach Boys' *Pet Sounds*, an album held in high regard by McCartney. Saltzman included a photo of Horn playing flute for Harrison in *The Beatles in India*.

A year after their shared experience in Rishikesh, Horn and Donovan reconnected and embarked on a concert tour that included a gig in Vancouver. On a day off, Horn visited Victoria and decided that's where he wanted to live.

Horn was 40 when he, his wife and their two sons moved to Victoria. By 1973 he hosted the *Paul Horn Show* on *CTV* and it was there he met his third wife, Juno-nominated Canadian singer and composer Ann Mortifee. The two divided their time between a home on Cortes

Island, part of Vancouver Island's Sunshine Coast, and Arizona. Horn also formed a band that provided musical scores for the National Film Board of Canada films. Horn, who died in Vancouver in 2014, had spoken of Mortifee as the truest love of his life.

The same sentiment could not be said for John and Cynthia Lennon. Married to Lennon for only six years, Cynthia had hoped the visit to India would be their second honeymoon but it wasn't even close, as the seeds of marital discord had been sown before they got there. Even Saltzman sensed something was amiss with the Lennons … and he was right. John had already begun an intense affair with the Japanese-American conceptual artist and exhibitionist Yoko Ono back in England and any hope of reconciliation seemed dashed. Of their time in India, Cynthia told *Rolling Stone* magazine: "John was becoming increasingly cold and aloof toward me. He would get up early and leave our room. He spoke to me very little, and after a week or two he announced that he wanted to move into a separate room to give himself more space. From then on, he virtually ignored me, both in private and in public."[78]

The article continues, "She later learned that every morning, her husband would visit the post office to check if Ono had sent him a letter."

Which brings us to The Ballad of John and Yoko and Cynthia and Canada.

Harrison's Ottawa Scouting Trip

George Harrison's high-profile visits to Canada included three tours as a Beatle and, later, a tour as a solo artist in 1974, but in between he made a much quieter, little-known visit to Ottawa in late February 1969.

He was in the nation's capital on a recruiting mission for The Beatles' Apple Records label. Harrison had a decent track record as a talent scout having recommended James Taylor to Apple after hearing him audition in London, and in fact even borrowed Taylor's song title "Something in the Way She Moves" for the opening line of his hit "Something".

Harrison stayed at the Chateau Laurier Hotel and was in Ottawa to catch American folk singer-songwriter Eric Anderson performing at the city's large Capitol Theatre, and Ottawa-based jazz-rockers the Modern Rock Quartet, at Le Hibou Coffee House.

Neither act was ever signed by Apple.

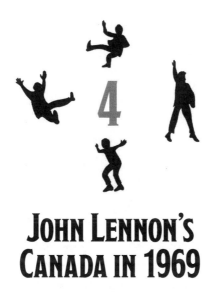

JOHN LENNON'S
CANADA IN 1969

The Ballad of John and Yoko and Cynthia and Canada

Born in Liverpool on October 9, 1940, John Winston Lennon lived both a tortured and a remarkable life during the brief time he spent on Earth. A gifted songwriter, artist and musician, his inspired and euphoric creativity relied as much on his suppressed anger and general state of unhappiness as it did on his constant journey of discovery. In the second half of his forty years, the so-called "First Beatle" was perhaps the most public, oft-quoted, photographed and controversial artist and rock star personality in the world.

How does a man go on to become who he is? At nearly every stage of Lennon's musical career, there was a connection to Canada or Canadians.

It began with his Quarry Men teenage audition for Carroll Levis, and again as the John-Paul-George trio of Johnny and the Moondogs, and over in Hamburg he was on stage when the Canadian Infantry tore up the club in which he and the early Beatles were playing. Three touring years with The Beatles included nine shows in Canada and, he closed out the 1960s lighting up his causes and music under Canadian skies.

Similarly, at nearly every stage of his marital life, Lennon also had Canadian connections.

It began with his mother-in-law Lillian Powell and a rather peculiar set of very personal circumstances for Lennon. It's 1962 and The Beatles are on the cusp of fame, working at a feverish pitch throughout Britain but especially in the northwest and also Hamburg to raise both their game and the brand to become a better and better group.

Then John's girlfriend and steady since meeting at the Liverpool College of Art five years earlier, Cynthia Powell, informs him she is pregnant.

So when the couple announced they would marry, family reactions ranged from severe to downright peculiar. This in stark contrast to the more caring response by Jim McCartney who quickly offered to plan a wedding when he learned his son, Paul, had fathered a child with future Canadian citizen Dorothy Rhone; not surprising as the McCartney brothers were raised within the constructs of love in a family environment.

Lennon's situation was radically different; he feared being loved. His father was bound to a career in the merchant navy and away for months at a time, and his mother Julia was tragically killed in a road accident in 1958. Lennon was psychologically damaged at a young age, bearing many scars as an adolescent and lacked any true sense of family, although he was surrounded by strong women in the form of his aunts, cousins and stepsisters.

His guardian, aunt and de facto mother, Mimi Smith, declared neither she nor any member of the Stanley (her maiden name) or Lennon families would attend John and Cynthia's wedding and rejected the entire premise of her 21-year-old John getting married— this despite the fact that Cynthia had at one time lived under the same roof as Mimi.

Which brings us back to Cynthia's mother, the widow Lillian Powell. With Aunt Mimi opposed to a wedding, Powell was the only remaining matriarch to offer any semblance of support. But it wouldn't materialize. Powell disapproved of Cynthia's boyfriend—a common theme in Lennon's relationships, as Lewisohn explains Powell merely "formed the same instant opinion of John as almost every parent since his infancy; she didn't like him at all ... John didn't much care for Lillian either."[79]

On August 22, 1962, the day before her 22-year-old daughter's wedding to Lennon, Lillian Powell set sail for Canada. As incredible as that sounds, there is an explanation.

So while at first glance you could be forgiven for thinking Powell's departure to Canada the day before her daughter's wedding to Lennon was an act of protest, the truth is she likely had already booked a return ticket long in advance; you see, Powell no longer held an address in England because she was living in Toronto.

Recalled Cynthia, who dropped the "I'm pregnant and marrying John Lennon" bomb only days before Lillian was to set sail:

> I was so afraid she would be disappointed in me. She was staying with my brother Tony and I went to see her the night before she sailed back to Canada. When I told her about my pregnancy her only concern was for me: she felt terrible that she was leaving the next day and couldn't stay to look after me. But she put her arms around me, told me that we all make mistakes and that it would turn out all right in the end.[80]

On her departure to cross the Atlantic by passenger ship, Powell was met at the Liverpool docks by her daughter and soon-to-be son-in-law who waved goodbye.

In the grand universe of Beatles fan pages, blogs, chats, and historic reviews and overall obsession in social media there exists a *Facebook* page dedicated solely to *The Beatles Wives and Girls.*

That particular source confirms that in as early as the spring of 1961 Powell was living in Toronto (around the time Louise Harrison, George's mom, was in Ontario). Powell had moved to the city to be with her niece (Cynthia Lennon's first cousin), and her niece's husband as the couple left England with their newborn child to study and become teachers in Canada.

The Beatles Wives and Girls tells us that soon after her mom's return to Toronto, Cynthia began "receiving packages of homemade knitted baby clothes" from Canada. Not long after Julian Lennon's birth in April 1963 Powell ended her two-year Canadian residency, returning to England for good and, by all accounts, enjoyed babysitting her grandson as The Beatles rise in the music industry put the Lennons on the road with increased regularity.[81]

The Lennons' marriage survived the early goings of Beatlemania and parenthood but would dissolve by November 1968. Cynthia would take three more trips to the altar before her death in Spain in 2015. Lennon's new love interest, Yoko Ono, was married three times before she met John (twice to the same husband). When she and Lennon went down the aisle (or more accurately the registry office in Gibraltar) in March 1969, it would be a transformative, final union for them both and Canada was to become their go-to destination during their first year as husband and wife.

The Three Lennon Visits That Changed Canada

Peaceful Prelude: Relaxing in his suite at Toronto's King Edward Hotel,
John made three event-filled trips to Canada in 1969, recording "Give
Peace a Chance", performing at Varsity Stadium and having tea with Prime
Minister Pierre Trudeau. His experiences in Canada emboldened him to
leave The Beatles. Photo by *Toronto Telegram* (York University Libraries,
Clara Thomas Archives & Special Collections, fonds ASC 00296).

Lennon and Ono were popular music's power odd couple of the latter 1960s. Seemingly mismatched, the truth couldn't be further. Through their music, art and celebrity, they sought the media spotlight to spread a very simple, unambiguous message of peace. Let's remember that in the late 1960s peace didn't seem all that impossible and while the Lennons didn't invent the peace movement, they wrapped themselves around it as a core belief; it became their mission and their message throughout their travels including an unprecedented three visits to Canada in less than eight months in 1969.

The Lennons spent a total of 22 days in Ontario and Québec, which surpassed all previous nights John slept on Canadian soil while touring as a Beatle (The Beatles played a total of nine concerts in Canada from 1964 to 1966 with only a handful of overnight stays as they pinballed from city to city across North America). For her part, Ono had previously visited Montréal in 1961 to participate in a music and performance art festival.

The Lennons were still in honeymoon mode when they visited Canada for the first time as a married couple in late May 1969. As wedding gifts go, Lennon must have appreciated the gift of time above all others. The Beatles awarded themselves a considerably long lull from recording during this period.

Their *Get Back* sessions—ostensibly songs for the later-released *Let it Be* album—ended on January 30. The next four months were basically time off for the boys, although punctuated with two relatively brief studio sessions—"Hey Bulldog" on February 11 and a John-and-Paul-only pop-up session for "The Ballad of John and Yoko" on April 14. Their next prolonged, full-time studio session work didn't happen until May 30 as they began recording the double *White Album*.

To appreciate the scope of the freedom granted to Lennon and his band mates from early February to late May 1969, and at other downtime junctures in their careers, consider that until that moment in time the world's hardest working rock 'n' roll band had, in barely nine years, given around 1,300 live performances, released 18 newly recorded or re-issued albums—participating in all the publicity that entails—sat through scores of photo sessions (they were perhaps the most photographed people on the planet), wrote and produced songs for others, tried to run their business after Epstein's death in 1967, made countless radio and TV appearances and media interviews, and starred in three movies.

"Our days off were sacred," McCartney once recalled.[82]

Their intensive work schedule was cited by Elmira, Ontario, author and journalist Malcolm Gladwell as their path to glory and it became one of the premier examples of a specific behavior to support the thesis in his 2008 book *Outliers*, that behavior, he construed, involves mightily blazing a trail of hard labour with 10,000 hours of repetitive, intense work to shape future success; in essence, The Beatles flowered in Hamburg:

> They were the house band in a strip club in Hamburg, Germany and they would play eight-hour sets, seven days a week for months at a stretch. The idea there is we think of them as these geniuses who come out of nowhere and who are naturally brilliant, but in fact they put in an apprenticeship of thousands of hours before … We sometimes look at people and think they must have this great innate talent and we forget the enormous amount of work that went into what looks like genius.[83]

(McCartney acknowledged Gladwell's research in *McCartney 3 2 1*, a July 2021 documentary on the streaming service *Hulu*. Asked by host Rick Rubin how many hours The Beatles played together before making their first record, McCartney offered this nod to the Canadian: "At least 10,000, according to the man.")

Interesting how Gladwell describes The Beatles earning their bones as an apprenticeship. Lennon's decision to stretch his legs in Canada in 1969 was an important continuation of that apprenticeship both musically and politically; he also put a great distance between himself, Paul, George and Ringo, endearing himself to a country he viewed as clean canvas, an experiment of just how far he could carry his celebrity. Still very much in the throes of love, he helped find a fertile and perhaps less judgmental place to showcase his new partner and her voice.

It's a wonder he chose Canada at all. His history with the place and its people wasn't exactly stellar. Even if we dismiss several of Lennon's earlier ghosts of Canada past like Carroll Levis or the conduct unbecoming of our armed forces in Hamburg or that it was once home to his mother-in-law, there remain negative incidents during The Beatles' 1964 tour like death threats, immigration snafus, deejays stepping up on stage to interrupt their show, and mad, unplanned panicked dashes from both Vancouver and Montréal—late night, desperate escapes because the band wanted the hell out of these cities in a hurry.

Instead of dismissing the place, Lennon saw safe haven in Canada, like Holland, France and Gibraltar were during his widely publicized honeymoon. He called Canada "a young country" that wasn't negatively interfering with other nations. What he couldn't have known was that the RCMP was keeping tabs on the Lennons and sharing their data with the FBI.[84] Moreover, Canada's immigration department seemed also deferential to the United States' security apparatus as a constant source of tension for the Lennons and their entourage whenever they visited.

Nevertheless, for media savvy, extroverted John, 28, and astute Yoko, 36, their extended honeymoon would be anything but normal. The lazy Beatle who once demurred "I'm So Tired" took his post-nuptial celebration lying down, literally, in bed, a lot, with Yoko.

Not just any bed, though, but a bed large enough to serve as a metaphor for the cause of world peace. Far from simply lazy rivering in a sack, the Lennons crawled under the sheets to take a stand in the global peace movement; in their own wacky way, John and Yoko used their bed as a public service announcement, inviting the world media, hippies, yippies, rabbis and popeyes and all manner of human kind to join in.

And so was born the Bed-In for Peace, part flower power offensive, part sit-com spectacle that saw first light in the presidential suite (Room 902) of the Amsterdam Hilton in late March. When they arrived at the hotel, their room was emptied of all furniture (except for the bed) and filled with flowers, posters and people. In some ways, the Lennons' Amsterdam suite looked like a scaled-down version of the "All You Need is Love" studio setting from the band's *Our World* performance beamed over a global satellite in 1967 but also very much a canvas aligned with Ono's performance art.

For the next seven days the Lennons invited a steady flow of free-wheeling media to cover their "product" as Lennon recalls it being akin to a marketing campaign:

"We thought instead of just being 'John and Yoko Get Married,' like 'Richard and Liz (Burton) Get Married,' (it should be) 'John and Yoko get married and have a Bed-In for peace.' So we would sell our product, which we call 'peace.' And to sell a product you need a gimmick, and the gimmick we thought was 'bed.' And we thought 'bed' because bed was the easiest way of doing it, because we're lazy. It took us a long train of thought of how to get the maximum publicity for what we sincerely believed in, which was peace—and we were part of the peace movement."[85]

The following month, the two began work on their *Wedding Album,* which included a 25-minute spoken word and acoustic sing-a-long called "Amsterdam" which was recorded in their Hilton suite. The *Wedding Album* released later in the year, would be the couple's third and (mercifully) final vocal-and-sound-effects experiment which began with the November 1968 release of *Two Virgins* that stretched the boundaries of free expression with a cover photo of John and Yoko, naked and demure.

The Lennon-Ono circus of 1969 was in full swing.

The couple's second Bed-In got off to a shaky start. Sights were set for New York City but the Big Apple would be a non-starter with the Lennons effectively barred from entering the United States. Historians have pointed to the Richard Nixon White House itself as taking a personal interest in the rabble-rousing Beatle with President Nixon and his inner circle, with the help of the FBI, labeling him a political agitator and systematically harassing Lennon with a goal of deportation.

One wonders why, with New York off this list, the Lennons chose the Bahamas, where they arrived on May 24 ready to prepare for a second Bed-In under the tropical sun at the Sheraton Oceanus Hotel.

The Bahamas fell short of expectations as the Lennons were either unhappy with their accommodations or found the heat too oppressive. Whatever the reason, after barely a day in the tropics they were on the move again as captured in an interview with Derek Taylor, the Lennons' de facto publicist on loan from The Beatles: "(The Bahamas is) not a good place. It's not that the hotels are bad, they're just not hotels. John and I both didn't like it, but we said, 'Let's go to bed and see what it looks like in the morning.' John called me at 7 and said, 'It doesn't look any better.' Then we decided on Canada. Looking back, it was really Canada all the time. Apart from the hotels, it was so damn hot down there, and not close enough to the States."[86]

In making the course correction, Taylor's "close enough to the States" comment is telling. The real problem with Freeport really came down to the fact that in a pre-internet world, it was too far away from the major North American media centres, ergo less coverage for a Bed-In. So the decision was made to move the entire enterprise to Canada. On the day of their flight to Toronto, Lennon took a moment to serenade Ono who was lying next to him in their Sheraton bed with his yet unrecorded song "Oh Yoko". He also strummed the basic construct of "Give Peace a Chance", trying to make his new wife laugh with silly verses in between the chorus. Roughly three hours later, they were in Canada.

1. "We all thought it was sort of like home … "

On May 25, 1969, the Lennons, Taylor, Ono's five-year-old daughter, Kyoko, cinematographer Nic Knowland, and a second cameramen flew directly to Toronto, met with airport immigration officials in what would be multiple visits to follow, and checked in to the King Edward Hotel. Lennon was familiar with this Toronto landmark, the same downtown hotel mobbed by fans when The Beatles arrived from

Detroit to play their first Toronto concert on September 7, 1964, and the King Edward also hosted the band during subsequent appearances in the city in 1965 and 1966.

During the two-day Toronto stay, and also during their entire time at their next stop Montréal, Lennon or his people made multiple visits to Canadian immigration officials but failed to convince them to grant Lennon visitation status as a desirable alien. The frosty welcome by the Department of Manpower and Immigration never really thawed— but, as a compromise, Lennon was told he could stay for ten days.

Canada was not the open country Lennon and his people had hoped: "We all thought it was sort of like home. Sort of like popping into Ireland only a bit farther,"[87] quipped Lennon who harboured no hard feelings and decided Toronto would serve as a stopover, a peace prelude as it were, to the Montréal Bed-In and a strategic city to drum-up some pre-publicity since most US news outlets had bureaus there.

Back at the King Edward, an archaic scene unfolded in Room 869 and Ritchie Yorke was there. A ubiquitous and influential figure in Lennon's Canadian visits, the Juno Award-winning Yorke was an Australian-born author, biographer, journalist and music publicist who, after moving to Toronto in 1967, launched his Canadian career by writing Brian Epstein's obituary for the now defunct *Toronto Telegram*. Here's what he saw at the King Edward:

> The press conference, attended by several dozen, was held in Lennon's hotel suite. Police had been posted along the corridors to keep back the 20 or so fans and to scrutinize press, radio and TV credentials.
>
> Inside the suite, Lennon and Ono were surrounded by pink and white carnations, record players, film equipment, empty glasses and ringing phones.
>
> The Lennons sat on a sofa holding hands. Ono wore a white blouse and cream slacks, no shoes; Lennon—his feet folded under his seat most of the time—had a white T-shirt with a green stripe, cream trousers, and white socks with red and blue stripes, no

shoes. A pair of white sneakers lay on the floor in front of him. He wore a gold chain around his neck.[88]

Enter Jerry Levitan. Impersonating a local news reporter, the fourteen-year-old Torontonian snuck in to the Lennon's suite.

It wasn't Levitan's first imposture as a journalist. A year earlier, the determined young man photographed and met Jerry Lewis in New York during the 1968 *Labor Day Telethon* under the guise of a contributor to the make-believe *Canadian News* agency.

Levitan's fanaticism for the Fab Four was more, much more than an adolescent phase; it was at another level entirely. He regularly waited in the alley behind his go-to downtown record store, Sam the Record Man, for the Capitol Records truck to deliver the latest Beatles album and be among the first to buy it!

So when word spread, likely on the radio, that the Lennons were in Toronto, a determined Levitan dusted-off his *Canadian News* persona and sprung to action, arriving at the King Edward Hotel at sunrise on May 26.

In his wonderful book, *I Met The Walrus*, Levitan describes what happened next:

> I took a deep breath … The door opened … I marched right in staring at my feet as I followed the carpet of the (hotel) suite into the living room. The base of a tripod was where I decided to sit down. I slowly looked up, there about four feet in front of me sat John Lennon and Yoko Ono.
>
> John looked down and smiled … John (dressed all in white, cross-legged) was barefoot and had a big bushy beard, exactly like the *Abbey Road* cover. Right then and there I knew my life would be changed forever.[89]

And change it did. He secured an interview with John and Yoko and, in the interim, radio station *1050 CHUM* loaned him a tape recorder, legitimizing Levitan's efforts to meet the walrus, Lennon's alter ego from his 1967 composition "I am the Walrus". And then it began, a marathon interview with 51 questions, song observations, rock 'n' roll contextualization and informed comments by Levitan; thanks to his intensive study of Beatles music and culture, the teenager was in many respects more qualified than some of the accredited journalists hovering in the hotel suite to pursue an interview with the Lennons.

Lennon seemed relaxed and in no way blunted the youngster's enthusiastic questions. At around questions 26 and 27 came Lennon's most provocative responses:

> **Levitan**: George (Harrison) is sort of the only one who's thinking of breaking out of The Beatles ... he's the one who's sort of dwelling into his own ...
>
> **Lennon**: What do you think I'm doing with Yoko? ... They're always blaming me for that. Ringo Starr is making these films all the time. I'm writing songs, you know. We're all doing, I mean, I was writing them books years ago. We're all doing our own gig now as well as Beatles. You know, one is The Beatles and the other is four individuals.[90]

It's worth pointing out that although on-and-off tensions among members of The Beatles began brewing during their final concert tour of 1966 and steadily grew from then, John and Yoko's first of three visits to Canada in 1969 was nine months before the official break up of the band in April 1970.

It's not to say young Levitan had the scoop of the century, far from it as Starr had already briefly walked out on the band, Harrison pursued solo projects and both he and McCartney had been writing songs for others; but to hear Lennon spell out to a kid in Toronto no less, that the band was "doing our own gig" as "four individuals" ranks among the earliest public hints or presage of a future filled with The Beatles as solo artists, and no more.

(Back to Levitan. In 2007, he teamed up with writer-director Josh Raskin, and animators James Braithwaite and Alex Kurina to produce a six-minute short film based on *I Met The Walrus*. The Toronto-based team earned multiple international awards and platitudes for the film, which starred Levitan and Lennon, including an Oscar nomination for Best Animated Short Film. In 2021, Levitan co-produced the *I Am The Egbert* series of short black and white animation film loops written and directed by John and Yoko's son Sean Lennon).

And wouldn't you know it, the madness that contributed to The Beatles' decision to stop touring after 1966 was on full display again that evening in Toronto as the Lennons and their entourage tried to make their way out of the King Edward Hotel, only to be met by a mob of fans which Toronto police struggled to contain.

They eventually got in a car and sped off to the airport for a 9:55 p.m. flight. An hour or so later, the Lennons, Taylor, Kyoko and their cameramen arrived in Montréal where local police drove them to the outskirts of the city to rendezvous with taxis that completed the trip to the Queen Elizabeth Hotel, checking into Rooms 1738, 1740, 1742 and 1744 for a seven-day, historic stay. Now known as Fairmont The Queen Elizabeth, the hotel is also referred to by its French name Le Reine Élizabeth, or as some local Anglophones call it, "the Queen E."

Why didn't the Lennon-Ono slumber party happen in Toronto? A legitimate question for certain, and it seems the Ontario capital was considered until Taylor was advised Montréal would be a better setting.

Lest we forget that for the best part of the 20th century, the Island of Montréal was Canada's pre-eminent international city and the hub for style, arts, sports, tourism and much of the nation's world profile. The Montréal Canadiens were the toast of the NHL, the Expo 67 world fair brought global attention to the city and its mayor, Jean Drapeau, was a visionary who later brought Canada's first major league baseball team and 21st Summer Olympic Games to his city.

And while Toronto has since overtaken Montréal as Canada's first city, in the late 1960s it was perhaps considered by some to be more staid and conservative by comparison; that said, Toronto would figure large in two additional visits by the Lennons later that same year.

While Montréal was an easy sell, whoever convinced Taylor to consider the city missed a key qualifier. Whether he chose to ignore it, hoped it would pass over, or perhaps was just doing what the boss told him to (as in get him and Ono to a major media centre as close to New York as possible without actually setting foot in the United States), Taylor seemed unperturbed about the very real and potentially dangerous undercurrent of political unrest in Montréal at the time.

Only five years earlier that unrest directly impacted The Beatles with potentially disastrous results. It was while they were preparing to play in Montréal in September 1964 that city police informed the band that Starr had received a credible death threat from a growing separatist's movement in the province. The threat was particularly sinister in that it also contained an untoward (and inaccurate) racist slur describing the drummer as an English Jew. The threat drove police to set-up sharpshooters and plain-clothes security at The Forum and, in an unusual but perhaps desperate move, Starr himself created a layer of protection while playing: "Once The Beatles took the stage in Montréal, Ringo—on his drum riser—purposely turned his symbols outward toward the audience for whatever little protection that afforded him ... The Beatles spent a total of 10 hours in Montréal and never returned."[91]

Lennon would become the first Beatle to return to the city and by 1969 the separatist movement had gained significant momentum, stirring up the status quo with nationalist objectives peppered with organized acts of violence, and all the while working to gain a legitimate political foothold.

The format of the Montréal Bed-In would be similar to the event in Amsterdam with the Lennons taking up the corner suite and looking like two gurus, donning white pajamas and sitting in bed at the centre of attention. They took questions, posed for photos, talked endlessly on the telephone, gave interviews, rambled, nagged and rejoiced in the power of the human spirit. It seemed like everybody and anybody showed up—reporters mostly, but also an eclectic group of intellectuals, faith leaders, supporters and fans.

Everyone had an opinion on war, conflict, political leaders, society and the establishment. That made the Lennons, and their activism, fair game to any and all that arrived in their hotel suite that week in May

1969, including two politicized and personal confrontations, one with an American cartoonist Al Capp and another with a Québec radical.

That Québec militant was a 35-year-old former journalist and activist named Jacques Larue-Langlois. After being fired by public broadcaster Radio-Canada, Larue-Langlois would become a member of the Front de Libération du Québec (FLQ). A year later during the so-called "October Crisis" of October 1970, the FLQ—a Marxist-Leninist separatist group—kidnapped and murdered Québec Deputy Premier Pierre Laporte.

Local photographer Roy Kerwood, who was 19 at the time, spent the entire week with the Lennons and recalled how John, who long stood for non-violent confrontation, bristled at the Québecker from the moment Larue-Langlois launched into his vision of an independent Québec nation: "John had absolutely nothing in common with him and said, 'You're talking about overthrow and violence, we're talking about peace, why are you here?'"

Added Kerwood, "There was no direction in the conversation where anything was moving forward."[92]

An amusing aside, Kerwood recalled being at the Queen Elizabeth and sharing a joint with Tommy Smothers, the American comedian-singer visiting the Lennons. They offered some to Lennon who, aware he needed to keep his wits about him with an impending arrival of a local group from the Krishna temple, declined the offer. Lennon was also perhaps mindful of how his mate Harrison might react should word travel across the Atlantic of a stoned Beatle meeting with local Krishnas.

But what Kerwood, who moved from Montréal to Burnaby, British Columbia in 1991, recalls best was "how absolutely wonderful John Lennon was. He and I struck up a friendship that was very, very good."[93]

People just kept arriving.

Ripping pages out of Jerry Levitan's book on how to impersonate reporters, two friends from Montréal's Northmount High School, Tommy Schnurmacher and Gail Renard, set out to catch a glimpse of Lennon—or at best to snag an autograph—by concocting fake media credentials before boarding the bus to Dorchester Boulevard with a box of crayons in hand and a date with history.

It was Schnurmacher's idea to visit the famous couple and he convinced a reluctant Renard to make their way to the hotel. He picked up the crayons as a gift for little Kyoko along the way. That simple enticement, along with cleverly getting off the hotel elevator on the 18th floor and using the stairs to descend to the 17th, was part of Schnurmacher's master plan and it got them to the Lennons' door.

Knocking on the door of Suite 1742 they were met by George Urquhart. Employed by the hotel for 32 years as a security guard, Urquhart walked shoulder-to-shoulder alongside kings, queens and heads of state but on this particular occasion he was given the assignment to guard the Lennons. In 2008, from his home in Calgary, he told *Canadian Press* what happened next:

> 'I remember it clearly,' recalled Urquhart, 73. '(Schnurmacher) walked by and I grabbed him by the scruff of the neck and asked him where he thought he was going. It was a funny deal, I'll tell ya.' Ono told Urquhart to allow the teens into the suite and they were able to stay.[94]

Schnurmacher, the son of Holocaust survivors who five years earlier pleaded with his dad for four dollars to buy his first Beatles album, was 18 at the time. Over the phone, he picks up the story: "Standing in the doorway, were Yoko and her daughter Kyoko who was eyeing the shiny box of crayons in my hand and asked for them. I obliged and then Yoko asked if we wanted to meet John. Meet John! We could barely believe it, nodded and said yes."

The forged media credentials never left his wallet. Whether rewarding their chutzpah, or perhaps looking to the young Canadians to fill a need, Lennon conferred with his wife and they asked Schnurmacher and Renard to look after the little girl for the balance of the week. The arrangement was informal; the young Montréalers were neither screened nor supervised and the Lennons didn't ask for any details. Instead, Schnurmacher and Renard would arrive to the hotel every morning and take Kyoko to Schnurmacher's home where they passed the time drawing in colouring books, drinking chocolate milk, and enjoying the playground at a nearby park; Schnurmacher also intro-duced Yoko's child to his sister Cynthia, who was the same age.

They returned Kyoko back to the Queen Elizabeth each night and, like *Groundhog Day*, repeated the mission for a week as casual employees of the famous couple in the spring of 1969. "We were the Lennons' unofficial babysitters. When it was over, one of John's people paid us $150 each for our efforts."

British-born radio personality, Roger Scott spent considerable time with the Lennons in that hotel suite, providing a daily afternoon broad-cast from the couple's bedside for *1470 CFOX AM*. On May 28 an enthusiastic Scott overstayed his time at the Queen Elizabeth and missed the start of his own show back at the station. He was reprimanded, his pay docked $50 and told it would be his last warning in a scathing memo from his boss Frank Gould, with a copy sent to station owner Gord Sinclair, eldest son of legendary Canadian journalist Gordon Sinclair.

At some point, Scott showed the letter to Lennon. Lennon read the letter and wrote this note to Scott's boss: "Dear Frank. I asked Roger to stay as a personal favour to me—which he did. I'm sorry it inconvenienced you but I hope you will understand his situation and not be THAT hard on him ($50)! With Love, John Lennon."[95]

It's unclear if the letter assuaged Gould, but just as he took teenagers Levitan, Renard and Schnurmacher under his wing, Lennon's actions illustrated acts of kindness and maturity well beyond his years in the chaos of his peace campaign in a country that ostensibly was more wel-coming to his ex-mother-in-law than to he and Ono. He even took time to ask a radio station in Edmonton to locate a Cree woman that Lennon had read about in a Montréal newspaper. The woman was named Lillian Shirt and she was protesting on the steps of the Alberta Legislature against poor living conditions for First Nations people. She had a remarkable conversation with the Lennons and evoked words that may have, even in the smallest way, inspired their signature song "Imagine".

The Lennons ate a lot of fish during their eight days at the Queen Elizabeth. Their diet consisted of broiled filet of sole, halibut and salmon, scrambled eggs with crisp bacon, brown rice, sirloin steak and lamb chops, along with comfort food like turtle soup, rice pudding and lots of tea.

Give Peace A Chance

Montréal Bed-In: John and Yoko were popular music's power odd couple of the latter 1960s. Seemingly mismatched, the truth couldn't be further. Through their music, art and celebrity, they sought the media spotlight to spread a very simple, unambiguous message of peace. The two were enamored with Canada as a country but also its proximity to getting their message across to the United States media. Photo courtesy of The Beatles Story, Liverpool.

If New York was Lennon's America, Montréal was his Canada. It's a wonder the city was never named nor formed a lyric in a Lennon song. It rolls off the tongue so rhythmically like "Old Montréal was the belle of the ball until Charles de Gaulle ruined it all" *mais (malheureusement) pas de chance!* The other Bed-In city, Amsterdam, made the cut as a track from Lennon and Ono's *Wedding Album* and references to New York City abound throughout his solo recording career.

In fact, there are zero Canadian place names or cultural references in any Beatles compositions or films unless Harrison's wry quip about Canadian geese crapping on the shores in "Pisces Fish" counts. Oh, and a shivering Starr asked "are we practicing to be Canadians?"—a reference to Starr freezing his Beatle buttocks during a Toronto winter in the 1970s—in McCartney's film *Give My Regards to Broad Street.*

Lest we get our northern knickers in a twist, consider that The Beatles rarely used foreign places by name or as adjectives in their songs. At my count only seven Beatle songs contain the names of places outside of the United Kingdom: Paris, Amsterdam and Vienna in "The Ballad of John and Yoko"; Ukraine, Moscow and Georgia in "Back to the U.S.S.R."; Tucson in "Get Back"; Los Angeles or "L.A." while waiting for Derek Taylor in "Blue Jay Way" and, in "Rocky Raccoon" the Black (Mining) Hills of (South) Dakota make the grade. In "What's the New Mary Jane", Lennon offers delectable morsels of Mongolian lamb, Mexican beans and Patagonian pancakes and stirs in references to Bahrain and an African Queen. Lennon was also dreaming, more or less, when he sang "On the Road to Rishikesh" (a song sliver which morphed into "Child of Nature" and much later as "Jealous Guy"). And there's a bootleg recording of something called "Commonwealth" a playfully hysterical song fragment where McCartney and Lennon manage to rhyme off several member nations like India, Pakistan, Australia and New Zealand too, but not Canada.

But it matters not. Lennon's greatest gift to Canada was the completion, recording and production of the world's most iconic peace anthem on Canadian soil! Montréal gave birth to "Give Peace a Chance" and the three-chord song offers the most hands-on, nurtured Canadian content of anything ever released by a Beatle. The phrase "Give Peace a Chance" was something Lennon had used as a sound bite in media interviews. It came to him rather spontaneously and, befitting the master of words, strung together the song in creative bursts of internal energy and external pleas. He finished the song during his time at the Queen Elizabeth; it's believed Lennon always wanted to craft a sing-along protest song with a particularly simple hook, as in "We Shall Overcome".

So how did its recording come to pass, and why?

To understand the hippie chaos unfolding in Suite 1742 in the moments leading up to the recording of "Give Peace a Chance" in 1969, let's hear from two eyewitnesses: *Montréal Gazette* writer and Juno Award recipient Dave Bist, and Allan Rock, the Ottawa-born future Canadian cabinet minister and ambassador to the United Nations.

Bist had a premium seat to the events in that room as he was literally squished with others at the foot of the Lennons' bed. He sets the scene with a colourful description moments before the reel-to-reel recording machine was turned on:

> There are about 40 people in the room (including reporters, hotel and entourage staff, celebrities ... and curious hotel guests), radio station *CFOX* is set up in the corner of the room and, frankly, it's hotter (than) hell. The tension, as they say, is mounting ...
>
> Some representatives of the local Krishna Consciousness Temple have been regular visitors and have brought along their instruments—drums, cymbals and tambourines—to accompany their Hare Krishna chants.
>
> The lyrics are pasted on the wall, (Tommy) Smothers perches on the edge of John and Yoko's bed and Leary and his wife, Rosemary, take up positions at its foot. The rest of us stand or sit on the floor and Lennon gives us his marching orders: he'll sing the lead and the rest of us can join in the chorus.
>
> Tony Hall, a bellboy who'd been assigned to the room, is handed a tambourine and (Timothy) Leary a pair of sticks to whack together. I'm ordered to guard a microphone stand. Hand clapping is encouraged.[96]

Here's what Allan Rock saw: "I walked into this suite it was complete mayhem. Over in the corner there was a group of Hare Krishna devotees chanting, in another corner was somebody broadcasting live for a Montréal radio station, somewhere else (cartoonist) Al Capp and Tommy Smothers were arguing over some political issue, and noise, and people coming and going, and things flying up in the air, and they were getting ready to record 'Give Peace A Chance', and they were bringing in instruments ... madness."[97]

Add these images to complete the setting: White carnations in white vases, white bed sheets and pajamas, strewn sections of newspapers (Lennon began reading daily newspapers as a teenager and seemed to add the city's English-language dailies, the *Gazette* and *Star*, to his regimen while in Canada), ashtrays and blue and white Gauloise cigarette packages, Coca-Cola bottles, wafts of cigarette, cigar and marijuana smoke, snow globes, coffee cups, half-eaten room service, telephones, wiring, microphones, cameras, television lights, Lennon's 1964 Gibson J-160E acoustic guitar and a cacophony of endless bits of unstructured chatter from the star struck, the curious and the media; and there, propped on a queen-size bed, were John and Yoko. What a scene!

Bist brings the familiar moment to its historic denouement:

> John counts, then launches into the song:
>
> Two, one two three four. Ev'rybody's talking about Bagism, Shagism, Dragism, Madism, Ragism, Tagism. This-ism, that-ism, is-m, is-m, is-m. Then the chorus is almost deafening:
>
> All we are saying is give peace a chance. All we are saying is give peace a chance
>
> This goes on for seven or eight minutes and everybody's having a great time, rocking back and forth, clapping and goggle-eyed ... [98]

The song ended with cheers and applause from the assembled crowd.

The Remarkable Story of Montréal's André Perry

Peace Team: Montréal's André Perry and John closely collaborated on the recording of "Give Peace a Chance" from Suite 1742 of the Queen Elizabeth Hotel. The two bonded instantly and forged a relationship based on mutual respect. Asked if he ever dreams of John, Perry said: "The spirituality you get from someone stays with you." Photo courtesy of André Perry.

In their colourful recollections of events in Suite 1742, neither Bist nor Rock mention the presence of a subdued 32-year-old French Canadian going about his business. In the warm, dreamy chaos of that hotel suite stood Montréal-born former jazz drummer turned recording engineer and producer André Perry, sporting a goatee, and wearing a cream turtle neck sweater covered in a brown corduroy jacket and crowned with earphones over his head.

On that day, June 1, 1969, Perry would work around the clock to make modern history as the Canadian to play the weightiest role in the music of The Beatles, either as a band or individuals.

Perry hit his stride in the 1960s in the Montréal and New York music scenes, recording and producing traditional and experimental acts. He opened his first recording studio in the Montréal suburb of Ville Brossard and built a solid reputation for his work with, among others, well-loved French-Canadian singer-songwriters Jean-Pierre Ferland and Robert Charlebois.

His fond recollection of working with John and Yoko 52 years ago is as crisp as the diverse sounds he brought to life in the recording studio. "It was a wonderful adventure," says Perry, 84 at the time of our chat, looking back on the experience that put him on a collision course with history.

He rebukes the suggestion made by countless sources that Derek Taylor hired him to record the song. "It wasn't Derek Taylor; it was the late Pierre Dubord, the A&R man for Capitol Records in Canada (The Beatles' Apple Corps distributor). I had worked with Pierre and Capitol on various projects and he knew I was capable, that's what put me at the centre of recording 'Give Peace a Chance'.

Why you, André?

"When I was called to do this recording, it wasn't a recording engineer that showed up, it was a musician and producer. But it is also worth mentioning that I wasn't really a total fan of The Beatles. I appreciated their talent but, to tell the truth, at the time I was more a Miles Davis guy."

And then there was the question of equipment. Perry revealed for the first time that his four-track recording equipment, required for the task, was not available.

"I accepted the job knowing full well my four-track recording gear was sitting at Place des Arts, as we were busy that spring for (the upcoming) production of *Tommy*," he says. Perry's company was hired to enable a quad playback version of Ferdinand Nault's world-premiere ballet interpretation of The Who's just-released *Tommy*. The dance-based adaptation by Les Grands Ballets Canadiens of the 1969 rock opera—that produced rock classics "Pinball Wizard", "We're Not Going to Take it" and "See Me, Feel Me"—was unique and another world-class achievement of the city's thriving arts community.

"In those days, four-track equipment was very bulky and as heavy as a refrigerator, so moving it from Place des Arts to the hotel wasn't an option so I rented a Scully four-track recorder from RCA Victor Studios."

Perry, and his life and business partner Yaël Brandeis, arrived in the Lennons' suite with their equipment and three assistants on June 1, 1969.

> It was a real zoo. You would think there would have been a lot of security and control with the overflow of people but in this instance it wasn't the case. There were a lot of people with fake press passes saying they were journalists just to get in. It was totally disorganized.
>
> My concern was about the audio quality—not so much from the noise, but from the room's low, 7-foot ceiling and walls made of sheetrock which create 'standing waves,' a type of bouncing effect. I also asked the Hare Krishna guests (members of the Radha Krishna Temple on Boul. Pie-IX in Montréal) to stop clanging their bells as the microphones I used were quite sensitive.

Bringing considerable technical and audio heft to the project absent of any fawning, star-struck admiration, says Perry, was crucial to establishing, and preserving, his integrity with Lennon.

"John Lennon was an extremely intelligent man," says Perry. Lennon wanted to raise the volume on his anti-war message and realized the Montréal Bed-In needed more firepower to attract attention.

"John had this idea that the song would make a bigger impact; one that the world's media couldn't ignore.

"We looked at each other eye to eye and two minutes later he gave me complete liberty to do what was necessary. And that made sense because at that moment he was more concerned with the lyrics, which he was modifying, and having people learn the chorus, and instructing (Tommy) Smothers to change his finger-style guitar playing to more of a strumming style."

Perry acknowledges, "My relationship with John Lennon was based on respect. You could say it was not unlike the kind of relationship he had with George Martin."

The reference to George Martin is striking. Martin was an extraordinarily talented producer and, in my estimation, for all the layers and texture he added to raise the art of Beatles recordings, is the real fifth Beatle. Perry, like Martin, was schooled in diverse genres of music. Both held deeper, wider musical roots. Perry was also a bit older than Lennon and possessed a keen understanding of songwriting, instrumentation and above all, audiophile-like precision when it came to the production of music.

Perry's team set up their recording equipment in the suite's dining area and placed four microphones: one next to Lennon for his vocals and acoustic guitar, another for comedian and peace activist Tommy Smothers, who also sang and played acoustic guitar, and two others to capture the wildly eclectic assemblage of guests like singer Petula Clark, comedian Dick Gregory, beat poet Allen Ginsberg, Taylor, Scott, anti-war activist Rabbi Abraham Feinberg and space cadet extraordinaire Timothy Leary.

Bed-In Bedlam: John Lennon's greatest gift to Canada was the completion, recording and production of the world's most iconic peace anthem on Canadian soil. But getting "Give Peace a Chance" on tape proved a challenge in the chaos of their Montréal hotel suite. André Perry and his team worked around the clock determined not to let the Lennons leave Canada without a release-ready song. Photo courtesy of André Perry.

The nearly five-minute recording ended with John's, "Ok, beautiful," and then cheers from the packed hotel room.

"We recorded it in two or three takes. It was a wonderful thing. I still wasn't overwhelmed that I was recording a Beatle, but I respected the hook he wrote."

Lennon asked everyone to leave the room save for Perry who played back the recording, which, he recalls, left much to be desired.

"I said, 'It's not good, right? Referring to the crowd sound,' and he agreed, 'Yes.'" Perry reassured Lennon he would "sweeten" the raw recording but before getting back to his studio he was asked to stay and record the B-side called "Remember Love", a four-minute song featuring a soft, falsetto vocal by Ono while John picks and strums chords that, at times, are reminiscent of "Dear Prudence".

Recording aside, Perry was struck by how caring the newlyweds treated one another:

> They both sat on the floor in front of the bed. I stood there about four feet away, put one mic on John and the other on Yoko. It was a wonderful experience and the song was quite beautiful. I was with them for about four hours and it was obvious they were madly in love. He was so patient with her and I was struck by how caring he was because it was difficult for her to sing this song in falsetto and we did many takes. After a while they would stop, return to bed and he would tickle her just to help her relax and we (finally) ended up with this wonderful take, very pure and without edits.

Perry didn't leave the hotel suite until early the next morning and headed straight for his basement studio in Brossard. His producer's instinct kicked in; determined, he didn't want Lennon leaving Canada without a release-ready song.

In studio and without delay, he transferred the four tracks to his Ampex eight-track recorder to allow room for overdubs, then Perry made a few calls and soon a steady stream of talented, even famous,

Québeckers arrived. They included Robert Charlebois, Mouffe (pop star Claudine Monfette), arranger and conductor Buddy Fasano and bassist Don Habib.

"I told them I needed their help with a John Lennon recording and they thought I was joking. But they heard he was in town and knew it was for real."

He tasked his friends to sing the now familiar chorus "all we are saying is give peace a chance" in a basic, unpolished way to blend with Lennon and the many voices in the hotel room. The group he assembled were all professionals so it didn't take long to achieve the desired result.

Next, he dealt with the controlled chaos of people banging on doors and ashtrays thinking they were keeping beat but in truth the sound was all over the place. He reduced those wayward sounds, swept them to the back of the recording and decided to introduce "a big bottom sound, a thump if you will."

"I was alone in the studio and grabbed my Rubbermaid garbage bin because, being a drummer, I knew it would give me the low thumping sound I was looking for."

To hear Perry's rubber trash bin, wait about a minute into the recording for the distinctive ba-dum thump sound, and soon afterward ba-dum is interrupted by a triplet of ba-dum-ba-dum-ba-dum every eight or sixteen beats. (Fans of Led Zeppelin have long theorized that drummer John Bonham tapped on a plastic pail, garbage can lid or guitar case for the song "Ramble On" in October 1969.)

Perry then took a shower and rushed back to the hotel with tapes in hand. When Lennon saw him he once again asked that the room be cleared. "He sent everyone out of the room and it was just me and John. Just the two of us."

As he thread the tape through the recorder he explained to Lennon that his "sweetening" retained the live, raucous, ensemble feel of the recording, but with much of the residual clutter cleaned up and that he also reinforced the chorus and, generally, achieved what he thought he was looking for. Before playing it, Perry offered Lennon two options: Use the mixed-down master that you're about to hear, or rework the original, unedited tracks when you get back to England.

"So I played it for him and he said, 'Extraordinary.'"

For Perry, the best was yet to come. Five weeks after "Give Peace a Chance" was released in North America, his phone rang.

"I got a call from Bill Rotari, president of Capitol Records, who said, 'André you're not going to believe this but the label copy on the 45 (rpm single) reads like your business card, it has everything but your telephone number.'"

Unheard of in the record industry, ever, and a demonstration of the fellowship he had achieved with Lennon, Perry's name and address appeared on the single; just below the printed song title was this commemoration: "Recorded by Le Studio, André Perry, 7585 Malo, Ville de Brossard, P.Q., Canada." Perry saw it as a message from Lennon:

> Of course that was John's way of thanking me. I didn't make much money, as some people might believe, for my work on 'Give Peace a Chance'. I was paid $2,500 for playing a role more as a co-producer than just an engineer and this included payment for my personnel, equipment, studio time and tapes. And I would say that yes, I saved the day on this recording.

In an instant and since then, the address of the yellow bungalow where Perry housed his studio was known to the estimated nearly 1.5 million buyers of the single "Give Peace a Chance". Years later, when *Mojo Magazine* asked McCartney to name his favourite Lennon song he gave the nod to "Give Peace a Chance" saying: "I love this song for its vibe, for its sentiment, and for its vocalist. He had a copy, played it to me and I was just blown away by the rhythm section of just everyone stompin'. It's just so John, you know."[99]

André and Yaël would go on to establish Le Studio as one of the world's first environmentally sensitive recording studios, relocating it in a forested lake setting near the town of Morin Heights in Quebec's Laurentian Mountains in 1974. By the time Perry sold Le Studio in 1988, it had become the go-to recording location for the world's most famous recording artists, welcoming David Bowie, Chicago, The Police, Keith Richards, The Bee Gees, Cat Stevens, The Cult, Sting and Nazareth as well as Canadian bands Rush, April Wine, Kim Mitchell, Bryan Adams, Corey Hart, Glass Tiger and Jeff Healey, including the late guitarist's version of "While My Guitar Gently Weeps".

Perry estimates 250 million albums were sold of recordings made at Le Studio.

Asked if he's ever dreamed of Lennon, Perry admits that he has, perhaps not of Lennon the person but the spiritual force he observed in the short time of their collaboration. "The spirituality you get from someone stays with you."

Less than six months after it was recorded, "Give Peace a Chance" became the protest song adopted by the Moratorium March on Washington, D.C., where an estimated 500,000 people gathered to call for an end to the war in Vietnam.

Led by singer Pete Seeger, the half million demonstrators were gathered across from the White House singing Lennon's just released "Give Peace A Chance" for ten minutes or more while Seeger implored, "Are you listening, (Richard) Nixon? Are you listening (Spiro) Agnew? Are you listening Pentagon?" Guided by the song, the demonstration would become the largest of its kind in American history and on that day Lennon's composition became a new rallying cry for the entire peace movement. For the past five decades it continues to be the English-speaking world's de facto song of protest, hope and change.

Even Lennon took notice: "I like 'Give Peace a Chance' for what it was. I couldn't say that was the best song as a song I'd ever written, but I'm always proud of it. I think one of the highest moments was hearing all those people in Washington, when the whole anti-war group was singing it. That was an emotional moment for me."[100]

Come Together's Montréal Origins

Less remarkable, but certainly worth a mention is that in addition to "Give Peace a Chance" and "Remember Love", a third Lennon song would materialize—although less directly—from his time in Montréal that spring. You'll recall that American Timothy Leary, an eccentric psychologist, author and psychedelic drug advocate, sang and banged sticks during the recording of "Give Peace a Chance" along with his wife Rosemary Woodruff—by the way, when the two married in California in 1967 all wedding guests and witnesses had ritualistically consumed LSD. With a colourful and controversial career that included overt drug use and experimentation plus several stints of incarceration and even a prison escape Leary, naturally, announced his candidacy for governor of California in late 1968 with a goal of defeating the incumbent Ronald Reagan!

A 48, Leary was one of the oldest participants in the Montréal Bed-In. While there he mentioned to Lennon his campaign slogan was the very clever "Come Together, Join the Party" and asked the Beatle to compose a theme song along those lines to bolster his election chances. In the 2020 release of *Gimme Some Truth*, a four-disc boxed set of Lennon songs and re-mixes released to coincide with what would have been his 80th birthday, a 124-page booklet offers the background to The Beatles' "Come Together" in Lennon's words:

> 'Come Together' was an expression that Tim and Rosemary Leary had come up with for his attempt to be president—or whatever he wanted to be—and he asked me at the Montréal Bed-In to write them a sing-song campaign song.
>
> I tried and I tried and I tried and I couldn't come up with it. But I came up with this 'Come Together', which would have been no good to them. You couldn't have a campaign song like that, right. It was a funky record—it's one of my favourite Beatle tracks, or one of my favourite Lennon tracks, let's say that. It's funky and it's bluesy, and I'm singing it pretty well.[101]

So let's again turn to Wyman's invaluable song-ranking abacus for a subjective assessment of "Come Together", the seed of which was planted in Canada. Wyman says it's the 44th best composition in The Beatles' 213-song catalogue, calling the swampy, bass-heavy and instantly satisfying tune a "quintessential" Lennon song and "everything a rock recording should be" that "remains the band's most perennially popular, a rock radio behemoth that is played more often even than 'Stairway to Heaven.'"[102]

On June 3, 1969, the Lennon entourage would return to Ontario. A story in the *Ottawa Citizen* headlined "The Beatle is Coming" told of how University of Ottawa student union president Allan Rock confirmed Lennon would "appear at a public meeting on the lawn of the Uof O administration building a 4 p.m., then take part in a seminar kicking off a three-day conference on peace … "[103]

Rock, and his student union friend Hugh Segal, met Lennon and Ono at the train station. Arriving at the University of Ottawa around 5 p.m., they participated in the impromptu peace conference, spoke with media and took-in a crowd of approximately 300 students gathered in front of the school's Tabaret Pavilion. The visit lasted approximately 90 minutes and, all the while, Montréal-born Segal, a future political strategist and Canadian senator, would pick up where Renard and Schnurmacher left off when tasked with looking after Kyoko.

College campuses in the United States were key rallying points for anti-Vietnam War protests—ground zero of the world's most vigorous peace movement, but what the Lennons saw in Canada was a comparatively tame University of Ottawa; perhaps representative of a country not at war that, at best, was comprised of people who openly sympathized with the predicament of young people south of the border. To be sure, there were anti-war protests attended by thousands in Vancouver, Edmonton and Toronto the year earlier, and the Canadian government did call for a cessation of US bombing of Vietnam and renewed its call for both sides to enter into peace negotiations but, despite its proximity to the United States, Canada didn't have a lot of skin in this game.

All that to say it was as if the couple were conducting their campaign in exile, which may have left the Lennons unsatisfied at the seemingly detached reality of playing out a peace movement in a country at peace. If that emboldened their resolve to take their message directly to the United States, the nearest they got was the border city of Niagara Falls, Ontario, on June 4—which turned out, like millions of newlyweds before them, to be their photo op in a conventional honeymoon destination.

And then, poignantly, in the hours leading up to the end of their negotiated 10-day stay, they had a final immigration hearing on June 5 and were promptly asked to leave, as Taylor would concede: "They were in fact deported from Canada at the end of the Bed-In because their appeal ... had failed. They'd done the whole Bed-In during an appeal period (and) were put on the first plane out to Frankfurt, which is not where we were going, we were going to London. So that, again, is something people forget! Doing a Bed-In and being deported when it was over."[104]

In a historic parallel, their deportation flight from Canada to West Germany would be Lennon's second international expulsion since he and his band mates were hastily removed from West Germany in 1960 for conduct unbecoming of foreign nationals. But despite all the chaos, missed opportunities and confusion surrounding his first solo visit to Canada in the spring of 1969, the Lennons would launch a cultural cottage industry of peace-making events, peace-intending songs and, above, all, the words "Bed" and "In" would jointly enter the peace lexicon for all time to come.

And, by the way, that seed of a song that Leary planted in Lennon's head on a bed in Montréal took root as The Beatles began recording "Come Together" a mere 46 days after Lennon's departure from Canada. Leary, incidentally, who famously videotaped his death from cancer in 1996 at age 75, was buried in the cosmos when his ashes were flown by Pegasus rocket to Earth's orbit where they remained for six years until flaming out.

When Peace Was Denied a Chance

André Perry noted he did not become rich from "Give Peace a Chance", but another Montréal associate of the Lennons did.

Gail Renard was the 16-year-old who, with her crayon-toting high school friend Tommy Schnurmacher, cleverly made her way into the Lennons' Queen Elizabeth Hotel suite and ended up spending eight days babysitting Ono's daughter, Kyoko.

In the aftermath of the recording of "Give Peace a Chance", Renard and Schnurmacher arrived in the famous hotel suite to find a mess. It was then, Schnurmacher recalls, Renard took a poster board that was lying around. This was no ordinary "Hair Peace" or "Bed Peace" board but the actual paperboard where Lennon, in a flash of anti-war inspiration, jotted the lyrics of "Give Peace a Chance" so as not to forget them while singing it.

In his hand, at the top of the board he wrote: "Everybodies talking bout" and below a neat row of four equally spaced columns devoted to each verse in the song. The left column listed various nonsensical Lennon made-up isms, like "Bagism, Shagism, Draggism ... " The next column had "Ministers, Sinisters, bannisters, cannisters," and then "revolution, evolution, masturbation, flagellation," and so on before listing a random group of personalities from Bobby Dylan to Norman Mailer and Alan Ginsberg. At the bottom, the Beatle scribbled the refrain, "All we are saying is give peace a chance."

You can probably guess the rest. In 2008, Renard took the vellum-textured, 22x28-inch board on which Lennon scribbled his lyrics and sang them while André Perry worked the tape machine, to London's Christie's Auction House and it sold for $841,000. Soon after the sale, she spoke with *CBC News* recalling what Lennon told about the paperboard memento: "He kept on saying, 'These things are going to be worth something someday. Have them.'"[105]

Schnurmacher remembers things differently. In fact the former Lennon babysitters have vastly dissimilar recollections of the events leading up to and during their time with the Lennons.

In his 2019 book *Makeup Tips from Auschwitz: How Vanity Saved My Mother's Life* author Schnurmacher devotes two chapters of his memoir to entering the Lennon's world in 1969, and the decades-later aftermath that caused the bitter end of a cherished teenage friendship.

Born in Budapest, Hungary, and raised in Montréal by his concentration camp surviving parents (his book is based on his mother's survival at Auschwitz), Schnurmacher passionately lays out his version of the facts relating to the board containing Lennon's hand-written lyrics and how, ironically, while that piece of paper held words to encourage peace it created nothing of the sort—more like a prolonged and personal dumpster fire of discord and petulance.

Let's back up.

Schnurmacher and Renard became friends while attending high school together in Montréal. As teens, they shared a passion for Monty Python and explored their creative sides, particularly around television and radio, writing scripts for *CBC Radio's Funny You Should Say That* national broadcast.

While Renard did not respond to questions and interview requests for this book, Schnurmacher did and offered these kind words toward her: "She was hysterically funny with a spectacular sense of humour. We got along very well as writing partners and friends."

Now back to that fateful meeting with the Lennons in May 1969. At the conclusion of their babysitting assignment, the two received payment of $150 each and also came away with souvenirs—Lennon signed and doodled on a black and white photo of himself for Schnurmacher, and Renard got the aforementioned poster board. She claims Lennon gave it to her with his best wishes, although Schnurmacher disputes this and said she grabbed it from the messy remnants of that hotel room after the raucous "Give Peace a Chance" recording session, which neither of the two attended.

At the time, such details were inconsequential and their friendship continued; they even travelled to Toronto on December 17 of that year to reacquaint themselves with John and Yoko who were visiting the Ontario Science Centre (Lennon was at the venue to announce an Ontario "peace rock festival" he was organizing for July 1970, although it never transpired).

Fast-forward to 2008 when Christie's announced the docket for its upcoming auction in London would include Renard's "Give Peace a Chance" poster board. When Schnurmacher heard of the impending auction, he received a couple of opinions suggesting something was amiss, including a lawyer friend who urged him to intercede and file a claim of unjust enrichment. The basis of the claim would be that he and Renard were partners in the events that led to her receiving Lennon's lyrics. And more to the point, it was Schnurmacher who hatched and planned the operation to meet the Lennons, bringing a reluctant Renard along for the ride.

In the end, Schnurmacher trusted his instincts and turned the other cheek, declining to take any legal action.

The sale happened and Renard received the tidy sum. Sometime later, the two sides squared off in a very public way, as Renard was a guest on Schnurmacher's *CJAD-AM* morning radio show. The back and forth between the two has been lost in the archives but it likely made for great radio. Renard, whom Schnurmacher claims offered him a cappuccino and piece of cake as recompense, went on to chronicle her life-altering adventure at the Queen Elizabeth in a book called *Give Me a Chance, My Eight Days with John and Yoko* without mentioning Schnurmacher, her friend, Bed-In accomplice and the man whose decision to bring Kyoko a box of crayons changed both of their lives.

These days, Renard has fulfilled a life-long ambition of living and working in England where she has made a name for herself as an award-winning TV writer for *BBC* and *ITV* and is the Treasurer of the Writers' Guild of Great Britain.

Now retired, Schnurmacher grew a successful career as a columnist with the *Montréal Gazette* newspaper and talk radio host, and had this to say about the whole episode: "If the tables were turned I would certainly have given her a percentage of it."

While Renard is outwardly proud of her Bed-In experience, crediting it and the glow of her time with Lennon as the impetus to pursue her dreams in England, Schnurmacher attributes none of his many accomplishments to what transpired in May 1969, stating, "Lennon had nothing to do with it."

As for the friendship that led two young Canadians into Lennon's orbit? Well let's just say it's over; the two haven't spoken since. "I got the photo and she got the lyrics, that's life," says Schnurmacher.

Bed-In Revisited

The Lennons' springtime in Montréal all those years ago has endured in ways perhaps no-one thought possible, putting an indelible cultural stamp on events and history. Here is a small sample of that endurance—nine modern-day highlights that depict what has spawned from the power and resonance of the Bed-In events.

1. Pop music references to the activities and recording during the Montréal Bed-In abound, including a chorus of "all we are saying, is give peace a chance" in the 1971 release by British progressive rock band Yes on their six-minute "I've Seen All Good People" single. A 1996 lyric by The Beatles-influenced band Oasis, "going to start a revolution from my bed," forms part of their song "Don't Look Back in Anger". Cover versions of the song "Give Peace a Chance" have been recorded by Louis Armstrong, Hot Chocolate and Mitch Miller. In a cartoon protest parody of Lennon's famous Montréal composition, SpongeBob Square Pants and Patrick are objecting to the construction of an underwater super highway when they sing 2010's "Give Jellyfish Fields a Chance".

2. In 1985, a reunion of sorts occurred during the Northern Lights for Canada's fund-raising response to Ethiopian famine relief with the song "Tears Are Not Enough". Two Canadians involved in Lennon's 1969 visit, "Give Peace a Chance" chorus singer Robert Charlebois, and Lennon's Ontario host Ronnie

Hawkins, would sing on the record that raised an estimated $3.2 million.

3. In early 1986, the release of the *John Lennon Live in New York City* album—based on the recordings of two charity concerts Lennon, Ono and their Elephant's Memory Band performed at Madison Square Gardens in 1972—featured "Give Peace a Chance" as the encore song. The Lennons invited dozens to join them on stage during an extended, saxophone-laden version of the Bed-In song, which fans spontaneously sang on the streets of Manhattan as they poured out of the venue after the concert.

4. On the 40th anniversary of the Montréal Bed-In, an organization called World March for Peace and Nonviolence set up a "peace bed" near Lennon's Strawberry Fields memorial in New York's Central Park, near where John lived and died. The organization's Chris Wells told *NPR* "John and Yoko had the vision to turn their honeymoon into a call for peace. They asked us to imagine a world without violence. It's a call that remains unfulfilled."[106]

5. Also on that same anniversary, Ono returned to Montréal to open a three-month art exhibit called "Imagine: The Peace Ballad of John and Yoko" at the city's museum of fine arts. "Montréal means very much for me because it was a place where John and I created a very important statement," said Ono who remains active in promoting peace.[107] The exhibit, which both Perry and Schnurmacher attended, was free to the public and included drawings, photography and art from Ono's private collection tracing the couple's time together from 1966 until their 1969 Montréal Bed-In.

6. In 2011, a now grown-up film producer Jerry Levitan reunited with Ono to produce a short film entitled *My Hometown*. The animated film follows the journey of young children creating places on Earth they identify as home. Levitan, who teamed

with Toronto's Eggplant Media on the project, used John and Yoko's "Remember Love"—the "Give Peace a Chance" B-side recorded in their hotel suite by André Perry—as part of the film's soundtrack.

7. Fairmont The Queen Elizabeth Hotel chose the UN's International Day of Peace in 2017 to unveil its exquisite recreation of Suite 1742 in the spirit of the original Lennon event 48 years earlier. For $3,000 plus taxes and gratuities, guests can book the "Bed-In for Peace Package" and stay in the suite that hosted the Bed-In and Perry's recording of "Give Peace a Chance". In addition to overnight accommodation and breakfast, guests receive white flowers, Bed-In themed pajamas, lyrics to the famous song, and various souvenirs. In launching the Bed-In Package, the Canadian-owned Fairmont Hotels and Resorts noted: "Nobody could imagine at the time that this event would play such a key role in the peace movement and that their suite would become one of the most mythical in the world."[108]

8. Actor Jeff Bridges and Starr jumped into bed with Ono in 2018 at an outdoor, staged Bed-In replica event in New York to support a local charity.

9. On May 23, 2019, to mark the 50th anniversary of the Bed-In, the Royal Canadian Mint issued a $20 pure silver coin featuring a rendering of John and Yoko sitting in their Montréal bed wearing pajamas and holding roses. The reverse is a portrait of Queen Elizabeth II. The Master of the Mint, the traditional title of the head of the Canadian crown corporation, Marie Lemay, said, "The Mint has captured that special moment in Canadian and music history with a pure silver coin celebrating Lennon and Ono's artistic talent and social activism ... We are delighted to have crafted a coin celebrating Canada's special connection to John and Yoko, and their lasting message of peace."[109] What the news release doesn't mention, but later

confirmed by the Mint, is that the images of John and Yoko represent the first time rock or pop music personalities appear on a Canadian coin. "We've featured writers and visual artists before, but this was the first for contemporary music," said the Mint's Alex Reeves in an email. Based in Ottawa, the Royal Canadian Mint has been producing all of Canada's circulation coins since 1908.

2. Vulnerabilities, Vagabonds and The Eaton Brothers

The precise origins of Lennon's post-Beatles group, Plastic Ono Band, are somewhat scattered. Lennon credited "Give Peace a Chance" to Plastic Ono Band but it's unlikely he meant to initiate all 40-or-so singers, foot-stompers, ash-tray banging and clap-a-long revelers in Suite 1742 in his new outfit. A fluid ensemble, Plastic Ono Band was actually formed after the Montréal recording (while The Beatles were still together) as an Apple Records concept band.

But in its most tangible form, that is as a performing group, Plastic Ono Band took shape in the back of a Boeing 707 somewhere left of Greenland—and all of it the result of a telephone call from a 22-year-old Toronto concert promoter John Brower who somehow got Lennon to pick up the phone on the other end of a desperate transatlantic call. Here's the story about that telephone call, its profound implications in The Beatles' history and the reason for Lennon's second visit to Canada in 1969.

First, step back. In the months leading up to the call, Brower had successfully organized concerts including the Toronto Pop Festival yet was striving to create a larger event that would put the city on the music festival circuit map, along with Monterey, Newport, Isle of Wight, Fantasy Fair and Magic Mountain Music, and Woodstock. He envisioned an event that would be known as the Toronto Rock and Roll Revival, and set his sights on Saturday, September 13.

With help from investors, Brower and friend and business partner Kenny Walker, 23, secured Varsity Stadium on the University of

Toronto campus for a promised 12 hours of non-stop entertainment from a virtual who's-who of rock 'n' roll pioneers including the likes of Chuck Berry, Bo Diddley, Little Richard, Gene Vincent, Jerry Lee Lewis plus Alice Cooper, Chicago Transit Authority and The Doors. In today's context, if just half of these immortal rockers were on the bill, they would have filled any venue, anywhere.

Enter rock impresario Kim Fowley, a California-based record producer and songwriter who was tapped to emcee the event. Fowley is credited with coming up with the seemingly impossible idea of adding Lennon on that Toronto concert bill. Just how that happened has grown into one of the most legendary stories in the history of late 1960s rock 'n' roll.

The slow pace of Revival concert ticket sales made Brower and his investors nervous and they faced the very real possibility of having to cancel the ambitious outdoor event. This was especially imminent because their key backers, members of the retail giant Eaton family, Thor and John David Eaton, were talking about backing out. That's when Fowley came up with the Lennon idea, actually less of an idea and more like a do-or-die Hail Mary pass. The Hail to Mary went something like this: Contact Apple Records, ask for Lennon, and casually inquire if he would like to come to Canada! Tell him all he would have to do is replace Fowley as the event's emcee and lend rock star credibly and heft on stage when introducing his childhood heroes, Berry, Vincent, Richard et al. Simple, right?

Brower vividly recalled the extraordinary details of that telephone call with music journalist Juliette Jagger, beginning with him imploring the Apple employee in London to write down the names of all the confirmed acts for the Revival concert in an effort to impress Lennon until, magically, Lennon himself picked up the phone:

> 'Hello. This is John Brower from Toronto, Canada and this is very important. I need you to write these names down.' The receptionist on the other end of the line wrote down the names of the artists and I said: 'I want you tell John Lennon they are playing and that we're inviting him to come and be the emcee.'

The next thing you know Lennon comes on the line. He goes, 'So all these bands are playing?' and I said, 'Yeah, this Saturday at the University.' He said, 'Well, we wouldn't want to come unless we can play.' I said, 'Do you mean The Beatles?' To which he said, 'No, just me … and Yoko. We'll put a little band together.' So I of course said, 'Yeah we'll squeeze you in,' which I realized sounded like the stupidest thing in the world because the show was going to be canceled, but he said, 'All right, well I need to get off the phone so I can get a band together.' We were on speaker phone so everyone was just thinking, 'Oh God how much is this going to cost?' But before he left I said, 'Listen, we can't pay you but we'll get you first class plane tickets and we'll put you up somewhere nice.' He said, 'That's all fine no problem.' I told him I'd call him back for the names on the plane tickets tomorrow and that was it. Click. And he hung up. I just looked at Thor and said, 'Okay, so do we have a show or what?' And he finally said, 'Okay, we'll do it.'[110]

Brower and Eaton couldn't believe what had just transpired: The founding member of The Beatles not only accepted their invitation but insisted on playing! To add to their astonishment, for a brief, existence-on-Earth defining moment, those listening on speaker-phone that Tuesday morning actually believed he meant The Beatles would be coming as a band!

Lennon clarified and said he would bring Ono and, in his even-tual recruitment of other musicians, essentially formed Plastic Ono Band. He attached a second condition that provided Apple the right to record a live album of the event or, more specifically, Plastic Ono Band's performance. He could probably have asked for the world and got it given the impact his appearance would have on the event's stature and financial success.

Sales of tickets, which were priced at $6, grew at a faster clip as con-firmation that Lennon would be performing on the bill was promoted on local radio—although some media refused to believe it, perhaps seeing the disconnect of a Beatle performing on stage without his three mates. And where was he? With the concert only a few days away, why hadn't Lennon been spotted in Toronto? The debate and uncertainty became inconsequential—the concert sold out!

Truth is, Lennon was still in England and in the process of trying to cobble together a band was having second thoughts. Harrison provided the first stab when he took a pass on Lennon's invitation to come to Canada; he was feeling a tad unsure of Ono's role in the whole affair. "When the Plastic Ono Band went to Toronto in September John actually asked me to be in the band, but I didn't do it. I didn't really want to be in an avant-garde band, and I knew that was what it was going to be."[111]

Harrison's rejection fed Lennon's misgivings about his spur-of-the-moment decision to play in Toronto; his uncertainly grew, and he decided to call the whole thing off:

> By the next morning, however, the enterprise looked doomed. Lennon had woken up to the reality of what he had got himself in to, and was scared to death. He called their assistant, Anthony Fawcett, still bleary-eyed from making all the travel arrangements, and told him to apologize to Brower and send flowers instead.[112]

What Lennon didn't know was that behind the scenes, his handlers worked around the clock and successfully secured the services of Eric Clapton on guitar, Hamburg friend, *Revolver* cover designer and Manfred Mann bassist Klaus Voorman, and a 20-year-old Alan White, future drummer for Yes—all of whom hurriedly agreed and were actually waiting at Heathrow Airport to board the pre-arranged flight to Toronto.

But there was no sign of their leader, or his new wife.

Huddled together at an airport pay phone, Fawcett and Clapton called Lennon, begging him in no uncertain terms to keep his commitment. It worked. They proceeded to book a later flight while Lennon and Ono made their way to the airport.

Five days after Brower's call, the hastily recruited Plastic Onos arrived in Toronto with a roar. On the day of the concert, September 13, 1969, Lennon, Ono, Clapton, Voorman and White arrived from London and were escorted straightaway to Varsity Stadium in motorcade-style by a fleet of Harley-Davidsons driven by members of the Vagabonds, a local motorcycle club that became bedfellows with the Eaton brothers as investors in the Rock and Roll Revival concert.

The unimaginable was about to transpire but the magnitude of the situation—which began to sink-in as the plane soared high over the Atlantic—was taking its toll on band leader Lennon; he had never played to a large audience without The Beatles, ever.

Fowley knew fans would be fascinated to see a Beatle in a non-Beatle situation but what he probably didn't anticipate was the extent of the 28-year-old Lennon's deteriorating psychological and physical condition. In a poignant exchange with Lennon minutes before he was introduced to the crowd, Fowley offers these chilling details:

> Everything is on and John Lennon summons me to the apron of the stage on the side by the canopy. I was dressed in a purple suit. He was in a white suit.
>
> Then John threw up. And he started to cry. He said, 'I'm terrified. Imagine if you were in The Beatles as the only band you've only been in your life. The first time you are to step on stage with people that weren't in The Beatles. You're about to go on stage with your wife, a friend, a friend, and a complete stranger with songs you had learned acoustically on an airplane on the way over from England with jet lag. You would be terrified. Do something so the kids don't know how scared I am.' He was that vulnerable.
>
> That's all he knew. 'Do something! Please, do something so people won't know how afraid I am to go out there.' He went ahead of his band. They were behind him. He was in a bad way."[113]

Fowley approached the microphone and asked the crowd of 22,000 to provide a special welcome to Plastic Ono Band by raising lit matches, lighters and candles, not unlike a religious experience where followers offer the glow of a heavenly welcome to their deity. Here are Fowley's words captured on the *Live Peace in Toronto 1969* album:

"Ladies and gentlemen, Plastic Ono Band; Toronto welcomes the Plastic Ono Band. Toronto, Brower and Walker present the Plastic Ono Band. Give peace a chance, give peace a chance." (Sadly the album, which was released several months later, removed this Fowley reference in editing: "Plastic Ono Band, please say hello to John and his friends with your matches and your lighters.")

Then Lennon walked on the stage.

Sporting a big bushy beard, he approached the microphone, resplendent in white on a warm Toronto night, and said: "Good evening ... okay we're just going to do numbers that we know, you know we've never played together before"—perhaps apologizing in advance as the band's only preparation was strumming and harmonizing through a selection of songs in the economy section of the 707 that delivered them to from England to Canada that same day. (Apparently, Brower's promise of first-class seats evaporated due to Lennon's delays and uncertainty requiring a later, last minute flight with only steerage seats available).

Flashing peace signs and yelling their support, the Toronto fans welcomed the Lennons and their band with gusto. Fowley would later describe Plastic Ono Band's sound as "sloppy," showing its lack of preparation and proper rehearsal time but he added "sloppiness is a charm ... it's night-time outside and people are drunk and stoned."[114]

After performing three rock standards including "Blue Suede Shoes", "Money" and "Dizzy Miss Lizzy", the band gave the audience a Beatles *White Album* tune "Yer Blues" before launching into two recent Lennon songs including the debut performance of his (later) solo hit "Cold Turkey".

Then came the turning point that would lead to a bizarre final act in Toronto. Lennon announced: "Now Yoko's gonna do her thing." What followed was nearly 18 minutes of an alarmingly disquieting vocal performance captured on side two of *Live Peace in Toronto 1969*. Was it art? Well maybe on some level, but not something people expected during a rock concert.

The crowd was understandably confused but generally respectful with only occasional amounts of jeering. That Ono's shrieking and yelping was even released on the album said a lot about Lennon's love, and indeed loving tolerance, for his new wife and her unusual form of expression art. Predictably, her performance in Toronto didn't sit well with critics and remains, for her detractors, to this day a touchstone of negativity toward the now 88-year-old Japanese-American artist.

Things returned to normal and the crowd responded with a massive vocal accompaniment when Ono's noise ended and the band closed their set with "Give Peace a Chance", some 105 days after André Perry recorded the song in Montréal.

Years later Lennon had this to say about his wife's part in the concert: "Yoko did a number which was half rock and half madness, and it really freaked them out."[115]

The Doors followed the Plastic Onos as the final act in the marathon concert, the first time ever rock gods Lennon and Morrison shared a stage. And while there are no photos of the two together, writer Richard Maxwell, who was watching the show from the edge of the stage, saw Morrison emerge from wherever he was hiding and join his band mates backstage to watch the legends Lennon and Clapton play. It would be both Lennon and Morrison's last time performing in Toronto.

As principal backers of the Toronto revival concert, the brothers Eaton, direct and wealthy descendants of department store baron Timothy Eaton, hosted the Lennons and their band in their King City, Ontario mansion following the concert—there exists a photo of Plastic Ono Band members sporting their white "Toronto Rock & Roll Revival" T-shirts while lounging on the edge of the Eatons' swimming pool—and then it was back to England, concluding their second visit to Canada, albeit a quick two nighter, in four months.

It has been said that Lennon privately considered ending The Beatles while en route to Toronto. That the show actually happened, despite his initial fears and apprehensions, perhaps provided the final push he needed—and the reassurance that there could be life after The Beatles. Toronto was essentially where Lennon took a stand to end the band. Before throngs of cheering Canadians, he got The Beatles out of his system and mustered the courage to end the enterprise he had begun as a schoolboy.

On his return to England, Lennon was said to be absolutely giddy about pulling it off in Toronto with new musicians, and perhaps a new lease on post-Beatles life: "Lennon's decision to form a new band, in retrospect, was his first unilateral decision of independence from The Beatles."[116]

Presented entirely in their own words and a superb source of the band's history, *The Beatles Anthology* book of 2000 offers this telling quote from Starr:

> After the Plastic Ono Band's debut in Toronto, we had a meeting in (Apple headquarters in London) Savile Row where John finally brought it to its head. He said: 'Well, that's it lads. Let's end it.' And we all said 'Yes.'[117]

Toronto was Lennon's Last Paid Concert Gig

In 1980, Lennon gave one of his last major media interviews to *Playboy* magazine. Among the questions, Lennon was asked the time-honoured query of whether he would consider reuniting with the others for a benefit concert. He responded by lashing out at the concept of third-party benefit concerts and added the Toronto concert was the only performance for which he was paid in the 14 years between The Beatles' last show in San Francisco's Candlestick Park and the time of the interview.

"Because they're always rip-offs. I haven't performed for personal gain since 1966, when The Beatles last performed. Every concert since then, Yoko and I did for specific charities, except for a Toronto thing that was a rock and roll revival. Every one of them (benefit concerts) was a mess or a rip-off. So now we give money to who we want. You've heard of tithing?" [5]

And what were John and Yoko paid to sing, play and screech at Varsity Stadium on September 13, 1969?

"According to the promoter, John Brower ... the Lennons were in fact paid union scale. There are documents in the possession of the AFM Toronto (American Federation of Musicians of the United States and Canada) office stating that John and Yoko received union scale—a grand total of $265." [6]

Thirty-nine years later, an intriguing contrast of riches reveals the province of Nova Scotia covered the advance fee for McCartney's outdoor concert at the Halifax Common urban park in 2008—a grand total of $3.5 million. [7]

3. December: "Canada is Canada. Show us the way"

November and December 1969 were busy months for John and Yoko. Hot off the glow of their concert in Toronto, they had a blur of projects on the go: They took part in two UK television documentaries; gave a series of interviews; appeared in a televised debate about religion; made the film *Apotheosis 2* featuring a helium balloon floating skyward; released the *Live Peace in Toronto 1969* album; performed as Plastic Ono Band for the second time at a Christmas concert at London's Lyceum Ballroom; and in mid December packed their bags for another return trip to Canada to promote their "War is Over" poster campaign.

Simmering beneath the surface of the couple's next phase peace campaign was the great unmentionable: The hush-hush reality that The Beatles had already broken up. While careful to keep the news to himself, Lennon slipped up (at least once) to a journalist during his final visit to Canada.

British journalist Ray Connolly was with the Lennons when they arrived in Toronto on December 16 and recounts John discussing The Beatles' dissolution: "(He) gleefully let me in on the secret of how he'd destroyed the band ... He hadn't planned to say that but, once spoken, and although news of the split wasn't going to be announced until the *Let it Be* album came out the following May, the words were never withdrawn."

But on Lennon's request, Connolly didn't write the article. When McCartney took the initiative to announce the break up the following April, Lennon was incensed that his band mate beat him to the punch and regretted asking Connolly to hold-off on the story, telling the journalist he absconded from his duty as a reporter irrespective of any agreement the two had reached:

> 'Why didn't you write it when I told you in Canada?'
> John demanded when he realized that Paul earned the
> dubious honour of announcing the end of the world's
> number one group. As (Lennon) started the band, he
> thought he should be the one to end it. 'You asked me
> not to,' I said. He was scornful. 'You're the journalist,
> Connolly, not me,' he snapped.[118]

For at least six days of their two-week December visit the Lennons were guests of performer Ronnie Hawkins at his ranch in Streetsville (now Mississauga), Ontario.

Arkansas-born Hawkins moved to Ontario in 1964 and the grass-roots rocker has made it his home ever since, touring across the province and earning the title Rompin' Ronnie for his unique, foot-stomping brand of rock 'n' roll and as a founding member of The Band.

Hawkins, who didn't know the Lennons before their arrival at his home, gave the couple a truly Canadian winter experience. A photographer snapped a photo of Lennon driving a bright orange, Québec-made Moto-Ski snowmobile while Ono sat shotgun bundled head-to-toe in a winter coat. Lennon was comparatively underdressed for the Ontario winter wearing a British Army military-style jacket.

It wasn't all fun and games. The Lennons' visit coincided with a 12-nation marketing campaign using billboards, posters and hand-bills to communicate a simple, black and white message in large all caps print: WAR IS OVER while stacked below IF YOU WANT IT in smaller type and then the polite greeting "Happy Christmas from John & Yoko." They also spent considerable time on the telephone, giving interviews to media outlets ranging from the *CBC* to the *Village Voice*, in the warmth of the Hawkins ranch.

Toronto, which erected up to 30 roadside billboards alone, joined major cities like Hong Kong, London, Tokyo, Paris, Helsinki, Rome, West Berlin, Athens, Rome, Amsterdam, Montréal, Los Angeles, and New York in the campaign. While at the ranch, Lennon enjoyed listening to Hawkins' latest songs and also kept his hands busy signing some 3,000 lithographs of his sketch art drawings, often erotic in nature, for art gallery exhibits and sale.

Whatcha Doin' Marshall McLuhan?

On December 19, Lennon and Ono pulled up to the University of Toronto's Centre for Culture and Technology in a white Rolls Royce dressed entirely in black, with John sporting some bling—a bright silver oversized belt wrapped twice around his waist. Their mission was to meet with 58-year-old Marshall McLuhan, the Edmonton-born and Winnipeg-educated philosopher and world authority on media theory, at the behest of the *CBS TV* network. The 45-minute interview took place in McLuhan's office. Calm, agreeable, fun and forthcoming, the three seemed intellectually synchronized and respectful of each other's point of view. Lennon seemed particularly intrigued by the Canadian's theories as the interview bounced around concepts and ideals for a free society on the cusp of a new decade. Lennon's friend, political activist and Chicago Seven member Abbie Hoffman, embraced McLuhan's theories, once describing the Canadian as being more relevant than Karl Marx.

Before McLuhan joined in, *CBS* reporter Desmond Smith asked Lennon to describe the reception he and Ono were getting in Canada. Said Lennon:

> We get a different response in each country ... the response in Canada, just from the media, they give us a chance, you know. They don't make fun of us for the sake of making fun, criticism is valid ... In England they just sort of refuse to hear anything we say even if it's one word 'peace' because it comes from an entertainer and his wife or an avant-garde artist and her freaky pop star husband.

When McLuhan arrived in the interviewer's chair, he enticed the Lennons with key observations and a particularly interesting theory, telling Lennon rock 'n' roll was the "aggressive music of the Empire." Lennon countered with an analysis that the end of mandatory military service in Great Britain in 1960 pushed the advent of rock 'n' roll in his country: "The Beatles and their ilk were created by the vacuum of non-conscription for the army ... from then on the whole music thing burst out; we just knew we were the army that never was ... we were the generation that were allowed to live and the music came from that."

On the issue of global Americanization, Lennon observed Canada was a self-aware country and, perhaps to the surprise of McLuhan, more impervious than other nations caught in the economic and cultural grip of American influence:

> I think you have a good protection against it by being aware of Americanization. Whereas a country like Britain (and Japan) who thinks it's independent from America is more American than Canada. I mean Canada has the skyscrapers and the radio but apart from that it's less American than Britain.[119]

Always lyrical and creative, Lennon closed the interview with a question in the form of a musical ditty for his esteemed Canadian host, singing "Whatcha doin' Marshall McLuhan".

McLuhan, whose mother was American and father a Canadian Army veteran, died just 23 days after Lennon on December 31, 1980.

On day seven of their Toronto visit, the Lennons packed and travelled with Hawkins and his wife Wanda by "peace train" (actually the CN Rapido—the express train that once served the Windsor-Québec City corridor) with the goal of meeting Prime Minister Pierre Trudeau in Ottawa but not before a planned stop in Montréal. It was there, in a familiar city, that Health and Welfare Canada officials, including Heinz Lehmann—a noted Canadian psychiatrist and psychopharmacologist who was an early proponent on the decriminalization of marijuana—and Ian Campbell, boarded their private train car and spoke with the Lennons for some five hours.

Lehmann and Campbell were not there to harass the celebrity couple, nor did they request autographs, inoculation records, or whether the famous couple had visited a farm within a fortnight. On the contrary, it was probably the first time the Lennons met Canadian government officials who didn't threaten some type of deportation or flag their troublesome travel status due to a previous marijuana possession charge. Ironically, Lennon's worldly experiences and legal troubles with marijuana made him exceptionally qualified as Lehmann and Campbell were there to record and take notes as representatives of the *Le Dain Commission*—a federal inquiry into the non-medical use of drugs. In a remarkable quirk of history, a Beatle and his wife would provide evidence for government use in the 40th Royal Commission since Canada's founding.

Lennon's testimony was unclassified in 2003, consistent with Canadian rules to wait at least 20 years after the death of a witness (rendering Ono's contribution still classified). His 76-page testimony was also made public thanks in no small part to the efforts of John Whelan, chief researcher at *beatles.ncf.ca*, the Ottawa Beatles Website.

The two commissioners offered an array of empathetic, streetworthy questions, points and counter-points to their famous celebrity witnesses, adding depth to a wide-ranging discussion on social issues and drugs. In an often rambling, fervent series of observations and anecdotes, Lennon discussed his views on marijuana, government, big business, the establishment, conspiracies and other points of view—all very '60s and pretty much what you would expect from the 29-year-old millionaire rock star's fertile, passionate mind.

The transcript shows Lennon was keen to place marijuana in the political, social and, interestingly prescient, economic context. He then spends considerable time overtly praising Canada; frankly, in all his vocal cynicism of international governments, Lennon took a kindler and gentler approach to Canada, perhaps buoyed that his opinion meant enough to a foreign government that he could potentially influence legislation. Here is Lennon, aboard a train, gushing about Canada to Lehmann and Campbell:

> And we honestly think a place like Canada looks like the only hope, because the only hope or help we've had is from Canada. The ... only people like you that we've ever been approached by, or the only people we've heard of that are doing anything like this, is going on in Canada, and Canada is America without being American, without that mighty—we are the mighty whatever scene.
>
> And the only hope is for a country like Canada that has the wealth and all the cars, and all the whatever it is that we all seem to think we want ... This is the opportunity for Canada to lead the world.
>
> This is it, and the youth are—just in youth talk it's like—when you mention Canada it isn't like "What! Australia!" That image is changing. You sell a country on image, like the Greeks, desperate to have an image, you know, and—image is how we sell our cigarettes and Coca-Cola, and Canada's image is just about getting groovy, you know.
>
> ... but all I mean is, forget Britain. Canada is Canada. Show us the way. You are the new country.

> Instead of us—the rest and Europe envying America
> its wealth, let us envy Canada (and) its progression.

Lennon offered more forward-thinking comments on marijuana but also pivoted to same-sex marriage:

> The one thing can be said about marijuana is it's non-violent, and if any government wanted to use it to calm the people, they have got the ultimate weapon. Tell the government how much they're going to make out of it. When the machine understands that it can make money from it, that's all it wants to know. We had an answer to Britain's problem. It was to legalize pot and let homosexuals marry, and Britain would be the richest nation on Earth.[120]

With their testimony concluded, the Lennons made their way to the Château Champlain Hotel—a large, sprawling downtown property that opened in 1967 to coincide with the Montréal's Expo 67 world fair—where they met informally with local media to roll-out their sign campaign. The schooling Lennon received five years earlier by Janette Bertrand seemed to have paid off with "*La Guerre est Finie! Si Vous Le Voulez*" etched on the global poster campaign in the heart of French Canada.

Lennon also learned an esoteric fact about the province's favourite sports franchise. In a quintessentially Canadian photo published in the now defunct *Montréal Star*, a bemused Lennon is seen holding the jersey of four-time Stanley Cup champ Gilles Tremblay, the Canadiens' sturdy left-winger. Lennon, like the pleasantly smiling Ono next to him, is wearing a toque and pointing to the "H" at the centre of the team's crest, which, he learned stood for *Habitants*, and hence the team's nickname Habs.

The couple overnighted at the familiar Queen Elizabeth Hotel and the following day, putting their toques to good use, boarded a train to Ottawa on a bitterly cold Québec morning. Six months after leaving an impromptu note at the front door of the prime minister's residence of 24 Sussex Drive, the time had come for John and Yoko to share in private tea with Pierre Trudeau.

Allan Rock re-enters the Lennon story in Ottawa, but on this occasion having ditched the Volkswagen for a limousine to drive the Lennons to the East Block of Canada's Parliament Building at around 11 a.m. for the closed-door meeting.

Shadowing the Lennons on their final visit to Canada was the ever-present Ritchie Yorke. He observed John's anxious state—approaching a near meltdown—in nervous anticipation of meeting a prime minister who was known, at times, to terrify others; famed American actor Marlon Brando once met with Trudeau to discuss Indigenous peoples rights, and said: "That's the most frightened I've ever been in my life. He's the most intimidating person I've ever met."[121]

Remembered Yorke: "I'd witnessed John and Yoko work their way through an assortment of difficult dilemmas and situations … but there'd been nothing quite like this frozen morning in the Canadian capital of Ottawa as (they) prepared for their first interaction with a world leader. I'd never seen John in the grip of such intense and restless nervous energy … pacing the bone-coloured carpet of his Ottawa hotel room … (lighting) one Gitane after another."[122]

The intended 15-minute meet and greet became a nearly one hour conversation. The Lennons and Trudeau shared mutual interests, discussed peace, the "War is Over/La Guerre Est Finie" campaign, the role of youth culture in society, marijuana, a planned peace festival the Lennons were to host at Mosport Raceway east of Toronto (although it never materialized) and generalizations comparing and contrasting policies in Canada and the United Kingdom.

Calm After a Storm: Without his Beatles wingmen, John struggled with severe bouts of anxiety in Canada in 1969. He wept and was ill before taking the stage in Toronto in September and, in Ottawa moments before he and Yoko sat down with Prime Minister Pierre Trudeau in December, a colleague said: "I'd never seen John in the grip of such intense and restless nervous energy ... pacing the bone-coloured carpet of his Ottawa hotel room ... (lighting) one Gitane after another." Photo by Duncan Cameron, Library and Archives Canada, a110805.

The media were alerted to the meeting while it was in progress and soon descended on the prime minister and his famous guests. Seemingly recovered from his nervous tension, a more relaxed Lennon appeared with Ono and Trudeau, but all the microphones were aimed at the famous couple.

Asked if he and Trudeau shared the same views, Lennon—looking dapper in starched white shirt, dark suit and tie and absent of any outward anxiety—skillfully responded with "We want hope for the future and in that respect our views are similar." For her part, Ono noted: "We're just overwhelmed meeting Mr. Trudeau because he is such a beautiful person, more beautiful than we expected."[123]

The Lennons remained on Parliament Hill for a second meeting, this time with Health and Welfare Minister John Munro under whose ministry the *Le Dain Commission* set out to research the implications of decriminalizing marijuana. Munro seemed a progressive minister in Trudeau's cabinet and once quoted The Beatles' lyrics in a speech. His meeting with John and Yoko lasted 90 minutes and centered mostly on the subject of drugs and youth culture. The Lennons left the meeting lifted at the prospects of spurring real change in Canada's attitude toward marijuana, with Ono particularly impressed with the reception she and her husband received: "We have great hope and love for Canada. It's the only place on earth where people have asked us for help in the cause of peace and where we've received tangible offers of help."[124]

As writer Robert Morrison noted on the 50th anniversary of John & Yoko's meeting with Trudeau: "It's now commonplace for pop icons and political leaders to meet and use their respective positions to champion progressive ideals. Half a century ago, when Trudeau opened his door to Lennon, that was not the case. Their extraordinary meeting marks the first time that a rock hero and a world leader met face to face to discuss the past, the present and the future. Their 50 minutes together highlighted the importance of peace to both men, as well as their shared commitment to raising political consciousness and mobilizing the popular forces of compassion and acceptance."[125]

That afternoon, the Lennons flew back to Toronto and, by coincidence, met Lester Pearson, Canada's 14th prime minister and Trudeau's predecessor, on the aircraft. Pearson, more than any Canadian prime minister of the era, may have achieved a certain, shall we say, undocumented synchronicity with Lennon. While Secretary of State for External Affairs in the cabinet of Prime Minister Louis St. Laurent in 1957, he received the Nobel Peace Prize for coordinating an international relief effort during the Arab-Israeli conflict in the Suez Canal; but more to the point, Pearson was deeply opposed to the Vietnam War. In an unprecedented act of unstatesmanlike bullying, he was physically roughed-up by President Lyndon Johnson in 1965 after calling for unilateral peace talks and a halt of US bombing. Pearson's pacifism opened a rift in the US-Canadian alliance that so angered Johnson he famously grabbed the prime minister by the lapels of his coat, lifted him off the floor and berated him with: "Don't you come into my living room and piss on my rug."[126]

The Lennons spent a final night with Hawkins (perhaps putting the finishing touches on a telephone bill speculated anywhere between $1,800 and $9,000) and the following day, Christmas Eve of 1969, would fly home to England; Lennon would not return to Canada again. His high-profile visits and consistent messaging around peace, equality and changes to marijuana laws received a lot of attention and several of the ideals he debated and discussed with politicians, bureaucrats (especially the *Le Dain Commission*), future diplomats, the media and generally people of influence in Canada would, in time, result in real change.

As for giving peace a chance, Canada's subsequent record was spotty. In recent years it participated in several regional conflicts under NATO auspices, most notably in Afghanistan but on the flipside also continued to permit Americans to dodge the Vietnam War draft with safe passage across the border until that war ended in 1975 and, under the backing of the United Nations, Canadian troops became globally recognized for their participation in peacekeeping missions throughout the Middle East and Africa, and also Cambodia, Croatia, Haiti, Bosnia and Herzegovina, and Kosovo.

In 2003, under the leadership of Trudeau's like-minded protégé Jean Chretien, Canada steadfastly refused to join the United States and its coalition invasion of Iraq because the military action wasn't sanctioned by the United Nations. Canada's ambassador to the UN that year was Allan Rock, the same former University of Ottawa student who shuttled the Lennons around town, first in a yellow Volkswagen and then a proper limousine, to help them pursue their peace mission in the nation's capital.

As for giving power to the people, Canada became the first country outside Europe and the fourth on Earth to legalize same-sex marriage when it passed the *Civil Marriage Act* of 2005. In 2015, the son of Pierre Trudeau, Justin Pierre Trudeau, would sweep to a majority victory to become Canada's 23rd prime minister on a platform that assured legalized marijuana. That promise was passed into law with the *Cannabis Act* of 2018 as Canada became one of the first nations anywhere to legalize pot.

First Light

Kim Fowley has said his Catholic school upbringing gave rise to the idea of encouraging the over 20,000 Toronto spectators to raise lit matches and lighters overhead in a welcoming sea of flickering lights to help calm a nervous Lennon before his first-ever stadium appearance without The Beatles. In school, Fowley recalled a classroom screening of the 1952 film *The Miracle of Our Lady of Fatima,* which captures the story of an apparition of the Blessed Virgin Mary witnessed by three shepherd children in Portugal in 1917. The children described seeing a woman "brighter than the sun."

Fowley saw Lennon that way and asked concertgoers to light the evening sky in his honour.

Will Vasquez at *vocal.media* says the practice of raising lighters is "a piece of concert culture and etiquette … It's a way of bringing people together during the most emotional parts of a concert, and also used by fans to request an encore or show their overall appreciation."

His research in the use of lighters at concerts suggests the Plastic Ono Band's Toronto gig ranks among the first times it happened.

You might not recognize the name Melanie Anne Safka-Schekeryk, but you'll know her simply as Melanie, the singer who wrote and sang "I got a brand new pair of roller skates, you got a brand new key" in 1971. When she performed in a rainstorm at the legendary Woodstock Rock Festival in Bethel, New York, near midnight on August 15, less than a month before the Toronto Rock and Roll Revival, "she saw the hillside light up with thousands of candles" notes Vasquez, likely the first time ignitable wicks were used to light up a concert song. (Coincidentally, Melanie would join Lennon on stage at Madison Square Garden for two charity concerts in August 1972).

When Fowley asked the Toronto crowd to raise their matches and lighters it was, says Vasquez, "almost certainly the first time a musical performance was welcomed on stage with lighters."[8]

The Beatles' legendary roadie and studio technician Mal Evans witnessed the first light in Toronto and said that Fowley: " … had all the lights in the stadium turned right down and asked everyone to strike a match. It was a really unbelievable sight when thousands of little flickering lights suddenly shone all over the huge arena." [9] Lennon agreed: "It was really beautiful and the vibes were fantastic." [10]

Evans died violently in Los Angeles in 1977 at age 40; Fowley was 75 when he died in 2015.

THE 1970s

Intermission

If *Us and Them* were a stage play, this is the part of the performance that follows the intermission. Your mind has temporality detached itself from a whirlwind of stimuli, your legs have had a stretch and breathing activity has returned to normal. Now the break is over, you take your seat and expect the story to unfold anew, picking up where it left off, but alas … it's light's out, for The Beatles are no more.

And chaos reigns as animosity among the four is raging, lawsuits are in full flight, and constant media reports fuel the fire between the warring parties; the lads from Liverpool are not dealing with their emotions particularly well.

But artistically, they're just getting warmed up, busting out of the gate like rock star racehorses.

From the arrival of Starr's George Martin-produced album of cover songs called *Sentimental Journey* in March 1970 and later a number one single in Canada "It Don't Come Easy", and McCartney's superb homemade album *McCartney* in April 1970—it reached number one on Canadian and US charts—the solo Beatles were spectacularly launched that year. Harrison's triple album *All Things Must Pass* was a monster hit and ranked by *ultimateclassicrock.com* as the finest Beatle solo effort, followed in December by Lennon's acclaimed *John Lennon/Plastic Ono Band* (reaching number one in Canada).

But for Lennon, the band's founder and de facto leader for most of its time together, his post-Beatles musical bounty would last only a decade. Lennon produced eight studio albums from 1970 to 1980 and during the last decade of his life did not visit Canada even after his protracted legal battle for a United States green card finally ended in a positive ruling in July 1976.

The tragic circumstances around Lennon's murder in 1980 haunt me, and millions upon millions of others to this day. Forty bewildering years later, while wintering in southeast Sicily, I stepped inside a Siracusa *mercato* and "Jealous Guy" began playing over the store's speakers. Grocery basket in hand, I took to chatting with a Sicilian at the checkout line and over the course of our chat I pointed to the song (actually it was the ceiling), he nodded solemnly and said, "*Sì, John Lennon*."

When it was clear he knew a little something about the song, it opened a conversational pathway for the author's typically self-indulgent party trick, as in plying Beatles knowledge to anyone with the slightest interest and then look for a reaction of genuine surprise, as in "I didn't know that" or total disdain as in "so what". In Siracusa that day I mentioned to him the beautiful tune was originally "On the Road to Rishikesh" and then "Child of Nature", both *White Album* non-starters. The Sicilian was nonplussed, only mildly interested when his thoughts turned again to Lennon; he slumped his head, shaking it to one side, "*peccato*" he said softly, Italian for "isn't it a pity or what a shame." He was right; Lennon's death was utterly senseless.

The Short Life of Curt Claudio

Curt Claudio was a lonely soul who crudely surprised Lennon at his Tittenhurst Park home in England in 1971 during the recording of the *Imagine* album (Harrison was among the musicians and houseguests at the time). As he had done countless times before, and ultimately leading to his death, Lennon warmed to fans in his post-Beatlemania liberation. He stopped for strangers in Toronto, Montréal, New York and even while sailing a 43-foot sloop from Rhode Island to Bermuda (where he wrote "Clean Up Time"), and wherever else to sign autographs, accept accolades and, all the while, paying too little attention to his personal security.

Claudio was born to a Canadian musician; his dad, Cesare Claudio Sr., was a cellist from Victoria, British Columbia, until he moved to Seattle and then to the San Francisco area where Curt was born. Curt's unapproved visit to the Lennon's estate was, remarkably, captured on film. In the scene, John and Yoko are standing at the door of their home talking to the weary and shy Claudio who, in his confused state, believed Lennon's songs were reaching out to him like a personal message.

Before making his way to England to seek out his hero, Claudio sent telegrams and wrote letters to Lennon. Knowing what we know today about unstable fan stalkers this story could have had a very different ending, but it didn't and, in the four-minute exchange with Claudio, Lennon tried to straighten him out by explaining that his song writing has nothing to do with Claudio or anyone: "You take a bunch of words, throw them out and see if they have any meaning, some do and some don't." Still unconvinced Claudio, who died in an airplane crash in 1981 at 31, turned inward and asked if Lennon is ever thinking of him in particular, when writing songs. "How can I be thinking about you? ... I'm singing about me and my life and if it's relevant to other people's lives, that's all right," Lennon responded.[127]

Perhaps realizing he wasn't getting through, Lennon then asked the sketchy, perhaps delusional son of a Canadian if he was hungry and invited him into his home for toast and coffee—an act of graciousness that is simply impossible to contemplate in today's context.

When he was in his mid-1970s self-confinement, baking bread, watching television and caring for son Sean in their New York apartment, Lennon regularly strolled through Manhattan's upper west side, ate, smoked cigarettes and wrote songs in Café La Fortuna, and took family walks through Central Park. People would stop them and they engaged, albeit briefly, in friendly banter, answering questions about a Beatles reunion and signing autographs.

On December 8, 1980, he signed an autograph and spoke to the embodiment of evil disguised as a fan outside his six-story, 100-year old Dakota apartment building; Lennon had no idea the degree of that fan's derangement for hours later he was murdered steps away from Ono, and outside the home the couple shared with their five-year-old son.

Peccato.

Winnipeg's Randy Bachman Asked Harrison for a Job

It's a little known fact that Randy Bachman once asked George Harrison to hire him as a guitarist in Harrison's post-Beatles session band. By 1970 both artists were without bands—Bachman left The Guess Who and, of course, The Beatles dissolved earlier that year.

Acting as Bachman's publicist, Ritchie Yorke was tipped off that Harrison might be looking for a guitarist to form his own band and suggested his client pick up the telephone and call the ex-Beatle. Bachman, who has since become a rock legend, radio host, guitar collector and certified Beatle-geek, shared the story with *Classic Rock's* Michael Hann:

> I never got to meet George, but I phoned him once. It was 1970 and I had left the Guess Who. The American Woman album and single were Number One, but I had a gall bladder problem and had to leave. Our publicist (the omnipresent Lennon liaison in Canada) Ritchie Yorke also worked with Derek Taylor, The Beatles' publicist. He said, 'The Beatles are breaking up. George is starting a new

band. Why don't you call him? Here's his number.'
Wow. So I phone him.

What 26-year-old Bachman hadn't counted on was Harrison's unwavering loyalty to his best friend, the half-Canadian Eric Clapton.

> A really nice sweet female voice answers, who I
> assume is Pattie Boyd. I say: 'It's Randy Bachman,
> and I got your number from Ritchie Yorke, and I'd
> like to speak with George.'

She puts down the phone, and maybe forty seconds later George comes to the phone. He's got this low growl. 'Winnipeg? Is that where Winnie the Pooh's from?'

He says he's heard 'American Woman'—'Good song, good solo'—but he says he's already got his band together. 'And my guitarist is my best friend, who I'm sure you know, Eric.'[11]

Despite the rejection, the Winnipeg-born rocker has never stopped believing in Harrison's underdog status within The Beatles, regularly flying against conventional wisdom by calling him out as the most significant member of the band. Around the time Harrison would have turned 75 in February 2018, Bachman toured across Canada to support his album, *By George—By Bachman*. The unique album concept includes 11 Harrison works that Bachman re-imagines by de-constructing tempo, keys and timing in a distinctive interpretation of tunes he wrote with and without The Beatles.

It would be among Bachman's many Beatles connections having also performed on stage with Starr, recorded a Beatles cover song with former Guess Who partner Burton Cummings and many more during his illustrious career.

Live and Let Live: New Brunswicker Battles a Beatle

The story of Herschel "Harry" Saltzman ranks at or near the top of Canadians in The Beatles' orbit. Born in Sherbrooke, Québec, in 1915 and raised in Saint John, New Brunswick and Cleveland, Ohio, Saltzman ran away from home as a teenager to join the circus and by his early 30s was living in Paris, studying political science and economics.

Saltzman parlayed these seemingly incongruous experiences into a budding career as a talent scout and agent and would live for most of his life in England. The life parallels between Saltzman and Carroll Levis are astonishing but could pass as coincidence if not for The Beatles; The Beatles, that is, and Paul McCartney.

If by now you're wondering if Saltzman missed a grand opportunity with The Beatles as Levis did with both Lennon and Johnny and the Moondogs, the answer is yes. But where Levis saw potential with unproven talent, Saltzman was dealt a much stronger hand and, as you learn, not only folded but upped his losses by also having a brush with McCartney as a soloist. What is it about Canadian talent scouts transplanting to England and dissing Beatles?

Saltzman was more, much more than a star maker. He was a member of the Royal Canadian Air Force stationed in Vancouver and in Trenton, Ontario, and is later believed to have carried out high-level espionage work in Europe with the Allies as a ranking US intelligence officer during World War II. *Vanity Fair* magazine asserts it's likely that in this capacity Saltzman met (and perhaps worked with) British naval intelligence officer and future James Bond novelist Ian Fleming. The Fleming-Saltzman Special Forces connection would, perhaps not coincidentally, travel full circle later in their lives.

Much of the wartime period in Saltzman's life is shrouded in secrecy, including redacted documents which only came to light when his daughter was asked to provide proof of her late dad's citizenship by Canadian authorities during her move from California to Québec in 2003.

What was revealed was proof of his clandestine missions either while with the RCAF or seconded to the US Army: Saltzman had "in the early years of World War II ... worked for the US Office of War Information, specifically its Psychological Warfare Division."[128]

After the war, Saltzman moved to the United States and built a successful company with the very Canadian name Mountie Enterprises, which installed coin-operated hobbyhorses in major department stores throughout the country. Not one to sit still, in the 1950s he was on the move again, taking his family to England to resume his pre-war career in the entertainment industry and this time aggressively pursued film and theatre projects.

It's unclear exactly how his alleged wartime association with Fleming landed Saltzman the film rights to the former's books, but in 1962 Saltzman joined forces with American Albert "Cubby" Broccoli to create EON Productions which held the monopoly on making James Bond movies and other very successful of films of the 1960s.

The Canadian was at the top of his game and, with Broccoli, produced the first of eight Bond movies beginning with *Dr. No*—released on October 5, 1962, which just happened to be the same day as "Love Me Do" went on sale in the United Kingdom. Flamboyant, energetic and at times volatile, Saltzman named his German Shepherds "James" and "Bond" and lived the high-life like of a Hollywood mogul (but in England) with a large mansion and friends with names like Michael Caine, Peter Sellers, Mick Jagger and Roger Moore.

So we have a larger-than-life Canadian showman with an impressive Rolodex at the centre of the 007 film franchise, but where is The Beatles' connection?

In 1963, plans were afoot for The Beatles to star in their first movie, *A Hard Day's Night*. When distributor United Artists went looking for a production company to back the film it approached, among others, Saltzman and, you guessed it, like Levis before him, Saltzman reviewed the script and turned down the studio's opportunity to work with The Beatles. Make no mistake, Saltzman was a master dealmaker and not a one-trick pony limited only to making Bond films. But there was something in the script, the terms, or perhaps his notoriously short attention span that got the best of him, and there was certainly something about The Beatles in film that didn't agree with the Canadian.

And so it came to pass, *A Hard Day's Night* became a critically acclaimed film (98 per cent approval on the review and aggregation film and TV website *rottentomatoes.com*) and a huge commercial success too—covering its production costs in only the first weekend it played in theatres. In today's US currency, *A Hard Day's Night* hauled $91 million at the box office yet cost only $4.5 million to make.[129]

Eleven years and several successful James Bond films later, Saltzman and Broccoli were set to produce their seventh Bond film, this time based on Fleming's 1954 *Live and Let Die*—the 1973 film that saw Roger Moore replace Sean Connery as Agent 007. George Martin was hired as the film's musical producer so it seemed a natural choice for him to pursue a Beatle to write the title track; McCartney was approached.

On Martin's recommendation, Saltzman and Broccoli formally invited McCartney to write the *Live and Let Die* theme song and sent McCartney a copy of Fleming's novel. "I read it and thought it was pretty good. That afternoon I wrote the song and (we) went in the next week and did it … It was a job of work for me in a way because writing a song around a title like that's not the easiest thing going," said McCartney.[130]

McCartney and his wife Linda wrote and recorded (with Wings) the superb *Live and Let Die* theme song, yet when the Wings' recording was given to Saltzman to review for his film, the New Brunswicker rejected McCartney's vocals. He would tell Martin that it was his preference to continue in the Bond film tradition of a female lead vocal for the theme song, perhaps someone like Shirley Bassey of Wales or American Thelma Houston singing "Live and Let Die" instead of the Beatle.

Here we go again: Canadians rejecting Beatles.

As an ex-Beatle on the cusp of a budding and indelible career on the horizon with his band Wings, 32-year-old McCartney possessed considerably more clout and negotiation power than he had, say, as a star-struck teenager with Johnny and the Moondogs and as such would have nothing of it. He informed Martin to tell the Canadian it would be the Wings' version or nothing. Pondering his options Saltzman was humbled, likely recalling the sting of passing up *A Hard Day's Night*, and capitulated, deciding never again to bet against a Beatle.

Saltzman's acquiescence was the right move.

"Live and Let Die" would become the first James Bond film song to be nominated for both an Academy Award and Grammy Award and it sold over a million copies. Also appearing in the film was Golden Globe winning actress Lois Maxwell who was born in Kitchener, Ontario. The talented and understated Maxwell played the role of M's secretary, Miss Moneypenny, for 14 Bond films from 1962 to 1985.

Saltzman's son, Steven, got into the spy film business too; in 2021, he co-produced *The Ipcress File* as a series for *ITV*, based on the Len Deighton cold war thriller novel. Harry Saltzman, who produced the original film version of *The Ipcress File* in 1965, died in France on September 28, 1994, at age 78. In 2012 *The Guardian's* John Patterson looked back at his career and had this to say:

"Saltzman seems to have stepped straight out of one of Mordecai Richler's novels about blazingly nervy and alive Canadian-Jewish bluffers and gamblers. Without him, British cinema of the 1960s—and ever after—would look decidedly different, and be a lot less fun."[131]

Spies Like Us

Continuing with the spy game, there was no quibble about who would sing the rocker "Spies Like Us", the upbeat McCartney-written-and-performed theme song for the film of the same name. The 1985 American comedy was written by Ontario-born actor and *SCTV* alumnus Dave Thomas and Ottawa's Dan Aykroyd. Aykroyd, who starred in the film with fellow comedian Chevy Chase, became the first Canadian to appear on a record sleeve with a Beatle when he, McCartney and Chase were photographed for the single. Moreover, Aykroyd was, and remains, the only Canadian to appear in a music video with a Beatle, mugging with McCartney throughout the nearly five minute "Spies Like Us" clip which featured the trio in disguise and doing a woeful job of being spies; it ends with them taking an evening stroll across London's famous Abbey Road crosswalk.

It was Aykroyd's second go-around in a film with Beatle connections. In 1978, Aykroyd played Brian Thigh, a record executive who turned down the fictitious Beatles satire troupe, The Rutles, in *All You Need is Cash*, an acclaimed Beatles spoof film co-directed and co-written by Monty Python's Eric Idle. The same film also saw a former drama professor from the University of Alberta, Henry Woolf, play a parody role modeled after Maharishi Mahesh Yogi. Woolf, who is 91, currently resides in Saskatoon, Saskatchewan.

After *Live and Let Die*, *Spies Like Us* is the second film involving a McCartney-written title song for a project involving Canadian talent. A third instance occurred in 2001 with the inclusion of his song "Vanilla Sky" in the Paramount Pictures film of the same name. Starring Tom Cruise—who spent several years living in Ottawa as an adolescent—*Vanilla Sky* was also among the first of several feature films to include Oshawa, Ontario-born model Shalom Harlow.

Up in Smoke

Harrison became the first member of The Beatles to take his solo act on an international tour after the band split in 1970. He opened his 26-city, 1974 North American tour with sitar virtuoso Ravi Shankar in Vancouver on November 2.

Despite placing Vancouver in the United States, author Graeme Thomson did a fine job of capturing the mood and all the historic firsts moments before Harrison stepped onto the stage, including a not-so-subtle jab at the performance that followed: "It is a night of firsts. Awaiting the first song of the first show of the first solo tour of the US by a former Beatle, the 17,500-capacity Pacific Coliseum is full and buzzing. The barkers selling the concert programs are calling the main attraction 'George ex-Beatle Harrison,' the music press are in full force, and it is not fanciful to detect the resurgent scent of Beatlemania in the air. What occurs in the ensuing two hours, however, might be expressly designed to puncture every last bright balloon of nostalgic reverie."[132]

Thomson's balloon-busting comments notwithstanding, the tour continued with two shows at Toronto's Maple Leaf Gardens on December 6, and two shows at the Montréal Forum on December 8, following the same west-to-east, multi-show Canadian tour pattern as The Beatles had done 10 years earlier.

Harrison used the tour to showcase some of the tracks from his newly released *Dark Horse* album. That album was recorded at Harrison's Oxfordshire home and also at A&M Studios in Los Angeles. Okay, hold that thought for a moment.

Tommy Chong, the Edmonton-born and Calgary-raised half of Cheech and Chong, met his cannabis consuming comedy cohort Richard "Cheech" Marin in the late 1960s in Vancouver. Chong ran a club and was a talented guitar player with the Motown band Bobby Taylor and the Vancouvers; Marin was in hiding, choosing to leave California and head north to British Columbia in order to evade the draft for the Vietnam War.

The lovable stoners, who performed together for the first time in Vancouver, were in Los Angeles in 1973 recording "Basketball Jones featuring Tyrone Shoelaces" during one of the sessions for their *Los Cochinos* album. During the recording session, album producer Lou Adler overheard that Harrison was coincidentally in the A&M Studios building and approached him, and his band mates, to play on "Basketball Jones" to which the Beatle and his friends obliged. Harrison's contribution was far more than a cameo; his electric guitar work can be heard from nearly start to finish on the 3:44 song which was co-written by Chong.

The website *songfacts.com* captured Chong's reaction to his collaboration with Harrison and, as one might expect, he added some sweet if not pungent cannabis flavour to his comments in the form of a rather eccentric Beatles bucket list:

> 'It was a big coming together,' recalled Chong ... 'It was a product of the times. That's what was happening then.'

Though they came from very different strata of the entertainment landscape, the comedic duo was no strangers to the world of the mega-stars.

'I must have smoked with George (Harrison) a good half-dozen times, maybe more, where we sat around and shared a joint, shared the moment,' said Chong.[133]

The website goes on to say Chong smoked weed with every Beatle except, oddly, McCartney—who has publicly embraced marijuana for most of his adult life and even served time in a Japanese jail for possession. Lighting up with McCartney remains on Chong's bucket list.

The *Los Cochinos* album won the Grammy Award for best comedy album during the same March 1974 ceremony where Martin and McCartney won for "Best Arrangement, Accompanying Vocalists."

So let's summarize. That winter night at the Grammys, McCartney takes home a statue for "Live and Let Die", a song he recorded for a Canadian film producer; the album *Los Cochinos* on which Harrison played with a Canadian comedian gets another statue. And there's one final connecting dot, the Montréal studio founded by Lennon's Bed-In recording engineer and co-producer André Perry, was among the three locations in which *Los Cochinos* was recorded!

Imagine This!

One of the great ironies of holding a peace conference is that its participants are afforded little or no peace of their own. A common thread in the comments and reminiscences of the many who witnessed the Montréal Bed-In was the constant ringing of telephones in the Lennons' master suite at the Queen Elizabeth Hotel; there were phones and tributaries of phone-lines everywhere with both John and Yoko constantly speaking to reporters and, in the astonishing story of Lillian Piché Shirt, it seems, some everyday Canadian heroes too.

Shirt, a 29-year-old Cree from Saddle Lake Cree First Nation, created headlines when she pitched a tipi at Edmonton's Winston Churchill Square to protest the scant housing opportunities afforded to Indigenous peoples. During her protest, she got word that a local rock radio station, *CJCA AM930*, had Lennon on the line wanting to speak with her.

Shirt, who was the same age as Lennon and had no idea who he was, arrived at the Birks Building in downtown Edmonton where *CJCA* was based. She listened as the Beatle described how he had read about her protest, wanted to hear in her words the reason for her demonstration, and whether he could help. The University of Alberta's Faculty of Arts picks up the story:

> Lennon told her he wanted to support her cause, asking if there was a message she'd like him to convey to the world. She thought of the Cree words her grandmother often recited to her: 'Keespin esa Kasakehetoyah, Kasetos-katoyah, Kawechehetoyah, Namoya Ka-no-tin-to-nanhoyo.'
>
> The phrase translates as, 'Imagine that if, there was no hate, if we loved each other, we loved one another, that there would be no war between us.'
>
> 'Lennon was moved and asked if he could use it,' recalled Shirt. 'Sure, go ahead,' she replied. At one point in the discussion, she remembers Yoko Ono chiming in to say, 'You look like me.'

Ono's comment likely referred to a newspaper photo she'd seen of a smiling Shirt speaking at a podium with long, raven hair parted down the middle. Shirt also recalls Lennon mentioning he wrote down her grandmother's vision of peace on the closest thing at hand—a pillowcase!

This incredible story came to light in 2016 when Alberta Indigenous scholar Corinne George revealed the research contained in her 2006 master's thesis that studied local Indigenous activists.

George spoke extensively with Shirt. Her research, including the incredible revelations of the telephone conversation with the Lennons, were fact-checked and defended by a University of Alberta historian and professor. During the verification process, an article in the *Montréal Gazette* archives was discovered with the headline: "Cree woman believes injustice in housing pitches a teepee." Published on June 2, 1969, the day after "Give Peace a Chance" was recorded, the *Gazette* story was likely what Lennon read in Montréal

It was not until she heard the song "Imagine" on the radio some years later that Shirt remembered the interview and giving permission to Lennon to use her grandmother's words.

If an Alberta Cree offered Lennon and Ono even a morsel of inspiration to write "Imagine" in early 1971, or perhaps help amplify the "Imagine" references found in Ono's 1964 art book *Grapefruit* or, as other sources suggest a Christian prayer book, the implications of an Albertan's role in Lennon's most famous, signature song are a stop-the-presses, too-large-for-words to convey nuance of music history.

Lennon had begun sketching the idea for "Imagine" during the *Let it Be/Get Back* sessions a few months before contacting Shirt. He and Ono completed and recorded the song—which reached number one in Canada to become the best-selling single of Lennon's solo career at nearly five million worldwide sales—about a year later in 1971.

But in the spirit of historical accuracy and fairness, it's prudent to impart a degree of restraint which is best summed by Corinne George (currently a regional school principal in Prince George, British Columbia) in her summary statement on the remarkable claim: "There's no doubt that she spoke to John Lennon, and that he was very interested. There's also no doubt that she told the story of her grandmother, and imagine is definitely in that. But whether this actually inspired him is open to interpretation."[12]

And thus it will always be. Shirt, who went on to champion many causes for Indigenous peoples in Alberta, passed away at age 77 on

July 18, 2017, and is buried at Sacred Heart Roman Catholic Cemetery in Saddle Lake. Shirt left a remarkable legacy, had six children, 31 grandchildren and 35 great-grandchildren.

A Bluenose Salute: Nova Scotians Cover The Beatles

On the subject of the Grammy Awards, Canada's Anne Murray has won four of them and in 1974 recorded a cover version of The Beatles' "You Won't See Me", which reached number one on *Billboard*'s Easy Listening charts in the United States, as well as "Day Tripper". Murray is fond of retelling the story of an impromptu visit Lennon made to her dressing room at the 1975 Grammys where she won "Best Country Vocal Performance" for "A Love Song".

According to Murray, the ex-Beatle popped his head in the door of her dressing room to say her version of "You Won't See Me" was the best cover of a Beatles song. "And then he was gone," she said. "I was in such shock."[134]

Murray, who recorded "You Won't See Me" again in 2007, wasn't the first Nova Scotian to record a Beatles cover to some acclaim. Nova Scotia-based artists seem to dominate Canadian bands that have covered Beatles songs. The first to do so was Halifax's Stitch in Tyme, which recorded "Got to Get You Into my Life" on the Yorkville label in 1967, the year after it was released on *Revolver*.

Waverley, Nova Scotia's April Wine paid homage to The Beatles and The Rolling Stones by alternating the guitar riffs from "Day Tripper" and "Satisfaction" during the coda of their 1980 rocker "I Like to Rock"—recorded at Perry's studio in Morin Heights; the band then recorded a relaxed, languid version of The Beatles' "Tell Me Why" in 1982.

New Brunswick-born and Nova Scotia-raised guitarist Kevin MacMichael got Beatles fever at age 13 when he saw the film *A Hard Day's Night* in Halifax, forming his first band shortly thereafter. Claiming he could play 200 Beatles songs on guitar, MacMichael was featured in a string of bands before moving to England in the mid-1980s. It was there he formed Cutting Crew and co-wrote their chart topping "(I Just) Died in Your Arms". In the years that followed, MacMichael took his stellar guitar work to new heights with Led Zeppelin's Robert Plant, and from 1998 to 2000 toured with the original Beatles drummer in the Pete Best Band. MacMichael died of cancer in Halifax in 2002 at age 51.

Also in 2002, Halifax's Sarah McLachlan delivered a mezzo-soprano delight with her version of "Blackbird" for the film *I Am Sam* that starred Sean Penn.

Victoria's David Foster

One of Canada's most valued treasures and musical exports, David Foster, is the only Canadian to produce, arrange, play or play on the same album with all The Beatles as solo artists. It's no wonder that, for Foster, the powder keg that ignited his interest in music was The Beatles. Growing up in a suburb of Victoria, British Columbia, he heard "She Loves You" on a transistor radio at age 14. "I could not believe this sound that I was hearing; it literally changed my life."[135]

A one-time Edmonton nightclub bandsman, Foster's astonishing career has earned him 16 Grammy Awards and recognition as one of the world's top music producers, composers and arrangers. A classically trained musician, Foster's unprecedented Beatles resume covered 15 years, beginning at age 25, and looks something like this:

With Ringo Starr
Foster played piano on *Goodnight Vienna*, a 1974 Starr album that also featured Lennon on piano, acoustic guitar and background vocals; Lennon also wrote the title track. Foster resumed his collaboration with Starr playing keyboards on the *Ringo The Fourth* album in 1977.

With George Harrison
Foster played piano, organ and synthesizer and arranged string sections on nearly every track on Harrison's 1975 *Extra Texture*, and added keyboards on another Harrison album, 1976's *33 1/3*.

With John Lennon

As mentioned, Foster and Lennon both played on Starr's *Goodnight Vienna* album.

With Paul McCartney

To round out his Fab Four work, Foster co-produced the song "We Got Married" on McCartney's *Flowers in the Dirt* in 1989.

Foster also holds the distinction as the only Canadian artist signed to a record label owned by a member of The Beatles. In the late 1970s, Foster's four-piece Los Angeles rock band Attitudes was under contract with Harrison's Dark Horse Records—named after his 1973 composition "Dark Horse", Harrison's post-Apple label that was initially distributed by A&M Records. Olivia Arias worked at A&M and handled the marketing activity for Attitudes; she would become Harrison's second wife in 1978.

Harrison and Arias were married until his death in 2001—a successful long-term union that stood in stark contrast to Harrison's first marriage to model Pattie Boyd. He met Boyd on the set of *A Hard Day's Night* and they married in 1966. Harrison's commitment to Boyd was shaky, and vice versa, and things took a bizarre turn in the late 1960s when Harrison became aware of his best friend Eric Clapton's infatuation with her. Soon enough, Boyd and Clapton developed an intense romance and a love triangle emerged until 1979 when Clapton married his "Layla", Pattie Boyd.

Harrison, along with Starr and McCartney, attended a reception for the just-wed couple at Clapton's country home in Surrey, England that spring; Lennon was stuck in New York and unable to attend on account of his long-running immigration battle. The occasion produced an incredible and rare impromptu jam session among the three Beatles who were joined by Clapton for a rendition of "Sgt. Pepper's Lonely Hearts Club Band".

When Pattie Boyd Harrison Visited Prince Edward Island

The George Harrison-Pattie Boyd-Eric Clapton soap opera is legendary in rock 'n' roll history. With the former model's love allegiance wavering between a half-Canadian guitarist and the only member of The Beatles with Canadian relatives, you would think something Canuck would turn up in her file. And it did, as the first Mrs. Harrison quietly accompanied her lover to Summerside, Prince Edward Island in late August 1974.

Although still married, Boyd and Harrison had begun a trial separation when Boyd, 30, arrived in Canada's smallest province for the funeral of Clapton's Canadian half-brother, Brian MacDonald, who had died at age 26 in a motorcycle accident in Miscouche, P.E.I. He was born to Clapton's mother, Patricia, and, her husband Frank MacDonald, a career soldier in the Royal Canadian Air Force. Like his father, Brian was an airman and stationed at CFB Summerside (which was closed in 1991) in St. Eleanors; the elder MacDonald was at CFB Gagetown in Oromocto, New Brunswick at the time. Brian's siblings were Clapton's Canadian half-sisters, Cheryl and Heather.

Clapton and Boyd's entry into Canada was not without complication. Their journey to P.E.I. began in Jamaica, where the two were vacationing and also where Clapton broke a toe trying to kick down a bathroom door. While there, they received word of Brian's death. Upon arriving in Canada, Boyd was red flagged by immigration authorities for a 1969 marijuana conviction slapped on her and Harrison after police raided their bungalow in Esher, England.

She recalled the incident to Clapton biographer Philip Norman:

> I remember Eric screaming drunkenly at the immigration people while I was put in a special holding area. Luckily when we got on to Robert (Stigwood, former Cream manager and the head of Clapton's record label), he knew someone at the Canadian embassy who managed to sort it out.[136]

Clapton and Boyd made their way to Summerside and checked into the Quality Inn Hotel. That evening the couple and Clapton's manager (possibly Robert Forrester) meandered over to the Brothers 2 pub and restaurant adjacent to the hotel where they met up with Patricia and Frank MacDonald, and the person who raised Clapton, his grandmother Rose Clapp, who had arrived from England.

(As a fascinating side note, that evening in Summerside Clapton mourned with his mother, grandmother and stepfather—all three of whom, history suggests, maintained their veil of secrecy by not revealing to Clapton the identity of his Canadian father. It would be another 24 years before the guitarist learned the name of his biological dad).

The sombre reunion of the Clapton/MacDonald clan occurred over dinner and drinks and, befitting his success, Clapton offered to cover the $150 bill at Brothers 2. Perhaps in the rush to fly to Canada from his Jamaican vacation, Clapton wasn't carrying Canadian cash or a credit card, so he turned to his manager (also bereft of local currency) who proceeded to ask the waiter to send the bill to his famous client's New York management firm.

It was an unusual request, perhaps viewed as sketchy by the waiter so he summoned the co-owner of both the hotel and restaurant, Don Groom, 30, at home to come and sort out the situation. On the telephone, Groom picks up the story from there: "I came in and stood at the bar when a guy who said he was his manager asked, 'Do you know who that is, it's Eric Clapton,' but I had no idea who Eric Clapton was. He was over by the table across from me with five or six people."

Against his better judgment, Groom agreed to bill the New York office although he wasn't quite sure how to do it or if it was even possible.

But Clapton's inability to settle the tab is not what made his brief visit to Prince Edward Island legendary; it's what happened next:

> Doug Gallant was our in-house musician and he was playing and singing in the bar. He was too busy performing to notice any commotion. He happened to have a new guitar that night and it caught Clapton's attention because he walked (hobbled, perhaps, given

his Jamaica misadventure) all the way over from the other end of the bar to ask Gallant if he could play a tune. Gallant says, 'Well, it's a new guitar so are you sure you know how to play it?'

It's not hard to imagine the expression on Clapton's face when posed with such an innocent but monstrously naive question but the guitar great didn't miss a beat, picked up Gallant's shining new six-string and played a couple of songs to the unsuspecting Islander patrons of Brothers 2.

Gallant would later tell Groom he had "never heard someone play like that in his life."

As we approach the 47th anniversary of Clapton and Boyd's visit to P.E.I., Groom is in a nostalgic mood and intends to write to Clapton to request the $150, or this option: In lieu of payment, the guitarist can return to P.E.I. and perform a concert at (and for the benefit of) Summerside's Celtic Performing Arts Centre. Some 70 per cent of Prince Edward Islanders are descendant from Scottish or Irish settlers dating back to the 1770s, hence Groom's and his community's interest in all things Celtic.

Brothers 2 is adjacent to the Quality Inn, which was built by Groom's father in 1952. Don Groom, who is 76 and retired, sold his share of the business to nephew David Groom. Located on Summerside's Water Street East and known for its local mussels and lobster, the family restaurant and hotel have hosted at least four prime ministers, multiple ministers from the Maritime provinces, entertainers and bygone Hollywood actor Dana Andrews.

Boyd and Clapton's union was tumultuous and they would divorce in 1989. A successful photographer and active in charitable work with Starr's wife Barbara Bach, Boyd is married to English property developer Rod Weston. Clapton married American Maria McEnery, 31 years his junior, in 2002; the couple have three daughters.

Harrison and Starr's Canadian Waltz Partners

The Canadian-American group that once backed Bob Dylan, The Band attracted the world's leading rock and folk musicians when it played its final concert, dubbed "The Last Waltz", on American Thanksgiving weekend in San Francisco in 1975, including guest drummer Starr. The concert, and the Martin Scorsese film that followed, was a moving performance second to none and critically acclaimed including *Chicago Tribune* film critic Michael Wilmington's description as "the greatest rock concert movie ever made—and maybe the best rock movie, period."[137]

Starr's participation in the concert put the Beatle drummer on the same stage as guest Canadian music royalty Joni Mitchell, Neil Young and Ronnie Hawkins, along with The Band's four Canadian troubadours Richard Manuel, Rick Danko, Garth Hudson and Robbie Robertson.

The Toronto-born Robertson, whose mother was Cayuga and Mohawk and raised on the Six Nations Reserve in Ontario, had several collaborations with Starr including the 1973 *Ringo* album, as well as keyboard, piano and clavinet on Starr's 1977 *Ringo the 4*th. Still with Starr's self-titled *Ringo* album, Band members Hudson and Danko also played on it, the accordion and fiddle, respectively, including the Harrison-written tune "Sunshine Life for Me"—the twangy country ditty, in some ways, paid homage to The Band's 1969 song "Rag Mama Rag". The Starr album would be a landmark event for other reasons too. Lennon and Harrison also appeared, marking the first time since their break-up that three Beatles appeared together in studio, in this instance to record the Lennon-written "I'm the Greatest".

Clapton was also on stage for "The Last Waltz", and once admitted he longed to be hired by The Band as an additional guitarist. He and Harrison were smitten with the mostly Canadian outfit but it was Harrison who made the first move to form a connection with Robertson and The Band after listening to their 1968 game-changing LP *Music from Big Pink*.

To Harrison, he and Robertson saw the role of guitar playing in a band the same way:

> Robbie's guitar style I always liked because, being in a band situation like myself, it was always the (guitar's) contribution towards the song or the recording it was not really (meant to be) a showpiece in itself, but it was always ... toward the sound of the band and the sound and production of the song.[138]

Apart from being the same age, the two had much more in common. Harrison and Robertson were highly integral members of large bands but not the principle singers. Driven by a fondness for the creative process and mutual respect, the two spent considerable time discussing their music when George and Pattie were invited to visit Robertson, Manuel, Danko, Hudson and Levon Helm at their upstate New York home studio in November 1968. Harrison was enjoying a break from The Beatles, having spent time producing an album for Apple artist Jackie Lomax.

"He came to visit with me and met a couple of the other guys. He wanted to see what was real ... He wanted to hang out and have some of this rub off on him," said Robertson.[139]

On that same visit and in nearby Woodstock, the Harrisons had Thanksgiving dinner with Dylan's family. The visit proved fruitful, as Harrison and Dylan co-wrote "I'd Have You Anytime" but more importantly he also penned his blockbuster "All Things Must Pass" after "seeking out the simple, soulful spirit that informed (The Band's) 'The Weight'"; Harrison wanted "the song to sound like something The Band would sound like."[140]

The *Facebook* page *Pop Goes the 60s* asserts there were 71 studio iterations, stops-and-starts and rehearsals attempted for "All Things Must Pass" when Harrison brought his Band-inspired song to The Beatles during the start of the *Get Back/Let it Be* album recording sessions in January 1969. In the end he wasn't satisfied The Beatles could pull off the distinctive Canadian sound he was seeking and decided to pull "All Things Must Pass" out of circulation on his own accord. "It's really George who put the brakes on this song."[141]

About six months later, Harrison and the late Phil Spector recorded the final version of "All Things Must Pass" at Abbey Road Studios (with Clapton adding acoustic guitar and backing vocals) to close the loop on Harrison's dogged determination to create, what author Simon Leng considers "perhaps the greatest Beatle solo composition," in the spirit of The Band.[142]

The Band's influence on Harrison extended beyond his songwriting. As it would do a year later for Lennon when he played in Toronto, Harrison's visit with the group's four Canadians and one American, and Dylan, strengthened his self-confidence and from it arose the notion that he could quite possibly pursue a solo career and take his art to a happier place.

Looking back, Harrison had this to say about that: "I had just spent the last six months producing an album of this fellow (English guitarist) Jackie Lomax and hanging out with Bob Dylan and the Band in Woodstock and having a great time. For me to come back to the winter of discontent with The Beatles ... (it) was very unhealthy and unhappy."[143]

Calling Occupants: The Strange Tale of the "Canadian Beatles"

In 1977, one of the all-time strangest Beatles controversies since the "Paul is Dead" conspiracy created international intrigue only to reveal the entire enterprise was squarely rooted in Canada. Capitol Records quietly released an impressive 1976 debut album called *3:47 EST* by three anonymous members of a band called Klaatu. The event would otherwise have hovered under the radar if not for a Rhode Island newspaper that speculated it could be The Beatles.

Klaatu's progressive rock sound was definitely Beatles-esque in a post *Revolver* kind of way; one hit in particular "Calling Occupants of Interplanetary Craft" seemed wrapped in the elements of "Across

The Universe", "I am the Walrus" and "A Day in the Life" in its lushly produced, dreamy glow with drum fills and harmonies at times reminiscent of The Beatles. And the lyrics held a "Strawberry Fields" sketch surrealism like something Lennon might conceive: "In your mind you have capacities, you know / To telepath messages through the vast unknown … "

More so, "Sub-Rosa Subway" held the recognizable sonic energy of "Martha My Dear", "Penny Lane" and "Hello Goodbye" with a bass line and orchestration that could have been delivered by the likes of McCartney and Martin. Again, lyrics evoked something akin to "Lucy in the Sky with Diamonds": "One station filled with Victoria's Age / From frescoed walls / And goldfish fountains / To Brahmsian tunes."

Klaatu's use of tempo changes, backward masking, horn stabs, harpsichord-like sounds, Mellotron, the London Philharmonic Orchestra and a host of rich production techniques made it all seem, well, plausible in a world obsessively awaiting a Beatles reunion.

Despite being paid an incredible compliment, Klaatu wasn't The Beatles but the latter's influence was so apparent it led Steve Smith, a staff writer with the *Providence Journal*, to wonder "Could Klaatu Be Beatles? Mystery is a Magical Tour" in a February 13, 1977 article. Newspapers, magazines and radio stations around the world took the bait creating a massive stir among Beatle fans and non-fans alike, and Klaatu album sales soared. What fueled Smith's misguided conjecture was the band's intentionally secret origins—wanting to be judged on the merits of their music alone, the band daringly offered neither names nor credits and zero background on that debut album. So who were these guys?

It wasn't until Klaatu's fourth album in 1980 that the band's core members were officially revealed: A trio of Toronto musicians and songwriters named John Woloschuck (bass), David "Dee" Long (guitar) and Terry Draper (drums). For a while the members of the "Canadian Beatles"—Draper and Woloschuck were neighbours and met Long in a high school battle of the bands competition—enjoyed a significant spike in sales led not only by the rumours but also the superb and familiar sound brought forth by the skilled and talented threesome. Bringing order and pace to their recordings was none other than Rush, Max Webster and Blue Rodeo producer Terry Brown.

After several years of feeling of weight of expectations to continue making music reminiscent of The Beatles, combined with declining record sales after their non-Beatle identities came to light, Klaatu disbanded in 1982 shortly after releasing its fifth album. Guitarist Long—who at 69 now resides in Hope, British Columbia—took a job working at George Martin's AIR Studios in London in the late 1980s. On one particular day, he recalls hearing an unexpected knock on the studio door:

> … and in comes Paul McCartney with two body-guards in pinstripe suits. He introduced himself (like he needed any introduction) and said, 'So you're the chap from The Beatles clone band.' He explained that he was on a TV talk show and the host played a bit of 'Calling Occupants' and asked Paul if that was him singing! Paul had never heard the song and said so … We talked for at least an hour, and I explained that we were never a clone band but just heavily influenced by The Beatles. We talked about music and life … He came back many times to hang out and jam and talk about writing songs. Again, he was just a wonderful person—easy to talk to, and full of positive energy. An experience I will always treasure.[144]

THE 1980s AND 1990s

Ringo's All-Starr Canadian Line-Up

Starrs Align: Ringo's All-Starr Band has been around for over three decades and has toured with musicians plucked from A-List bands including four Canadian groups that were at or near the top of the Canada's hit-making machine from the 1960s to 1990s: The Band, The Guess Who, Bachman-Turner Overdrive and The Jeff Healey Band. Photo by gaisler (licensed under CC BY-NC-SA 2.0).

An annual fixture in small- to stadium-size concert venues across Canada, the All-Starr Band has been touring for the better part of the past 30 years and has included no fewer than 48 permanent and guest musicians ranging from Peter Frampton to John Entwistle to Starr family members Zak Starkey (son) and Joe Walsh (brother-in-law). In many ways Starr was living his best life as a natural-born entertainer when he managed to assemble strings of revolving super groups of talented musicians and songwriters.

The All-Starr Band set-list would typically include several Starr songs from The Beatles and his solo catalogue, and then the left-handed drummer would get behind his right-hand configured drum kit to accompany the bevy of talent he assembled on stage as they played their own songs.

From Canada, Starr decided to pluck members from four Canadian bands that were at or near the top of the country's hit-making machine from the 1960s to 1990s, beginning with what was most familiar to him, The Band, and later The Guess Who, Bachman-Turner Overdrive and The Jeff Healey Band.

When Starr accompanied Canadians Danko and Hudson (plus Helm) on The Band's songs "The Weight", "The Shape I'm In" and "Up on Cripple Creek" in the first iteration of the All-Starr Band in 1989, it would become the first time a Beatle performed on stage to songs written by Canadians. Lennon, McCartney and Harrison hadn't ever performed made-in-Canada songs in a live setting.

It would happen again in the 1990s.

In 1992, Burton Cummings played keyboards, tambourine, harmonica, and flute and sang with Starr as a guest musician. When the Winnipegger blew familiar bluesy notes into the harmonica to introduce The Guess Who's signature hit "American Woman", Starr kept beat on the drums. Cummings also played rhythm guitar on "No Time" for Starr who in summer of 1992 recorded *Ringo Starr and His All-Starr Band 2*—a live album from the Montreux Jazz Festival in Switzerland that was released the following year.

Three years later, Cummings' writing partner with The Guess Who and noted Beatles fanatic Randy Bachman played guitar and sang

"You Ain't Seen Nothing Yet" and "No Sugar Tonight/New Mother Nature" with Starr on drums. Both songs appeared on *Ringo Starr and His Third All-Starr Band, Volume 1*—a 1997 limited-release live album recorded in Tokyo.

To date, 81-year-old Starr has assembled 14 versions of his All-Starr Band and, since 1989, no fewer than six Canadian musicians and one comedian (Newmarket, Ontario's John Candy once sang and played harmonica for Starr) have joined the Beatle on concert stages around the world.[145]

If ever a cultural, feel-good highlight existed during the dreaded COVID-19 pandemic, it happened when Starr and The Band's Robertson re-grouped, at least virtually, to lead a project called *Song Around the World*. Co-produced by Robbie's author and musician son Sebastian Robertson, the seamless nearly six-minute web recording of "The Weight" included 18 other musicians from five continents—places as diverse as Bahrain, Nepal, The Congo and Japan—all contributing to The Band's Canadian-written classic. In the opening frames, moments before the global entourage of musicians begins playing, Starr is captured on his cell phone asking Robertson: "What key is it in Robbie?" and then jokes to himself "F demented." The project was the brainchild of a non-profit organization called Playing for Change. Founded in 2002, it aims to bring musicians in diverse places around the world closer through the power of their music.

And speaking of made in Canada, Starr became the second Beatle—after Lennon's *Live Peace in Toronto 1969*—to release a full, live performance recorded in Canada. The All-Starr's *Tour 2003* was a concert and interview DVD lasting nearly two hours and recorded at Casino Rama Resort in Rama, Ontario, on July 24, 2003, and released the following year. Casino Rama was also the venue for the All-Starr's pre-tour rehearsals, including five days of preparation in 2014.

Cummings wasn't the only Canadian with the All-Starrs during that 1992 world tour. Toronto guitarist and songwriter Jeff Healey played on "Yellow Submarine" and "With a Little Help From My Friends". The blind Toronto musician was both an opening act for Starr and also joined the Beatle on stage as a guest performer.[146]

Jeff Healey's Harrison-Clapton Circle Route

On his 1990 album *Hell to Pay*, Healey included a superb, rockin' cover version of "While My Guitar Gently Weeps".

The icing on the cake was that Healey got more than permission to record the song—its composer Harrison also agreed to play on it which offers an interesting historic parallel: Only 24 at the time, Healey would become the second guitarist with Canadian bloodlines to play in a studio release of this Harrison song with its composer; the first, of course, was 22 years earlier when Clapton sat in on The Beatles' *White Album* recording session.

As the story goes, while at his home in Hawaii, Harrison was sent Healey's studio recording tape of "While My Guitar Gently Weeps" with several tracks deliberately left open with instructions for Harrison to do as he liked on any of them. Sometime later in Los Angeles, Harrison teamed up with Jeff Lynne to add vocals and acoustic guitar—both featured in Healey's hit release.[147]

Two additional events put a meaningful close to the very Canadian Harrison-Clapton-Healey loop: Healey released a blistering, riff-laced cover version of the Harrison-Clapton-written Cream song "Badge" in June 1995 and The Jeff Healey Band once toured with none other than Slow Hand himself, you guessed it, Eric Clapton.

Healey died of Sarcoma cancer at age 41 in 2008.

In His Life: George Martin, Celine Dion and Jim Carrey

The producer of every Beatle album except *Let it Be* is the celebrated fifth Beatle George Martin. Brilliant beyond words, Martin's role with The Beatles cannot be understated as the buttoned-down, focused counterpoint to the Fab Four's relative youth and naiveté in the studio setting, at least in the early years.

But for playing the seemingly straight man role, Martin possessed a keen sense of humour and was involved in recording comedy acts early in his career. In 1979, he co-wrote his biography and gave it one of the great Beatles-association-book-titles of all time, *All You Need is Ears!*

Martin had a great life and if he doesn't go down as the greatest music producer of all time, he certainly will always be recognized as one of the music industry's finest talents, a painter of sound. Over the span of 48 years he received many, many accolades including multiple Grammy and Brit Awards, three honorary doctorates or degrees and a knighthood.

In 1997, the year after he became Sir George, Martin was winding down his stellar career and decided to produce his final album by trying something a little different. He took 13 of his most loved Beatles songs and brought together an eclectic group of celebrities to record them, like Robin Williams and Bobby McFerrin combining for "Come Together", Sean Connery voicing the words of "In My Life" and actress Goldie Hawn (who summered in Muskoka, Ontario) providing a breezy, slow tempo and seductive version of "A Hard Day's Night." The album was called *In My Life* and, as Martin put it to *Rolling Stone* magazine, "the essence of making an album like this was to have fun, really. I thought if I'm going to have a last record, I might as well enjoy it."

Perhaps the funniest, well silliest, performance came from Newmarket, Ontario-born comedian and actor Jim Carrey doing "I am the Walrus" which Martin acknowledged:

> I needed someone who, first of all, could get their tongue around all these very difficult words. Someone who could sing with a good sense of rhythm, someone who'd give a bit of a zany quality to it, because it needed that. John Lennon originally did it fairly straight. I mean, there was no overt humor in there. But I think if you're going to do an alternative version, you might as well bring out the humor on it anyway, and Jim Carrey certainly did that.[148]

Carrey, incidentally, sings "Can't Buy Me Love" a cappella from the Hollywood Bowl stage in his 2008 film *Yes Man* and, also in Los

Angeles, in 2014 he joined a bevy of background singers with Starr singing "With a Little Help From My Friends".

Charlemagne, Québec's Celine Dion, whose late husband and manager once fronted a Québec trio of Beatles impersonators, was also featured in Martin's final project. The chanteuse was at the peak of her career when she recorded "Here, There and Everywhere" in a ramped-up orchestral version of a song McCartney considers one of his finest compositions.

Active until his death at age 90 in 2016, Martin handed the reins over to his son Giles to preserve and even improve on The Beatles' recordings in future re-releases. The son of the great producer has become the de facto custodian of The Beatles' recording legacy and would get his breakout international project working on *The Beatles LOVE*, an album and performance concept that was hatched in Canada.

Lennon, McCartney, Harrison and Neil Young

It was Canada's Neil Young who inducted McCartney into the Rock and Roll Hall of Fame in 1999. In his speech, the Toronto-born, Omemee, Ontario- and Winnipeg-raised Young referenced, obliquely, attending Kelvin High School in Winnipeg's River Heights neighbourhood. It was there, said Young, where "the first song I ever sang was (The Beatles version of) ... 'Money (That's What I Want)' ... at the school cafeteria and it didn't go over that good so we tried 'It Won't be Long', yeah, and that was better."[149]

At the Hall of Fame induction in Cleveland, Young went on to reference the first McCartney solo album, *McCartney*, saying he "stepped from the shadow of The Beatles and there he was, it kind of blew my mind and I said, 'Well, maybe I can do this too.'"[150]

There's every indication that both Lennon and McCartney were and are fans of Young's music, and you can add the late Linda McCartney to that list when she indicated the Canadian, along with Bob Marley and her husband, as favourite songwriters in the 1989

McCartney World Tour concert program. Certainly Young and Lennon shared an energy for penning anti-war songs and wrote the era's key protest tunes, Lennon's "Give Peace a Chance" and Young's "Ohio", within a year of one another. The tripartite dots of Lennon, Young and McCartney were wonderfully connected in 2016. In October of that year, Young smiled broadly as he joined McCartney on stage in California to perform a chorus-filled rendition of Lennon's "Give Peace a Chance" during the one-off Desert Trip rock festival.

With McCartney's erstwhile band offering accompaniment, he and Young alternated verses of "A Day in the Life" as a preamble before they transitioned to the Lennon world protest song that originated in Montréal. (As an aside, during the "the English Army had just won the war" line, McCartney turned to Young and added, "with a little help from the Americans." Sheesh, Paul, did you expect the Canadian to salute?)

In 2011, readers of *Rolling Stone* magazine ranked the pair in their Top 10 Songwriters of All Time. Young was ranked sixth, right behind McCartney at fifth and Lennon at third; the Lennon/McCartney tandem was ranked second and Bob Dylan took first prize.[151]

Young hovers in the path of The Beatles' orbit in a unique and special way—choosing a Beatles song to perform for the first time while in school and rounding out with links to both McCartney and Lennon ... and also Harrison. Young took the stage with Harrison, Clapton and others in New York on October 16, 1992, to play "My Back Pages" in a celebration of Bob Dylan's 30 years as a recording artist.

As wonderful as that collection of talent was on stage that night, it was not as amazing as the next big Beatles show, which was all about *LOVE*.

The Beatles, The Brick, Moosehead Beer and Long John Baldry

There exists a photograph by Michael McCartney (known as Michael McGeer) depicting his 20-year-old brother Paul McCartney standing outside Liverpool's Lime Street bus station with a tall, blond-haired singer named John William Baldry. Born in England and a year older than Paul, the two became friends after meeting at the Cavern Club where they both played. Baldry's superb voice would launch a successful career as blues singer Long John Baldry, involved with A-List artists such as The Rolling Stones, Elton John and Rod Stewart. In fact as a member of Long John's band Bluesology, keyboard player Reginald Dwight took the bandleader's first name as his last when he re-christened himself Elton John.

During the filming of a Beatles TV special called *Around The Beatles* on April 19, 1964, Baldry made a guest appearance and sang "Got My Mojo Working" with the camera occasionally switching to the seated John, Paul, George and Ringo enthusiastically singing along and encouraging their friend from the audience balcony.

Openly gay and suffering from severe bouts of mental illness, Baldry sought a change in his mid-30s and after a brief stint in the United States, moved to Canada, first Ontario but then, in search of warmer winters, settled permanently in Vancouver.

He continued to perform and record while in Canada and also made a lucrative living pursuing another career as the voice behind dozens of Canadian television commercials throughout the 1990s. From retailers Mark's Work Warehouse, Winnipeg Shell gas stations and The Brick, to utilities Edmonton Tel, B.C. Hydro and brands such as Thrifty's Bluenotes jeans, Irish Spring soap and Moosehead beer, Baldry applied his trade and also voiced-over many animated productions of *Star Wars*, *Sonic the Hedgehog* and *Merlin*, to name a few of many.

Baldry, who became a Canadian citizen, died in 2005 of a chest infection in Vancouver at age 64.

2000 TO TODAY

George Harrison: Love and Barnacle Bill in Montréal

In mid-June 2000, 17 months before his death, George Harrison attended what was then North America's only Formula One race at Circuit Gilles Villeneuve on Montréal's Notre Dame Island. Motor racing (and, later, gardening) ranked high among Harrison's non-music passions. He saw his first F1 race in England as a boy in 1955. His older brothers Harry and Peter also enjoyed motorsports.

During his visit, Harrison attended an annual Grand Prix weekend party at the sprawling, mountainside, south shore estate of Cirque de Soleil co-founder and billionaire space tourist Guy Laliberté. It was a warm, breezy evening with guests mingling in and out of the Saint-Bruno, Québec estate, which included a private lake, palatial gardens, a forest filled with tall, centuries-old trees and a massive outdoor fire pit. DJs spun dance music while jugglers and acrobats animated the atmosphere for an assembly of racing and business elites.

Befitting past and future guest lists of the wealthy founder of the surrealist circus troupe—whose reputation for merrymaking is legendary, Harrison would be among the likes of Robert De Niro and Sylvester Stallone visiting the Laliberté home. The former Beatle was suitably impressed with the billionaire's taste for entertainment as Olivia Harrison later told *Newsweek* how, after returning home from the event, her late husband described the scene in Saint-Bruno:

> George came home and said, 'You know, there was a man and a woman sitting in a lake. She had a tuxedo on and he had a ball gown on and they sat at a table all night long having a candlelit dinner with water up to their waist. There were people in feather costumes swinging in the trees like birds.' This really was right up George's alley. Guy was the visionary and so was George. They had a lot of excited conversations.[152]

Harrison and Laliberté were already acquainted—having met before over their shared passion for F1 racing. The two hatched the idea of Laliberté's acrobatic troupe performing to the music of The Beatles at that party. In time the idea took flight, spawning the enormously successful *The Beatles LOVE* franchise.

It has been suggested that initially they compared the concept to something akin to bringing *Yellow Submarine*—and its cast of characters such as Max, Old Fred and a Blue Meanie or two—to the stage. As well, Harrison told Laliberté he preferred two shows, one based on The Beatles' music, the other on his own catalogue, although the latter never happened.

It took six years of back and forth between Cirque, McCartney, Starr, and the families of Lennon and Harrison for the show to take shape. There were the performers to train, the lyrical apparition sets to design, and the eccentric characters—Father McKenzie, Doctor Robert, Lady Madonna, Sgt. Pepper, Mr. Kite—to bring to life, all based on lyrics in The Beatles' songs. The Cirque de Soleil performance of *LOVE,* written and directed by Sorel, Québec's Dominic Champagne, debuted at the Mirage hotel in Las Vegas on June 30, 2006.

In attendance was an extraordinary and rare ensemble of Beatles and their families: McCartney, Starr, Yoko Ono, Cynthia Lennon, Julian Lennon, Olivia and Dhani Harrison, and George Martin. It can be said a Montréal-based circus production company, and its Québec City-born co-founder Laliberté, were directly responsible for the largest and most public modern day reunion of the sometimes estranged Beatles family since the band's break up in 1970.

Moreover, what began as made-in-Canada idea catapulted the career of Giles Martin as a producer and re-arranger of The Beatles' music. The *LOVE* soundtrack was the younger Martin's first major Beatles project and went on to sell nearly four million copies in a landmark production of 26 re-mastered and mashed Beatle tunes. Since his father George's death in 2016, Giles has been at the forefront of every re-issue of The Beatles' music, responsible for the next wave of immortal fruit born from the band's recording sessions.

Well over eight million Beatle fans have travelled to Las Vegas to watch *LOVE*—which *Newsweek* described as a "$150 million surrealist spectacle" at the Mirage resort's theatre, and by 2020 Cirque de Soleil put on its 6,000th show.

Between the 69-lap Grand Prix de Montréal on Sunday (won by Ferrari driver Michael Schumacher after starting from pole position), and his revelry with Laliberté, Harrison took in more subdued race-related activities including an event at Canada's largest art museum, the Musée des Beaux-Arts on Montréal's Sherbrooke Street West.

Also attending was Dali Sanschagrin, a fashion journalist from *Musique-Plus* (French Canada's version of *MTV*). She was tipped off that Harrison would attend but was told he would not be doing interviews.

In one of the museum's five pavilions, guests gathered for a cocktail party. Either to avoid recognition or simply because it was raining, Harrison wore a white-brimmed rain hat and long dark raincoat like the one he wore to Linda McCartney's memorial two years to the month earlier. The Beatle stood alone in the crowded setting, not a handler or fan to be found. He had arrived on the atrium of the pavilion and was making his way to the second floor.

As he ambled toward the elevator Sanschagrin and her cameraman were waiting and entered the elevator car with him. They introduced themselves, tried to make small talk and asked if he would like to answer some questions. Moments after the elevator doors opened the camera began rolling and Sanschagrin could be heard asking Harrison in a pitched, excited voice what music he listened to on the way to the museum?

Sanschagrin's persistence paid off but what she didn't know was that the 84-second, six-question interview that followed would be one of the first Harrison gave after retreating to Fiji to convalesce from serious injuries sustained in a home invasion six months earlier and, sadly, among his last on-camera interviews—Harrison died the following year in Los Angeles.

> **Sanschagrin**: Mr. Harrison can you tell me, oh please please, what are you listening when you drive your car, what is the music that are you listening to when you're driving in your car?

> **Harrison**: Hoagy Carmichael, 'Barnacle Bill the Sailor' from 1929.

> **Sanschagrin**: Did you (ever) dream of becoming a Formula One driver?

> **Harrison**: Is he with you (glancing at the cameraman) … no I never. Not really.

> **Sanschagrin**: Then why do you like coming here so much?

> **Harrison**: It's just a hobby, because it's like a soap opera, it's a big soap opera so I like to see the soap opera and how it develops.

> **Sanschagrin**: Are you driving fast?

> **Harrison**: No, no, I used to when I was young but now I'm slow, very slow, now I just drive a wheelchair.

> **Sanschagrin**: Do you like Montréal?

Harrison: Montréal is very nice. Yes. It's a bit wet today, but it's nice, yes.

Sanschagrin: What do you like about the city?

Harrison: I like the croissants! Thank you, nice to meet you.[153]

Harrison's six responses were delightfully reminiscent of the offbeat and charming Beatles witticism that was so prevalent during the height of Beatlemania. It has been said The Beatles were reincarnated as Monty Python, or that Monty Python were The Beatles of comedy.

That George, who produced and appeared in Python's *Life of Brian*, snuck in irreverent, cheeky references to Barnacle Bill, cruising in a wheelchair, soap operas in racing and croissants in the Montréal interview was nothing short of magical.

Harrison was passionate about singer-songwriter Hoagy Carmichael who hit his stride in the 1920s and 1930s and during his long career collaborated with Jack Fallon, the Canadian who played his de-tuned his violin fiddle on the *White Album*.

Credit is due to the interviewer who, in a hurried moment, fired-off six spontaneous questions (and a very Beatles "please, please" plea) that drew Harrison's attention even though he was clearly trying to avoid being noticed. And who could blame him … not only was he was stabbed and seriously injured in that home invasion, but 18 months before that he was treated for throat cancer.

As Sanschagrin recalled, "We were told not to approach him but my director was a huge Beatles fan, so I decided to go for it. George Harrison was very cool, simpatico, you know, and thin. The questions came to me at that moment, I just went with a feeling and it worked."

Sanschagrin, who was born in Québec City, is also a writer and currently working on a fifth book, this one about being a parent and a coach with French soccer goalkeeper and coach Joël Bats. In her career, meeting Harrison and getting an on-camera interview ranks second only to bumping into Gerard Depardieu one night in Paris and securing him for an interview the following day.

She believes she is one of the last journalists with whom Harrison spoke for a stand-up, on camera chat and recalls the 84-second interview was re-played around the world at the time of his death.

Canadian Actors Play Ringo Starr, Heather McCartney

In 2019, the provinces of British Columbia and Ontario captured over $6.5 billion in film and television production revenue, the largest concentration of (mostly) foreign and domestic investment in Canada's annual $9.3 billion movie-making industry.[154]

It's no wonder both provinces squabble over which jurisdiction rightfully earns the title of Hollywood North. But there's no argument that each province can lay claim to the film setting for two important Beatle biographical films.

In March 2000, filming began in Vancouver for an American television biopic on Linda McCartney—the only Beatle wife for whom a film has been made. The life and times of the New York-born photographer, the former Linda Eastman, is captured in *The Linda McCartney Story*. The two-hour film follows her life as a single mother at the start of her career surrounded by the era's biggest rock acts, meeting and then marrying Paul, their long, 29-year run as a couple, inclusion in the band Wings, entrepreneurship, philanthropy, family and the breast cancer diagnosis that eventually cut short her life at 56 in 1998.

Released in May 2000, the film features a Canadian-born actor playing the role of a Beatle. Toronto's Mike McMurtry, a Gemini nominated performer and writer, plays Starr. Other Canadians in the cast include Ottawa-born and prolific voice actor Nicole Oliver who played the role of Eastman's friend, and Nanaimo, British Columbia's Jodelle Ferland, who played Linda's daughter, Heather See (later adopted as Heather McCartney). While the film was limited to TV release and was absent of high praise among critics, it did feature Golden Globe-winning and Oscar-nominated actor George Segal who played Linda's dad, Lee Eastman.

That same year, various locations in Ontario doubled as New York City as cameras and crew set up in the province for an acclaimed film that depicted the 1976 real-life get together of Beatles Lennon and McCartney.

Two of Us, a title lifted from the McCartney-written song about he and Linda on the *Let it Be* album, starred Aidan Quinn as McCartney and Jared Harris as Lennon. The film is regarded as one of the better Beatles films ever made. Despite its fictional dialogue, the 90-minute film manages to offer subtle, Beatle- and Liverpool-specific references between the two and superb, playful and sometimes heart-wrenching banter that seems a plausible dramatization of how they spent their time. The honest and genuine mood of the film is likely why it received a respectable 79 per cent audience score on *rottentomatoes. com* and was described by one film critic as "a little masterpiece."

Director Michael Lindsay-Hogg—yes, the same director who gave us the *Let it Be* film—took a strong script by Mark Stanfield and created an honest account of what might have transpired when McCartney paid an unannounced visit to Lennon in his Manhattan apartment in the years between The Beatles' break up and Lennon's death.

How Toronto's Lorne Michaels Nearly Reunited John and Paul

A second Canadian angle from the era is captured in *Two of Us*. Lorne Michaels, the uber-successful creator of *Saturday Night Live* and native son of Toronto, appears in the film. The Michaels segment involved actual footage of a hilariously mocking offer he made The Beatles on the show's first season in 1975.

Michaels took to the air to offer The Beatles a paltry $3,000 to reunite and play three songs on *NBC's Saturday Night* (as the show was then called before becoming *Saturday Night Live*). The film does a credible job of showing the two Beatles in Lennon's living room watching Michaels make the proposition on television. In real life, McCartney and Lennon actually considered the offer a short time later, gathering their guitars and pointing out the *NBC* studio was only minutes away.

It was, by all accounts, a close call. Michaels' antics very nearly led the pair to appear on the show. As the story goes, McCartney and Lennon lost interest when they realized the late hour and had a change of heart.

A year later, Harrison appeared on *SNL* and discussed with Michaels the earlier offer only to have Michaels raise the ante … to $3,200! McCartney has appeared multiple times throughout the show's 45-year run. One 2013 skit was with Canadian comedian Martin Short, where the singing Caleb (Short) restricts Monty (McCartney) to tapping a triangle insisting the Beatle remain quiet because "you can't sing … I have a million dollar voice and you are a lump." The duo separate and McCartney breaks into the crowd-pleasing "Wonderful Christmas Time".

Starr also hosted an episode of *SNL* in late 1984.

Sealing the McCartney's Marital Fate in Charlottetown?

During their four-year marriage, Paul McCartney and Heather Mills-McCartney took on a number of charitable, humanitarian causes. While they attracted a lot of needed attention on the insecurity and danger of active land mines, they also supported animal rights and, near the top of their list, was the controversial Canadian seal harvest. To make the point, they made a brief and daring March 2006 stop on a Gulf of St. Lawrence ice floe off Québec's Magdalen Islands, a 6.5-hour ferry ride straight north of Souris, Prince Edward Island.

Spectacularly, the McCartneys, backed by the United States Humane Society, staged the risky photo op landing by helicopter on the floe to pose with newborn harp seal pups while the cameras whirled.

Danny Williams, then the premier of Newfoundland and Labrador, expressed "disappointment and annoyance" at the negative attention the McCartneys were bringing to the region and, in a news release, invited the Beatle to visit his province to "lay out for McCartney why the seal harvest is important to the province, as well as to correct some of the inaccurate information in the public domain regarding the harvest."[155]

As expected, the daring event garnered international media attention but nothing like what transpired the following day on *CNN* as veteran US talk show host Larry King interviewed the McCartneys, who were in Charlottetown, and then patched-in Williams in St. John's to join the teleconference.

Paul's tone was diplomatic, respectfully disagreeing with the premier's position and even calling him by his first name, "Danny"; Mrs. McCartney, on the other hand, was overtly passionate, less kind and provided *CNN* and King the sensational television moment they had likely hoped would transpire.

The McCartneys and Williams kept King busy; as moderator, he repeatedly tried to break-up their interruptions, telling the three to behave, wait their turn, and not to speak over themselves. That's because Mills-McCartney came out swinging and soon learned she had met her match in a feisty Williams who was more than up for the challenge. Verbal blows were struck, points scored and wounds inflicted on both sides as more than 4,000 words were slung back and forth in the televised boxing ring.

Near the end of the exchange, a pitched Williams (who served as premier from 2003 to 2010) re-iterated his invitation, this time extending the offer to Mills-McCartney, to come to Newfoundland and Labrador for a first-hand look at the province's fishery, economy and people. It's at that point McCartney, who seemed otherwise quite informed about the situation, got his provinces confused, thinking he was actually in Newfoundland and Labrador but all the while he was sitting in a Prince Edward Island studio.

It's perhaps easy for foreigners to lump Canada's Maritime provinces together as one homogeneous group, ignoring their distinctive culture, character, geography and the fact Nova Scotia and New Brunswick, along with Ontario and Québec, represent the cradles of Canadian confederation when the nation was established in 1867.

Here's are excerpts from the March 6, 2006 *CNN* transcript of McCartney's cringe-worthy Canadian geographic faux pas, beginning with Williams speaking directly to Mills-McCartney until Sir Paul intervenes:

> **Williams**: This is about propaganda. This is about using superstars like your husband. I want you to come to Newfoundland and Labrador. I want you to know the truth and the facts. And I'm certain that you will partner with us and move this forward because I think we can convince you that this is a very humane undertaking.

> **McCartney**: Well, we're here, Danny. You don't need to invite us. Thanks for the invitation, but we're here. We're actually in the studio here. We are in Newfoundland. And we saw the seals yesterday.
>
> And the point we're making here is that this is inhumane. No matter how much you say it is humane, it isn't. This is a small percentage of the fishermen's income. No matter how much you say it isn't.
>
> This is nothing to do with the depletion of the cod stocks. That's due to human overfishing. And there are plenty of ideas that the Canadian people might be very interested in, in the same way as whale watching has become a huge industry, which used to be whale hunting.
>
> In the international arena, Canada is known as a great country, a great people. And this creates a stain on the character of the Canadian people internationally.

> **Mills-McCartney**: Why are you so against the seal hunt being stopped? Why do you not want to give the sealers an alternate income? There's no other justification on this. Why don't you want that to happen? Why don't you want to have peace talks? Why do you want to keep going to war and doing this to the animals?

Williams: … first of all, <u>Paul, you're in Prince Edward Island now</u>. And I'm in Newfoundland and Labrador. I'm inviting you to come to my province to see that. We are supported by the World Wildlife Fund, a very reputable organization. This is supported by the United Nations and the International Society for Conservation. These are worldwide policy speakers … they see nothing wrong with it.[156]

In time it was abundantly clear that the seal hunt debate didn't end in Charlottetown or on the Gulf of St. Lawrence. But another battle soon emerged, this one in the McCartney household as two months following the *CNN* interview, Paul and Heather announced their separation that was later followed by a turbulent divorce proceeding.

It didn't take long for Williams and a federal cabinet minister to take credit for the couple's break-up.

Canada's Fisheries and Oceans Minister, Loyola Hearn of Newfoundland and Labrador, mockingly, and perhaps unfairly, told reporters outside the House of Commons that Williams' firm position during the interview so raised the hackles of Mills-McCartney that it "likely changed the former Beatle's view of her," and added "we'll take some credit for that."

Hearn's rhetoric continued. He said Paul McCartney, an animal rights advocate, seemed to respectfully disagree with the Newfoundland and Labrador sealers' point of view espoused by Williams during the televised debate. His wife, an ardent anti-sealing activist was, said Hearn, "not so gracious."[157]

And while we're on the subject of McCartney's Canadian geographic gaffes, his much-hyped *Back in the U.S.* album of 2002 was the result of live concert recordings made during his *Driving USA Tour*, yet the 35-track album includes his heartfelt tribute to the fallen Lennon, "Here Today", recorded not in the US but in Canada's largest city, Toronto, on April 13; even the tickets to the Air Canada Centre show were embossed with *Driving USA Tour*!

Gratis

A flurry of Beatles-Canada activity closed the first decade of the 2000s.

For starters, the core members of The Guess Who, Burton Cummings and Randy Bachman, returned to the studio in 2007 to record an album of oldies called *Jukebox* and covered "Happy Just to Dance with You". The Lennon-McCartney composition, which Harrison sang and reached number one in Canada in 1964, was also covered by Nova Scotia's Anne Murray in 1980 and featured in a recent animated kid's television series for *Netflix* called *Beat Bugs* which includes music from The Beatles' catalogue with Vancouver's Atomic Cartoons providing the 3D animation.

In early 2008, singer and songwriter Cindy Gomez, of Mississauga, Ontario, was a last-minute recruit for a band assembled by the Eurythmics' Dave Stewart to back up Starr for a series concerts and TV appearances. When Gomez got the call to join Starr, she described her reaction to *Maclean's* magazine: "'Oh my God, it's a Beatle!' She didn't know all of their music, she admits: 'But I knew a Beatle was a Beatle.' (Musician and producer Mike) Bradford asked if she was free. 'And I said, wait, let me check my schedule.' She laughs. 'And I said, of course I am free. And then he said, 'You have to memorize four or five songs.' And I said I'll do whatever it takes. If I have to pay my way (to get to Los Angeles) I will. Don't pay me any money. I just want to do it.'"[158]

Gomez, who continued to work with Starr by providing background vocals on two tracks from Starr's 2010 album *Y Not*, wasn't the first Canadian to offer free services to a surviving Beatle.

In 2009, Paul Saltzman was asked if his Rishikesh photos be used as a backdrop for an upcoming McCartney concert appearance. Saltzman obliged and when asked his fee he graciously offered his photos *gratis*, on the house. An array of photos from India were projected on the rear wall of the stage while McCartney played his Rishikesh-written "Cosmically Conscious" with Starr on drums and a host of celebrities lending their voices like Eddie Vedder and Sheryl Crow—all raising money for the David Lynch Foundation at New York's Radio

City Music Hall. In what would be only the second time McCartney and Starr performed together without The Beatles in public, British Columbia resident Paul Horn and his flute joined the two on stage.

Bench Strength: Perhaps more than any other Beatle, Ringo has recruited Canadians to play on the many albums of his solo career, including David Foster, Cindy Gomez, Alanis Morissette, Robbie Robertson, Garth Hudson and Rick Danko. Photo by Schröder+Schömbs PR_Brands (licensed under CC BY-ND 2.0)

Anglo-Saxon Idol Crashes Québec City's Birthday Party

Macca The Magnificent I: Two weeks after 47 people perished in the horrific 2013 train accident at Lac-Mégantic, Québec, Paul offered 1,000 free
tickets to survivors and family of the deceased for his Québec City concert
where, in French, he dedicated "Let it Be" to the victims. The Beatle once
told *CNN*: "In the international arena, Canada is known as a great country,
a great people". Photo by Laura Staeger courtesy of the Tennant Family.

In the summer of 2008, McCartney played a free concert on Québec City's historic battlefield, the Plains of Abraham, as part of the provincial capital's 400th anniversary of its founding by French explorer and diplomat Samuel de Champlain. Celebrated as a major event, it nevertheless didn't sit well with some Québeckers. At least 35 prominent artists, writers and politicians, including two separatist members of the National Assembly of Québec, issued an open letter opposing the concert. They suggested that a celebration of Québec City's history should not involve "an international Anglo-Saxon idol."[159]

It would be the third and final brush for a member of The Beatles with Québec separatists—you may recall a death threat against Ringo in 1964 and Lennon's shouting match with a radical separatist in 1969. On the flip side, supporters of McCartney's appearance at the city's birthday party said his presence validates that Québec had two founding peoples, French and English.

Ill feelings aside, he spoke some French when he arrived on the massive outdoor stage, saying *"Bon soir les Québécois, bon soir toute le gang ... C'est ma premiere visite a Québec,"* to the delight of a staggering 200,000 fans who filled the park as well as nearby streets to catch the band play through 38 songs including 24 Beatles numbers.

A quirky fact that emerged from McCartney's visit to the provincial capital was that he gave the chef at his hotel, Auberge Saint Antoine, a hand-written recipe for his favourite omelet and the bartender another note on how to mix his preferred margarita!

Canada's Love Affair with Mull of Kintyre

Another word for goosebumps is the French word *frisson*, as in getting a shiver or chills when moved by the aesthetic of musical art: "A psychophysiological response to auditory and/or visual stimuli that often induces a pleasurable or otherwise positively-valenced affective state ... the sensation occurs as a mildly to moderately pleasurable emotional response to music with skin tingling."[160]

Macca The Magnificent II: For many years, Paul has made an emotional connection with Canadians including giving 10 local pipe and drum bands in six
Canadian provinces the once-in-a-lifetime hometown thrill of joining him on
stage to play "Mull of Kintyre". Pipe and drum bands from the Vancouver area,
Edmonton, Regina, Winnipeg, the Toronto area, Hamilton, Ottawa and Halifax
have taken part in the tradition between 1993 and 2016. Photos are courtesy
of Halifax 78th Highlanders Pipe Band, left, and Megan Conrad-Kindiak and
Blake MacEachern, Edmonton Police Service Pipes and Drums, right.

In the vast 213-song catalogue of The Beatles, many songs still give
me *frisson*. I can be mushy and sentimental when I listen to Lennon's
youthful reflection in "In My Life", which he recorded shortly after

his 25th birthday. My imaginary conductor's baton points and gestures its way throughout the orchestration in "Eleanor Rigby". And I can dwell on the admission of loss or blame in "For No One", tear-up at the beautiful construct of "Dear Prudence", or face the day with positive, uplifting energy listening to "Here Comes The Sun", written by Harrison in Clapton's home.

As individuals, Lennon's raw voice and lyrical plea to end the myth-making media machine in "God" and Harrison's awareness-raising for the plight of the poor and displaced in "Bangladesh" and his anguished, painful-to-listen-to, end-of-life clarity on "Stuck Inside a Cloud" and Starr's kind and sentimental "Never Without You" tribute to Harrison with Clapton on slide guitar, do the trick for me.

It's subjective, and quite personal, but for me these songs and others prove unmistakably The Beatles' ability to raise songwriting and production to an art form and, as art, has the potential to produce something approaching an emotional experience.

For McCartney as a soloist, my choice is the skin-tingling emotion raised by the music and lyrics of "Mull of Kintyre", a simple five-chord song and melody about the natural beauty and human kinship in a weather-beaten corner of southwestern Scotland, separated from Northern Ireland by a channel and the stone steps of the mythical Giant's Causeway.

And yes, it's the bagpipes and drums in "Mull of Kintyre" that take my breath away but also the song's deep and storied Canadian connection.

Written with Wings band mate Denny Laine and recorded in Scotland, McCartney's "Mull of Kintyre" surpassed "She Loves You" in UK sales and stands as one of McCartney's greatest musical achievements and commercial success stories:

> At an estimated nine million copies sold world-wide—despite having never being released as a single in America—"Mull Of Kintyre" is among the 50 biggest-selling singles of all time worldwide, and a bigger-selling single than any other that McCartney has ever penned, the entire Beatles catalogue included

save for "I Want To Hold Your Hand". It spent nine weeks atop the chart, becoming the first UK single to sell over two million copies. It remained the biggest-selling British single of all time until usurped by Band Aid's "Do They Know It's Christmas?" in 1984.[161]

In "Mull of Kintyre" the cue for the lush bagpipe and drum section follows soon after the lyric "my desire is always to be here". And as it turns out, a Langley, British Columbia resident was actually "there"— yes, he lived in Campbeltown, Scotland, near the Mull of Kintyre, and helped the McCartneys and Laine recorded their masterpiece. It's also, incidentally, the place where McCartney wrote "The Long and Winding Road" and where Linda snapped the iconic photo of her bearded husband nestling daughter Mary in his jacket for the cover of his first solo album, *McCartney*.

John MacCallum has lived in British Columbia for the past 23 years; a Canadian citizen, he is married with two daughters, but in 1977 a 19-year-old MacCallum played the tenor drum with the Campbeltown Pipe Band, an ensemble McCartney hired to play on "Mull of Kintyre". MacCallum says the McCartneys were regulars in Campbeltown, a town of 5,000 people on the Kintyre Peninsula in southwest Scotland about a few kilometres from the famous couple's family farm.

The huge McCartney hit was laid-down in one take, with seven pipers and seven drummers, at his farmhouse studio known as the Spirit of Ranachan.

"Paul loved the area and Linda was particularly fond of the beaches and the outdoor family life including horseback riding, so he decided to write a song," remembers MacCallum on the phone from Langley. MacCallum left Scotland in 1984, falling in love with the beauty of Canada's western-most province.

Back in Scotland, MacCallum recalled that his pipe major, Tony Wilson, worked with McCartney to come up with the music for "Mull of Kintyre", noting McCartney played the melody on keyboard, and Wilson adapted it to pipe music.

The Campbeltown Pipe Band, and perhaps half the town's popula-tion, are featured on the "Mull of Kintyre" music video filmed on nearby Saddell Beach with the McCartneys and Laine. It includes a nearly three-second close-up of MacCallum. Look for the curly red-haired young man energetically twirling the soft mallets on his vertically held drum to the "Mull of Kintyre" score at 2:52 of the official video.

In the years that followed MacCallum's playing on "Mull of Kintyre", hundreds of Canadian musicians have had their own "MacCallum Moment," following his beating drum on a path to join McCartney at arena and open-air concerts across Canada.

While Scotland's Mull of Kintyre and Canada are separated by over 4,000 km of ocean, a musical bridge has linked the two places thanks to a decision made by McCartney himself.

He decided that Canada (or at least English Canada) would be one of only four countries where he would perform "Mull of Kintyre" (the others are the UK, Australia and New Zealand). Since 1993, he has tasked his team with finding local pipe and drum bands to join him on stage. It's for this reason that "Mull of Kintyre" holds a uniquely special place for Canadians attending his concerts.

The tradition began on May 21, 1993 when Winnipeg became the first Canadian city to join McCartney on stage. Over 40,000 fans at Winnipeg Stadium saw 24 members of The Heather Belles, an all-female pipe and drum ensemble, join Paul, Linda and their post-Wings band mates Hamish Stuart, Robbie McIntosh, Paul "Wix" Wickens and Blair Cunningham on stage. (Wickens, who is still with McCartney's touring band, would play a pivotal role in all future Canadian settings for "Mull of Kintyre".)

Said McCartney on that Winnipeg night: "I'll tell you why it's always good to come to somewhere like Canada because it gives us an opportunity to throw in an extra song. It was a hit here and it wasn't in some other countries."[162]

The Heather Belles were formed in Winnipeg in 1951 and achieved success through competitions and special events over the years. In 2001, 195 current and past members of the band gathered to celebrate their 50th anniversary of playing together at the North Kildonen Community Club. The celebration, however, would be their last as they disbanded six years later.

The other Canadian stop in 1993 was Toronto and it was there at CNE Stadium when the Peel Regional Police Pipe Band, from the nearby city of Brampton, marched on stage to join McCartney for that sultry bagpipe and drum part on "Mull of Kintyre" before 40,000 fans.

McCartney didn't tour for nine years after the 1993 concerts as Linda became ill and, sadly, succumbed to cancer in 1998, so his next visit to Canada was not until 2002. The Peel police band reprised their role at the Air Canada Centre in Toronto—the only instance during that year's 28-city North American tour that a pipe and drum band joined him on stage.

The Peel police band played their final accompaniment in 2005, again at the Air Canada Centre. Another four years went by before McCartney returned to Canada and began a nearly annual tradition of involving local Canadian pipers.

In July 2009, Nova Scotia's 78th Highlanders of the Halifax Citadel Pipe Band were part of a memorable outdoor concert that attracted some 50,000 fans. Just as he did a year earlier, McCartney played at the Halifax Common, an urban park located just below Citadel Hill. The 78th Highlanders took their name from Citadel Hill (also known as Fort George), a National Historic Site built in 1856. In the early 18th century, the British garrison established the city of Halifax at this site as it overlooks the harbour and offered a superb defensive location.

Halifax would be the only city in 2009's six-city mini tour where McCartney played his ode to Scotland but not before observing, "I'm just looking up and seeing moon over Nova Scotia"[163] providing a unique familiarity for Canada by way of a song the former Beatle reserves for places like it.

Canadian pipers and drummers in full tartan regalia would be featured in 2010 for two nights at Toronto's Air Canada Centre with the Paris Port Dover Pipe Band, which boasts over 100 members. In 2012, the Delta Police Pipe Band played at BC Place Stadium in

Vancouver and, in Edmonton for two nights, the Pipes and Drums of the Edmonton Police Service—which can trace its beginnings to 1914 when founding band members joined Princess Patricia's Canadian Light Infantry on the battlefields of Europe—played at the Rexall Centre.

The following year and in their 93rd year as an ensemble, the Winnipeg Police Pipe Band were decked in their traditional Royal Stewart Tartan to play with McCartney in front of 31,000 people. Also in 2013, celebrating its 20th anniversary, the City of Regina Pipe Band played to 40,000 at Mosaic Stadium, as did the Ottawa Police Service Pipe Band at Canadian Tire Centre—McCartney's first-ever concert in the nation's capital. In 2015, my wife Tamara and I and several friends rose up in our seats and cheered as the Paris Port Dover Pipe Band made its second appearance with McCartney at the Air Canada Centre.

On April 19 and 20, 2016, the Delta Police Pipe Band returned to the Rogers Centre in Vancouver to accompany McCartney for "Mull of Kintyre".

The last performance of the pipes occurred in Hamilton, Ontario, on July 21, 2016, where McCartney and the band were joined by the Argyll and Sutherland Highlanders of Canada at FirstOntario Centre—the first and only *military* pipe and drum band in Canada to join him on stage.

In introducing "Mull of Kintyre", which would be the third song in his encore set, McCartney said: "For all you ex-pats or families of ex-pats"[164] perhaps shedding light on why he only plays "Mull of Kintyre" in select Commonwealth countries. In the past, McCartney has also noted the song has sold well in Canada.

Record sales may have been the initial driver of McCartney's special concert treat, but in time the appeal of the song in countries that held a bond with the United Kingdom—or more specifically Scotland— became the principle motivation. The Scottish were among the first Europeans to arrive in Canada when they landed in the 17th century. By 2016, men and women of Scottish ancestry represented the third largest ethnic group in Canada at nearly five million. Indeed,

Canada's first prime minster, Sir John Alexander Macdonald, was born in Glasgow.

McCartney's last show in Canada before the COVID-19 pandemic was a two-night Vancouver stopover in July 2019. At age 77, he proved he was still every bit a rock 'n' roll legend performing for over three hours with ample credit due his band with whom he's been touring and recording since 2002—Abe Laboriel Jr. on drums, and a pair of dynamite guitarists Rusty Anderson and Brian Ray and stalwart keyboard player Wickens.

The band played an incredible 39 songs at each of four Canadian venues (Québec City, Montréal, Edmonton and Vancouver) that year, including seven songs during encores.

But here's the thing: "Mull of Kintyre" was missing from the regular and encore set list in that 2019 tour, and it wasn't performed internationally in 2018 either. With his 2020 tour dates cancelled due to the pandemic, for now we can accurately surmise that the July 21, 2016, concert at Hamilton's FirstOntario Centre is the last time (in a marvelous on-and-off 24-year run) that a local pipe and drum band played with McCartney anywhere in Canada.

It wasn't however the final "Mull of Kintyre" he performed live around the world. That honour goes to the New Zealand's Auckland & District Pipe band, which joined McCartney and his band mates at Mt. Smart Stadium on December 17, 2017 during a mini-tour that stretched across four Australian cities and Auckland.

While it's easy to get bogged down in Mull minutiae, there exists a key distinction for Canada in McCartney's history of performing the song.

The Hamilton Argyll and Sutherland Highlanders of Canada Pipes and Drums are part of the Canadian Armed Forces Reserve. As the bands that joined McCartney at the 2017 stops in Australia and New Zealand were either civilian or police bands … drum roll please … the Hamilton Argylls were the last pipe band to play with McCartney in Canada or the United Kingdom but, more to the point, were also the last *military* pipe band to join him on stage anywhere—not too shabby given the great history, Canadian and internationally, of the song.

Remembering Nathan Cirillo: The tragedy of Cpl. Nathan Cirillo's 2014
terrorist-inspired murder in Ottawa moved Paul's team to ask the pipe and
drum band of the late soldier's regiment to join him on stage in Cirillo's
hometown of Hamilton, Ontario. Before the 2016 concert, bandlead-
ers Scott Balinson, far left, and Ben Jaeckle, far right, met Paul who asked
if he could hold Balinson's bagpipes that have been with the regiment since
1916. Photo Courtesy of Argyll and Sutherland Highlanders of Canada.

However if you're reading this in 2022 and an octogenarian
McCartney is still touring (gosh, let's hope that's the case) and has
reversed his 2018 decision to cease with local pipe and drum bands
and goes on to include a military band, consider Hamilton's distinction erased and accept the author's humblest apologies. If it holds
true, Warrant Officer's Ben Jaeckle and Scott Balinson of the Hamilton
Argylls consider it an honour.

When told the news, Jaeckle was rendered speechless with pride,
and Balinson too until he said: "When I think of amazing artists like
Paul McCartney, you hope they'll go on forever." Balinson, a retired
police staff sergeant, is the Pipe Major and Drum Major Jaeckle is a
fire service captain who, along with 24 others, joined McCartney on
stage that fateful night in July 2016.

Balinson says the Hamilton Argylls have played multiple times for their Colonel-in-Chief Queen Elizabeth II, at the Edinburgh Tattoo and in other high-profile events but it was their solemn performance for a fallen comrade-in-arms during one of the most tragic events in recent Canadian history that brought them to the attention of McCartney's people.

It was October 28, 2014, and a veil of sadness stretched from coast to coast to coast as Canadians mourned the senseless, terrorist-inspired murder in Ottawa of Cpl. Nathan Cirillo, a member of the Hamilton Argylls Regiment, an infantry unit of the Canadian Army Reserve. On that day his funeral was broadcast nationally as his regiment paraded in solemn ceremony; these were soldier musicians, playing their bagpipes to lay to rest a fallen Argyll during a nation's outpouring of grief.

An employee of Live Nation Entertainment was so taken by the Argylls performance that he approached the band to play in a future McCartney show. Few details were shared and the Argylls ran the request up the chain of command and approvals were granted, but the date with McCartney would be a long way off.

Fast forward to June 2016, two weeks before McCartney would play at FirstOntario in Hamilton and Balinson gets the call from Live Nation: "It went something like this, 'Hey Scott, can you guys still do the McCartney gig?'"

Balinson and Jaeckle began assembling the musicians, in some cases writing to their commanding officers or pulling them away from their day jobs, for rehearsals. They were in direct contact with Wickens, McCartney's long-time keyboardist and band member who recommended the pipers use their B flat orchestral chanters (in order to tune their bagpipes to a flatter pitch to harmonize with McCartney's band) and that they prepare by watching the original 1977 music video starring, among others, MacCallum.

Preparations were well under way and nerves were building when the Argylls caught a break ... two of their members had previously played with McCartney: Retired Sgt. Glen Howie had played with the Paris Port Dover pipe band on its two previous concert dalliances with McCartney and university student, Cpl. Andrew Sandison, played joined McCartney on stage with the Ottawa Police Service.

The day before the show, with Howie and Sandison helping the musicians get through their part, the Argylls rehearsed with McCartney's band and then McCartney himself at the arena. At the end of his sound check, McCartney stepped off stage and approached both men.

"He walked over and shook our hands and we introduced ourselves," recalls Jaeckle who, with Balinson, tried to maintain a professional demeanor.

"He asked us a lot of questions about the Argylls and our instruments," says Jaeckle. Balinson's pipes, for instance, date as far back as 1916 or earlier and used by the Argylls in both world wars. The mace which Jaeckle carries is also quite historic and very ornate ... both relics vividly caught McCartney's attention.

McCartney mentioned he had never held a set of bagpipes and wondered if Balinson would oblige? The words barely left his mouth before Balinson, in a moment worthy of a cinematic period drama, thoughtfully handed the large and cumbersome woodwind instrument over. As his curiosity had taken him in to interesting places in the past, McCartney held the century-old pipes immersing himself in a relic of Canada's past glories.

It is a tale that still gives me *frisson*.

The Tennant Family

Super Fans: The Tennant family of Vancouver has joyfully achieved serial status as McCartney concertgoers. Led by dad Jody (right), and mom Helen (left) and kids Akaya, Solstice and Ocean, the Tennants even spent seven entertaining minutes on stage with Paul in 2016—the *YouTube* video of which has been seen by nearly 1.5 million people. The Sgt. Pepper costumes belong to Jody's band, The Fab Fourever, an internationally acclaimed Beatles cover group. Photo by Gerry Kahrmann Courtesy of the Tennant Family.

In April 2016, McCartney was on stage in Vancouver, waving a large Canadian flag. Before the Beatle began his encore set, he announced it was time to recognize the scores of fans waving signs with messages of affection. "Each evening we try and select one of the signs to bring them up on the stage, so let's see who we got tonight," he said.

Despite his kind invitation, it's likely not even McCartney could have prepared for the Tennant Family.

Six multi-generational members of a Vancouver family and three family friends, dressed in elaborate and remarkably authentic bright blue, red and rose-coloured Sgt. Pepper uniforms, walked single file onto the Rogers Arena stage and remained there for nearly seven minutes during a pause in the encore, creating an audience-loving spectacle not often repeated anywhere in the world of McCartney fandom.

The Tennant clan of Vancouver has achieved serial status as McCartney concertgoers and super-fans. With a bemused McCartney at the microphone making the introductions, they each got to say hello starting with Jody Tennant, then his wife, Helen (who introduced herself as "Helen Wheels"), followed by Jody's mom Lea, and then the kids, including 10-year-old Solstice, Akaya, 13, Ocean, 16, and Ocean's best-friend Tessa, 16.

"Very nice turn out, Jody ... that's a pretty nice brood you've got there," said McCartney, who proceeded to sign Jody's left arm and introduced each member, offered hugs, handshakes and more autographs.[165]

Helen curtsied, then wriggled and lowered the blue Pepper uniform to her waist—creating a stir from the audience—and offered McCartney, in a white collared shirt with Hofner bass guitar slung over his arm, a shoulder to sign. She got not only his autograph but also a kiss on the cheek. Moving on to sign Lea's arm, McCartney looked over at Helen and quipped, "and she begat this tribe of Abraham."

Through email, Ocean Tennant described the depth of the family's infatuation with Sir Paul: "We've all been going to Paul's concerts for basically our entire lives. I was just a toddler when I went to my first McCartney concert in Toronto. I believe I've been to seven or eight in my life. (The 2016 Vancouver show) was actually the second time that we've met Paul, as well."

Second time! There have been others?

"We've had many really cool experiences at his concerts. We've had seats upgraded, been recognized, and were once pulled backstage to meet him after a concert in Seattle. Other than that, we've just grown up being surrounded by Beatles music. It has honestly been a huge part of our lives forever."

Among the many highlights of the Tennant's on-stage appearance at Vancouver's Rogers Centre that evening, was family friend, Jennifer

Cormack, revealing a massive tattoo on her entire back depicting intricate, psychedelic-inspired Beatles art in the spirit of the *Sgt. Pepper's Lonely Hearts Club Band* and *Yellow Submarine* album covers; even McCartney (who you would think in some 60 years of performing has seen it all) seemed shocked and hesitated for a moment before he put sharpie to her flesh too, only to be followed by Jennifer's husband Terence who asked McCartney to sign his poster board.

"Jenn has a really cool Beatles tattoo on her back that she had been trying to get Paul to sign for years," explains Tennant.

Macca The Magnificent III: If you think that after some 60 years of performing Paul has seen it all, think again. Jennifer Cormack shocked Paul and a capacity crowd at Roger's Stadium in Vancouver when, in asking for an autograph, revealed her elaborate Beatles body art. After Paul signed her shoulder, Cormack arranged to have a tattoo artist trace over the signature to create a lasting, indelible McCartney moment. Photo by Laura Staeger Courtesy of the Tennant Family.

After Cormack finally got McCartney to autograph her back, she decided to make it permanent and arranged with a tattoo artist to trace over the signature to create a lasting, indelible McCartney moment. She wasn't alone.

"My parents, my grandma, and Jenn all got them tattooed," says Ocean.

The Pepper costumes were on loan from Jody's band, The Fab Fourever, an internationally acclaimed Beatles cover group where the Tennant patriarch plays bass guitar, left-handed no less! Like the Analogues, The Fab Fourever stress authenticity, from the throwback Vox amps, vintage instruments to mop-top haircuts and Ed Sullivan-era 1964 Beatles suits. Tennant's band twice represented Canada at International Beatleweek in Liverpool, performing 10 shows in seven days to worldwide throngs of Beatle fans at such landmark concert venues as the Cavern Club, the Casbah Club and the Locarno Ballroom.

While Jody's kids were spared the mop-top haircuts growing up, their fashion sense has, over the years, included a Beatles-esque flair, including period-specific Beatles clothing. Ocean notes they've had several hand-me-down costume varieties over the years, which they've worn to many of his shows.

"A lot of them were made for my dad's band, but some of them have been made individually for us as we grew up."

The once-in-a-lifetime Vancouver chapter of the Tennant's McCartney passion was followed by the band playing "Hi Hi Hi" and is captured on video. With over 1.4 million views on *YouTube* to date, the Tennant story illustrates the extent to which The Beatles have won the hearts and minds of so many Canadians.

Right Honourable Beatles Fan

The Beatles' story has had the participation of more than its fair-share of Canadian political leaders—we've heard about Pierre Trudeau, Lester Pearson, Danny Williams, Allan Rock, Hugh Segal, Loyola

Hearn, Philip Givens, John Munro and there was also provincial politician Russell Doern who invited Lennon to Manitoba's centennial celebration in 1970 (to which Lennon agreed but didn't attend).

But none have publicly demonstrated their love of The Beatles more than former Prime Minister Stephen Harper.

Harper was only five when The Beatles first played Maple Leaf Gardens, not far from where he was born in the Toronto neighbourhood of Leaside. In his rise from political aide to an Alberta Member of Parliament at age 26, to the highest office in the land by the time he reached 47, Harper has been a Beatles super fan. And not a quiet one—he has never shied away from an opportunity to perform Beatles songs, whether in the comfort of his home, with his accompanying band the Van Cats, or while serving in the duty of Canadians as prime minister.

Harper ranks as Canada's sixth longest-serving prime minister (2006-2015), and represented a riding in Calgary, Alberta. The first public expression of the passion he holds for The Beatles took place at Ottawa's National Arts Centre in 2009. Joined by renowned American cellist Yo-Yo Ma, the prime minister sang lead and played piano on "With a Little Help From My Friends". While on the election trail in 2011, he performed "Imagine" in the Winnipeg home of 11-year-old singer and Lady Gaga friend, Maria Aragon. The *YouTube* video of the Harper-Aragon duet caught the ire of Lenono Music and was subsequently pulled for copyright reasons.

In April 2009, his wife, Laureen Teskey, and children, Benjamin and Rachel, treated Harper to a tour of Abbey Road Studios and a walk imitating The Beatles on the famous *Abbey Road* album cover zebra crossing as a gift for the prime minister's 50th birthday; befitting a foreign head of state, London police on motorcycles and Harper's security detail on foot are seen in the photo of the first-family blocking traffic along Abbey Road in St. John's Wood.

He took his Beatles passion to an international stage while on a state visit to Jerusalem in January 2014 and entertained Israeli Prime Minister Benjamin Netanyahu (and a room full of social and political elites) with both "With a Little Help … " and "Hey Jude"—again on vocals and piano. Later that year, his seven-song set list at a Conservative Party Christmas gathering in Ottawa included "I Saw Her Standing There".

Demonstrating his varied musical interests, the rockin' former leader has also sung from the The Who, Johnny Cash, The Rolling Stones and Guns N' Roses song catalogues. Harper's electric guitar collection includes models signed by Carlos Santana and Gene Simmons and, while prime minister, he was visited at his home by Bryan Adams and Randy Bachman, both of whom jammed with the prime minister.

Harper, like the members of The Beatles, is a published author although the subject matter of his works of non-fiction—hockey and politics—have no ties to his passion for rock music.

The Harpers: In what other country on earth except Canada does its elected national leader stop London traffic to be photographed with his family walking the famous Abbey Road zebra crossing? Prime Minister

Stephen Harper's love of The Beatles is so legendary that his
family arranged for this moment as his 50th birthday gift in 2009.
Photo by Jason Ransom, courtesy of Jason Ransom.

Hey Grandude, My Illustrator is from Peterborough

Grandude's Canadian Artist: Ontario's Kathryn Durst was handpicked by
Paul to illustrate his latest series of children's books. "He said he was drawn
to my illustrations right away!" said Kathryn whose collaborations with the
Beatle (who has eight grandchildren) include *Hey Grandude* in 2018 and
Grandude's Green Submarine in 2021. Photo courtesy of The Bright Agency.

Lennon was the first Beatle-turned-author with his 1964 *In His Own Write*, and 1965's *A Spaniard in the Works*. Both titles offered quirky poems and short stories with the author having much fun with words and word associations.

Harrison followed in 1980 with a mild autobiography *I, Me, Mine*, containing original lyric sheets and background to some of his best-known compositions. Starr took visual approaches to book publishing and, consistent with his strong sentimentality for The Beatles, in 2004 produced *Postcards from the Boys*, which adds commentary to reproductions of dozens of postcards he was sent by the other Beatles and, in 2013 a photographic autobiography simply called *Photograph* and his most recent, *Another Day in the Life*, included his photo of Calgary's Peace Bridge.

McCartney, who fathered or adopted more children than the other Beatles at five, and currently holds the Beatles record with eight grandchildren (although Starr, who has seven grandchildren, recently became the first Beatles great-grandfather) wrote and performed a delightful children's song "We All Stand Together" with The Frog Chorus (literally, frog croaks, ribbits and glunks as part of the chorus!) in 1980. Released in 1984, "We All Stand Together" featured Toronto-born and now British Columbia resident Dee Long, founding member of Klaatu, as a sound effects contributor. McCartney would re-visit his fondness for children's entertainment in 2005 when he co-wrote a children's book called *High in the Clouds*.

He returned to children's writing in 2019—this time with the help of a Canadian—with an illustrated bedtime book, and drew inspiration from his many grandchildren with *Hey Grandude*.

Released in September 2019 by Random House books in Canada, *Hey Grandude*'s co-creator was Kathryn Durst, chosen by McCartney himself to illustrate his book. A graduate of Ontario's Sheridan College, Durst worked in animation for five years including a stint with Pixar Animation Studios, before setting off an a career as an illustrator, based in Peterborough, Ontario.

Approached in 2018 to work with McCartney, then 27-year-old Durst said:

> I couldn't say no to an opportunity like that! I sent off a few designs to the publisher who then sent them off to Paul for review. He said he was drawn to my illustrations right away! It was still a few months before I found out I had gotten the project, and once I did I then spent 2018 working on the illustrations for the book. Paul and I were actually able to speak directly about the illustrations over the phone.

The two exchanged ideas and concepts and communicated on a first-name basis. When it came down to the main character, "Paul said the design of Grandude didn't need to be a caricature of himself, though he did describe the character as a hippie-ish, quirky, older British gentleman who is a bit magic. There is also a scene where Grandude is playing guitar for the children, which was definitely inspired by Paul as a musician."

The 32-page children's book tells the tale of an adventure-seeking, slightly eccentric grandfather with a hip demeanor who takes his four grandchildren on magical quests.

They met in person backstage in Montréal during an early stop of McCartney's 39-city, two-year Freshen Up Tour concert in September 2018. A year later, at the *Hey Grandude* launch event at the large Waterstones bookshop in London's Piccadilly district, Durst and McCartney entertained a group of school children and other guests with drawing exercises and readings from within a life-sized rendering of the living room recreated from the story itself. In 2021, McCartney and Durst launched a sequel edition called *Grandude's Green Submarine*.

Durst loved the work: "He gave me full creative freedom about the look of the characters. It's one thing to idolize your favorite artist, but quite another to collaborate with them directly, so I feel very lucky."[166]

Emma's Cape Breton (My Unama'ki)

At the tail end of the same Freshen Up Tour, 77-year-old McCartney performed in Vancouver in September 2019. It seems Vancouver takes the cake as the Canadian city where McCartney's most notable live performances have taken place.

On a warm summer's night, July 6 at BC Place, he described to the packed house his feelings upon hearing a stirring, heart-pounding version of his 1968 Beatles song "Blackbird" by Emma Stevens, a First Nations teenager from the other side of the country; he chose that night in Vancouver to give tenth grader Stevens a shout-out heard around the world.

At about the halfway point (an hour and 33 minutes, into McCartney's typical marathon concert), he launched into his familiar, jangly "contrary motion" acoustic fingerpicking intro of "Blackbird" and, when the applause waned into the light of the dark black night, he returned to the microphone to say:

> Thank you. I'll tell you what, this evening's special in Vancouver. Because I don't know if you've heard it but there's a beautiful version on the Internet by a girl called Emma Stevens. She sings it in the native language. Have you heard it? It's a beautiful version and she's actually here tonight (he waved to the teenager). I met her before the show and I said, 'Listen, your version is so beautiful that I'm going to be nervous singing my version.' Anyway it's fantastic and it's in Mi'kmaq.[167]

Stevens is from Eskasoni First Nation in Nova Scotia, the largest Indigenous peoples community in Canada's Maritime provinces with nearly 4,000 residents; it's also the largest Mi'kmaq-speaking community in the world. So it follows that Stevens' version is entirely in Mi'kmaq and when it was released in April the reaction was swift and the Internet exploded with praise.

Eskasoni First Nation is located on the scenic island of Cape Breton in eastern Nova Scotia and boasts its own community-operated school system, including Allison Bernard Memorial High School where Stevens, fellow students and their music teacher Carter Chiasson, took on the unique project of interpreting The Beatles' classic song in Mi'kmaq.

Stevens told me she was well versed in Beatles music. "When I was a kid, my dad used to play songs all the time and The Beatles were one of the bands. I was singing Beatles songs for as long as I could remember."

There are elements of the song, particularly the lyrics "take these broken wings and learn to fly," that resonate with Indigenous peoples experiences in Canada. "The song is just like the type of gentle advice that we get from our elders when we feel defeated and when we feel down," she says.

Before the concert that night in Vancouver, Stevens and Chiasson met McCartney and presented him with a handmade Mi'kmaq medallion. The white, blue and black ceremonial pendant was made by Cape Breton artist Vivian Ann Googoo and featured an image of a blackbird. She told *CBC News* that in the few minutes they spent talking to McCartney he "expressed his appreciation for how the Mi'kmaq version of the song helps to celebrate culture."

Chiasson responded by thanking McCartney for drawing global attention to the Mi'kmaq rendition of "Blackbird" and in so doing he helped support the revitalization of the Indigenous language, which, like others like it, some fear could be lost forever if not sufficiently passed down to future generations. It's a point Stevens brings home too: "Before 'Blackbird' not many people knew our language which was slowly dying. 'Blackbird' made Mi'kmaq language and culture seen, and people finally started to see what was going on."

Momentum for Mi'kmaq cultural and linguistic preservation continued unabated throughout 2019 when the United Nations observed the International Year of Indigenous Languages with an aim to establish a link between language, development, peace and reconciliation. On the strength of "Blackbird" Stevens and Chiasson represented Eskasoni First Nations people at a UN assembly in Nairobi, Kenya that year.

McCartney has boasted about Stevens' efforts at shows outside of Canada too. At a show in Lexington, Kentucky he said: "There's an incredible version done by a Canadian girl. You see it on *YouTube* (over 1.5 million views and counting). It's in her native language. It's really cool, check it out."

Adds Stevens: "It's a beautiful thing that 'Blackbird' did, and with some time maybe more people will learn our language, because Mi'kmaq is a beautiful language and an amazing culture."

Pu'tliskiej Wapinintoq: That's Mi'kmaq for "Blackbird singing … " as in the opening line in "Blackbird" courtesy of Nova Scotia teen Emma Stevens. Emma, who lives in the Eskasoni First Nation, recorded a stirring, heart-pounding version of the 1968 Beatles classic to worldwide acclaim. So moved by Emma's voice, Paul was nervous about performing it on stage fearing his version would be inferior! Photo by Rockpixels, courtesy of Emma Stevens.

In Mi'kmaq, the word or concept of a blackbird is "Pu'tliskiej" and Stevens' opening verse goes something like this:

> Pu'tliskiej wapinintoq
> Kina'masi telayja'timk
> Tel pitawsin
> Eskimatimu'sipnet nike' mnja'sin

To hear her sing it is to be reminded of Canada's rich diversity. But don't stop there; give a listen to the equally gorgeous "My Unama'ki" by Stevens with a little help from her friends. An ode to her homeland, it literally means "My Cape Breton". The song is partially sung in Mi'kmaq and contains the natural sing-along strains of an open air, communal environment not unlike McCartney's "Mull of Kintyre". And quicker than you can say John MacCallum of Langley, there's a part in the song reminiscent of the bagpipe section except the gorgeous sound comes from a Celtic fiddle, an instrument that spiritually evokes Cape Breton's majestic mountains and naturally rugged coastline.

CONNECTING THE BEATLES' CANADIAN DOTS

The contribution of Canada and Canadians to the music, art, history and phenomenon of The Beatles in some ways was not unlike the stages of an efficacious long-term relationship between two people facing life's challenges, with equal parts of passion, innocence, drama, rejection, deception, tension, and indifference but ending with all parties being reasonably satisfied.

But we certainly had our moments.

What with Carroll Levis letting Lennon, and then Lennon, McCartney and Harrison, escape his grasp in 1957 and 1959, the boys bearing witness to our alcohol-fueled, out-of-control troops in 1961, Harry Saltzman passing on their film in 1963, a death threat in 1964, promoters scurrying to fill empty seats in 1966, an alleged unpaid and un-credited album contribution in 1968, Lennon's 1969 deportation, an immigration red flag for Harrison's wife in 1974, and McCartney's abhorrence of Canada's controversial seal hunt, it's reasonable to believe our welcoming shores were a little less than advertised.

But they kept coming back to play our hockey rinks, to enrich our lives and affect our history, and we kept loving them—at one time mustering the world's largest Beatles Fan Club. If we put in perspective the moments where Canada or Canadians gave The Beatles a hard time it certainly paled with other places in the world. Their inadvertent snub of President Marcos' family in the Philippines created rioting on the streets of Manila but when the mayor of Toronto and his wife were refused at The Beatles' King Edward Hotel door it didn't exactly trigger a sequel of the 1837 Upper Canada Rebellion; on the contrary, the citizenry carried on like nothing happened. Their records and books were burned in South Carolina, they were threatened in Dallas and Memphis, arrested in England, jostled and affronted in Tokyo and, years later, McCartney would be robbed at knifepoint in Nigeria and arrested in Japan.

It's also not lost on me that Canadians, who have altered the course of The Beatles' history, and their art, were perhaps entirely unaware they were making such an impact. If you're Cheryl Finn, then Sgt. Pepper took you by surprise! Her granddad Sgt. Randall Pepper was humbly doing his job protecting the band while in Toronto and yet it's possible his work ethic, demeanor, good natured-ness or none of the above but simply his rank and surname somehow could have inspired the most important album title and concept of the 1960s. Cindy Bury was keen to party with Lennon, Harrison and their partners and, with her boyfriend, thought it would be fun to turn them onto acid which she could not have predicted would gradually and dramatically change the sound and texture of their music and lyrics.

And Lillian Piché Shirt was going about her purpose-filled life of raising awareness for the plight of Indigenous peoples in Alberta when Lennon called her only to get an earful of Cree wisdom that could have carried forward with the Beatle when he composed "Imagine". Shirt's protest on the grounds of the Alberta Legislature Building may have brought her to the attention of Lennon but, more essentially, became the catalyst event that kick-started the eventual creation of a provincial plan for welfare housing in Alberta. It's also worth noting that her possible contribution to Lennon's song does not appear in her obituary and neither she nor her family have ever tried to capitalize on the connection. It was only through the work of respected academics that Shirt's conversation with Lennon came to light.

Just as Shirt was unconcerned about her connection to The Beatles because she was focused on her cause, Randall Pepper, like Art Ellefson after him, behaved indifferently to his association with the band, perhaps uncomfortable at the thought of being remembered solely as footnotes in a Beatles narrative; my guess is that it didn't mesh with their values and let's not forget that despite his date with destiny the remarkable André Perry wasn't really a fan—just going about his business dispassionately.

Youth was at the core of the band's pop music roots; pre-teens and teens gave The Beatles their initial lift in Canada. With youth comes innocence, pranks and risk taking—all appropriate explanations for the four Canadian teenagers, Decker, Levitan, Renard and Schnurmacher, whose boldness got them an audience with members of the band, although in Decker's case merely a peek through an aircraft door! As a measure in degrees of how profoundly they were affected by their encounter with a Beatle, Renard wrote a book on her experience while Schnurmacher dedicated two chapters to his time with Lennon in the post-Holocaust memoir he wrote about his parents, and his life. Levitan and Saltzman have not only written books on their Beatles experiences but were also driven to create films and Decker's barefoot airport dash is the stuff of legend in Manitoba.

Trudy Medcalf neither wrote a book nor made a film but the once enterprising 14-year-old would give back to society by co-launching the Ottawa volunteer committee "Aging by the Book" to support and understand older Canadians through group dialogue.

We also saw many curious Canadian connections to intimate Beatle histories like marriages, honeymoons, infidelities, childhood abandonment, divorce and pregnancies.

McCartney's teenage girlfriend Dorothy Rhone miscarried after wedding plans were arranged; she soon after fled to Canada to start a new life. Decades later, the engagement ring McCartney gave to Rhone would be returned to her in Toronto. No sooner had Cynthia Lennon announced her pregnancy with John's child did her mother leave for Canada, missing her daughter's wedding and the birth of the first Beatles child, Julian Lennon.

Beatle collaborator and friend Eric Clapton is a war child who never knew his Canadian father after a one-time fling with the mother of the future guitar great, and yet Clapton's mom would go on to marry another man, also a Canadian. And still with Clapton, his obsession and infidelity with Harrison's wife Pattie Boyd played out while attending a funeral in Prince Edward Island.

The Lennons, John and Yoko, invited the world to their Montréal bedroom and visited Niagara Falls while still on an extended honeymoon; forty years later smirking Canadian politicians took credit for McCartney's failed marriage to Heather Mills, their comments based less on fact and more on, shall we say, political karma.

Still on marriages, here is a list of the celebrity musicians in The Beatles' solo orbits that have married Canadians:

1. McCartney songwriting and recording collaborator Elvis Costello is married to Nanaimo, British Columbia-born jazz and pop vocalist Diana Krall. Krall recorded the mostly McCartney-written "And I Love Her" in a 1995 Beatles tribute album.

2. Long before he married former Toronto advertising executive David Furnish, Elton John recorded versions of Lennon songs "Lucy in the Sky With Diamonds" and "One Day at a Time" with Lennon himself providing harmonies. John also contributed vocals and piano on "Whatever Gets You Through The Night" and the two performed at Lennon's last ever concert appearance in 1974 where, like in Toronto five years earlier, the Beatle was sick with fear before taking the stage.

3. Singer Phil Collins and former wife, Vancouver's Andrea Bertorelli, have a Canadian-born daughter, the actor and producer Joely Collins. Dad Phil was an extra on *A Hard Day's Night* and played percussion on Harrison's "Act of Dying" in 1970's *All Things Must Pass*.

Lennon told Canada's Marshall McLuhan the existence of The Beatles was facilitated by the post-war end of military conscription in Britain yet, ironically, the history of The Beatles was invariably shaped by members of the Canadian military both in war and in peace. In fact Canadian soldiers, including some who remained in Britain after both world wars or served as peacekeepers, offered perhaps the single largest stream of subtextualization running through Beatle connections to Canada. Two branches of the Canadian Armed Forces, army and air force, saw the highest participation in The Beatles' history, and it's no wonder with some 750,000 army troops and nearly 250,000 airmen part of the allied effort in World War II while The Beatles were infants. Canadians Saltzman, Fallon and Fryer in fact were all members of the RCAF that by 1945 was the world's fourth largest air power.[168]

McCartney's debut as a singer and Starr's last gig with Rory Storm and the Hurricanes happened in summer camps owned by Billy Butlin. While living in Toronto, Butlin was among 3,327 Eaton's employees to enlist with the Canadian Army in World War I[169] with the company's promise of giving its workers one-half of their wages throughout the war. The store was run by the founder Timothy Eaton's son John Craig Eaton whose own son, John David Eaton, hosted Lennon (and his first Plastic Ono Band) at his King City, Ontario, estate a half century later after co-funding his first concert without The Beatles in 1969.

Carroll Levis wasn't a soldier but in 1945 he was part of a group of entertainers who put on a show for a war weary Canadian First Army who had successfully ended their campaign fighting on the vast Western Front of Europe during World War II.

We had our peacekeepers arrested for tearing-up a Hamburg club in which the boys were playing, a Canadian actor joining Lennon in a satirical war movie, a Canadian soldier who remained in England was a Beatles booking agent and even played fiddle on the *White Album*, alleged New Brunswick World War II superspy turned top film producer Saltzman came in from the cold to reject *A Hard Day's Night* but later commissioned McCartney's "Live and Let Die", and

Harrison's harmonica player Tommy Reilly was a Canadian who spent the war in German prison camps.

In modern times, McCartney's wonderful, long-time tradition of including bagpipe and drum bands on stage with him during "Mull of Kintyre" ended (at least for now) in Ontario with soldier musicians. The selection of the Argyll and Sutherland Highlanders—who also played with Nova Scotia's The Trews and their 2014 patriotic song for our warriors, "Highway of Heroes"—to join McCartney was inspired by the funeral of a Canadian soldier. And like the Argylls, several other bagpipe and drum bands he has welcomed on Canadian stages trace their origins to playing for soldiers on the battlefields of the First World War.

Not surprisingly, several Beatles connections to Canadians and drugs were also apparent; hey, it was the '60s and '70s—an age of trippy experimentation with many social and lifestyle constructs, so drugs simply went hand-in-hand with the leisure of the times. Whether talking-up legalized marijuana on a train with Canadian bureaucrats, drinking LSD-dosed coffee in London with the help of a Hamiltonian and dentist friend of one of Canada's most respected wine critics, partying with the Edmonton-born half of Cheech and Chong or, as Ronnie Hawkins infamously told the *CBC's* George Strombouloupoulos in 2013, smoking weed with the Lennons and Prime Minister Pierre Trudeau,[170] Canadians got high with The Beatles! While Hawkins' blockbuster claim has never been independently verified, the tale of Lennon turning down a joint because he needed his faculties for an impending Hare Krishna visit was a priceless snippet from the Montréal Bed-In and perhaps a nod of respect toward his mate Harrison. Indeed, it was while he hung-out with a spaced-out American gubernatorial candidate in Montréal that Lennon was first tinged with the idea to write "Come Together"—a hit which the songwriter himself considers one of his finest works.

Most enjoyable of all was re-telling the stories of ordinary Canadians and their extraordinary Beatles connections. Stories can be very powerful yet, over time, can lose their meaning. So it can't be overstated enough to declare that a definitive collection of stories that outline the roles of Canada and Canadians in The Beatles' history needed a proper place to reside, for the record and for generations of fans down the road. If nothing else, that's what *Us and Them* offers the world at large.

Emma Stevens' recording of "Blackbird" and McCartney's reaction to it may have permanently moved the goalposts forward for Mi'kmaq culture. Vancouver's Tennant family wore their radiant Sgt. Pepper uniforms on McCartney's stage perhaps unaware the real-life Sergeant may have been an Ontario cop.

P.E.I.'s Don Groom was stiffed by Eric Clapton and Harrison's wife Pattie at his Summerside bar but not before the collective jaws of his Island patrons dropped when the non-Beatle, who famously played on the *White Album* and co-wrote a song with Harrison, picked up a guitar and played two songs. That amusing tale from the country's small-est province would be one of several examples of comic relief in The Beatles' Canadian experience, but how's this for some smile-inducing silliness: So rich of character, diverse of age and background and, often, pure of innocence are the cast of Canadians in The Beatles' history that they would have rivaled the collage of 19th century humanity described in Lennon's carnival classic "Being For The Benefit of Mrs. Kite":

Consider a visual and sonic dreamscape of fairground organs and calliope music swirling as excited toddlers go round-and-round on one of Harry Saltzman's coin-operated horse rides, or become trans-fixed by the gaze of Carroll Levis' hypnotic suggestion as Billy Butlin busks the coin toss game and Tommy Reilly exhales notes on his har-monica; all the while, Jerry Levitan aims his 8 mm film camera and André Perry records the sound on a magnetized tape machine while a serene Lillian Shirt, her braided dark hair in beads and clutching an eagle feather, stands solemnly by her four-pole painted tipi looking up at Sgt. Randall Pepper who stands at attention in full parade dress uniform keeping order over the whole affair. A Utopian and wondrous carnival scene of several Canadians assembled in one magical place to celebrate their connections to The Beatles, re-telling their unique Fab Four stories, and chanting "All We Are Saying … " while John MacCallum keeps time by pounding on his highland snare drum.

To sleep, perchance to dream, now there's the rub.

For The Benefit of Us and Them: A beautiful and wondrous Utopian scene of Canadians Jerry Levitan, Lillian Shirt, John MacCallum, Randall Pepper, Tommy Reilly, André Perry, and a young Harry Saltzman, assembled in one magical place to celebrate their connections to The Beatles. Arcane words and concept by John Robert Arnone based on the poster for Pablo Fanque's Circus Royal appearance at Rochdale, England on February 14, 1843. Typesetting and design by Richard Arnone; Illustration by Michael Santi.

But returning to reality for a moment, we have all the pre-requisites in place to build a real and honest homegrown Beatles legend around Bruce Decker. Unconstrained by risk of injury or arrest, the barefoot kid from Winnipeg ran across an airport apron to embody the essence of *Us and Them*, and the soul of The Beatles' fandom.

While that scene paled in comparison to their tumultuous and historic arrival at New York's JFK Airport six months earlier, the Winnipeg stop-over was The Beatles' first Canadian moment and it was made memorable not only because delirious fans truly created an event out of what was merely a fuel stop without an associated concert in the city, but the screaming fans and Decker's Dash gave John, Paul, George and Ringo a taste of what to expect before taking the Cow Palace stage the next day in Daly City, California.

Handsome, talented and well-loved by his family and friends, Decker is even described as "musician-turned-historian" by the Manitoba Historical Society befitting a man who went on to make significant contributions to Canada's musical, cultural and Indigenous peoples history.

Beatles fans owe a debt of gratitude to another Canadian, Vancouver's Carroll Levis who, like Capitol Canada's Paul White, possessed a golden ear; *BBC* records suggest Levis' talent shows made professionals out of 45 amateur contestants. But Levis did the world a favour by not putting John, Paul and George on his popular television program in 1959; the boys simply weren't ready for an early shot at fame. They lacked more than a full-time drummer, the early Beatles were novices, unwashed, and undisciplined—they ate, fought, swore, smoked and even drank beer on stage with Lennon sometimes burping into the microphone—and they hadn't even begun to hit their stride as their development as songwriters and musicians would take a few more years.

Levis was raised in British Columbia, a province that certainly punched above its weight when it came to Canadians hovering in The Beatles' orbit with perhaps none greater than the global grand master David Foster who says his remarkable journey in music began with "She Loves You".

Foster's hometown newspaper, the *Victoria Times-Colonist*, was flooded with letters from readers when asked to provide their recollections on the 50th anniversary of the band's 1964 North American invasion. The mechanics of that invasion, as we learned, were potentially put into play when Ottawa's singing sensation Paul Anka heard The Beatles in France and pressed his management company to have a look at them—which they did, and launched The Fab's North American debut.

There existed a notable wave of ex-patriot Canadians crossing the Atlantic and becoming part, or landing on the fringes, of The Beatles' history.

Levis, Reilly, Saltzman, Ellefson, Fallon, Bury, Knox, Fryer, MacMichael *et al* were among them and Butlin lived in Canada before returning to England. In an article for *Commentary* magazine penned in 1965, the late great author Mordecai Richler implies England was the beneficiary of a significant post-war brain-drain from Canada—a pattern where some of Canada's finest made waves across the pond (Montréal-born Richler perhaps the most famous of them all).

It was more than music. British plays, cites Richler, were "unfailingly directed by Canadians." He further noted Canadians were active in British television production because "where Americans (who require work permits) are lacking, Canadians, some of them very gifted, are usually found to fill this office in British entertainment." He pointed out Toronto-born Sydney Newman, who was involved in the very early days of *Hockey Night in Canada*, moved to England and became "the most powerful drama producer in British TV" having been responsible for the *BBC*'s *The Avengers*, *Dr. No* and many other British television staples.[171]

Is it any wonder we find a rich history of Canadians in The Beatles' orbit? With the wave of Canadians making their mark in the British entertainment industry, my pick as the most captivating to make an association with The Beatles is Harry Saltzman. The man from Saint John had a touch of fairy tale follow him from the moment he left home to join the circus, to doing clandestine work for the Allies behind enemy lines, gave the world James Bond on film and then would go on and produce the McCartney-themed film *Live and Let Die*. How is it this intriguing and successful Canadian from humble beginnings wasn't bestowed a posthumous Order of Canada or, in the least, a BAFTA Fellowship or Special Achievement Genie for his body of work?

In a notable coincidence, when *The Guardian's* John Patterson wrote Saltzman's obituary in 1994 he brought both Canadian ex-pats—producer Saltzman and the novelist Richler—together, stating Saltzman's arrival on English shores was "straight out of one of Mordecai Richler's novels."[172]

For my money it's the other Saltzman, Paul, who ranks up there with his namesake Harry as the Canadian with the most remarkable Beatles connection. From his intimate, embedded time with The Beatles in Rishikesh, Paul Saltzman released his long-awaited film *Meeting The Beatles in India* in September 2020. Narrated by Morgan Freeman, the 79-minute documentary is filled with rich imagery, rarely seen footage and interviews with the likes of Lewis Lapham and Pattie Boyd, both of whom were with Saltzman in Rishikesh during his life-changing week in 1968.

For Saltzman, meeting The Beatles was not the highlight of his time in India … far from it. The young Canadian found much deeper meaning in the power of self-awareness and spirituality through meditation. It was perhaps that glow that he shared with The Beatles that made his connection all the more extraordinary—a Canadian connecting with The Beatles on a higher plane of consciousness. Saltzman was also witness to The Beatles' initial writing and rough development of songs that would appear on the *White Album* and elsewhere in their incredible discography—an unparalleled vantage point for anyone, let alone a young man from Toronto who quite by accident found himself at the centre of a prodigious moment in The Beatles' history.

To summarize, and perhaps to underscore the role Canada played as a bookend in the life and times narrative of The Beatles, here are 31 key firsts … and lasts—turning points, if you will—in 67 years of their history with varying degrees of separation and direct implications or involvement for Canada and Canadians:

1954: McCartney's first public performance occurs in a talent competition run at a Welsh campground owned by a one-time Toronto resident and member of the Canadian Armed Forces Billy Butlin.

1957: The first of two Canadian blood relatives of a Beatle is born: Harrison's nephew Gordon Caldwell Jr. of Ontario.

1962: The last gig Starr performed with Rory Storm and the Hurricanes before joining The Beatles occurred at an English campground owned by a one-time Toronto resident and member of the Canadian Armed Forces Billy Butlin.

1963: One of the first known uses of the term "Beatlemania" occurred during a performance in Scotland that was booked by an agency owned by Canadian Jack Fallon.

1963: The Beatles' first album released in North America is Capitol Canada's *Beatlemania! With The Beatles.*

1964: Ottawa singer Paul Anka claims to have played matchmaker between his American manager and Brian Epstein, resulting in the first appearance by The Beatles in North America.

1964: While en route to their first groundbreaking tour of North America, The Beatles held their first media interviews and the first outdoor mass encounter with fans on an airfield in Winnipeg.

1965: The first acid trip taken by Lennon and Harrison is aided and abetted by Ontario-born Cindy Bury.

1967: Lennon's first acting role without The Beatles occurred in a film that included veteran Canadian actor Alexander Knox in the cast.

1968: The first significant studio solo effort by a Beatle while still a Beatle, Harrison's *Wonderwall Music*, involved a Canadian harmonica player Tommy Reilly.

1969: The first live album recorded by a Beatle while still a Beatle was Lennon's *Live Peace in Toronto 1969* at Toronto's Varsity Stadium; it was also the last time Lennon was paid to perform on stage.

1969: The debut act of flicking lighters to welcome performers at stadium rock concerts occurred to assuage Lennon's fear when he approached a Toronto stage.

1969: The first independent single released by a member of The Beatles and the first song attributed to Plastic Ono Band, "Give Peace a Chance", was co-produced and recorded by a Canadian, André Perry, in Montréal.

1969: The first Beatle to have an extended meeting with a world leader was Lennon's time with Canadian Prime Minister Pierre Trudeau on Parliament Hill in Ottawa.

1970: Half-Canadian Eric Clapton played the first note of the first song on *All Things Must Pass*— Harrison's first, post-Beatles album.

1974: The first concert Harrison played in his first multi-city tour since The Beatles ceased to exist occurred in Vancouver.

1976: Apart from the star-studded mix of musicians in Harrison's *Concert for Bangladesh*, the first multi-disc live album by a solo Beatle—McCartney's *Wings Over America*—featured a song ("Bluebird") recorded in Canada.

1977: The first band to be widely mistaken for a Beatles reunion was Klaatu—three talented musicians and songwriters from Toronto described by McCartney as Beatles clones.

1984: The first studio album released by a Beatle child, Julian Lennon's *Valotte*, featured Port Dover, Ontario-born Rory Dodd on backing vocals. Toronto's Bob Ezrin would produce and play on a subsequent Lennon album.

1989: The first and only Beatle to publicly perform songs written by a Canadian is Starr who played drums on three songs written by Robbie Robertson.

1998: The first and only Canadian to play and tour in a group formed by an original Beatle—The Pete Best Band, is New Brunswick-born guitarist Kevin MacMichael.

1999: The first Beatle to enter the Rock and Roll Hall of Fame, McCartney, was inducted by Canada's Neil Young.

2000: One of the last on-camera stand-up interviews given by Harrison occurred at a Montréal art museum.

2003: Starr becomes the first Beatle to record a live concert DVD in Canada with *Tour 2003*.

2006: The first major Beatles mash-up, re-issued album, or studio project produced by George Martin's son Giles is a project initiated in Canada—the Grammy-winning *The Beatles LOVE.*

2007: The first Beatle-based film to receive an Academy Award nomination for Best Animated Short Film is *I Met The Walrus*, produced by Canadian Jerry Levitan.

2011: The first graduate of the world's first university degree program on the study of The Beatles is Canadian Mary-Lu Zahalan.

2014: The first Beatles songs performed by a world leader during a foreign state visit were "With a Little Help from my Friends" and "Hey Jude" by Prime Minister Stephen Harper in Israel.

2015: The last military pipe band in the world to join McCartney on the concert stage for "Mull of Kintyre" is from Ontario (claim is valid at the time of publication).

2020: The first documentary film about The Beatles' time with the Maharishi—*Meeting The Beatles in India*—is directed, produced and written by Canadian Paul Saltzman.

2021: The first project by a Beatle child to illustrate their dad's songs, Sean Lennon's *I am the Egbert* original animations, is co-produced by Canadian Jerry Levitan.

Some final words on my heroes John, Paul, George and Ringo

Between Shows: The Beatles pose for the cameras between their matinee and evening shows at Toronto's Maple Leaf Gardens on September 7, 1964. Cover photo reproduced in its original form. Photo by Joe Black, Graphic Artists.

George Harrison's Canadian kin, songwriting collaboration and relationship with Eric Clapton, palatable inspiration from The Band, and friendship with Guy Laliberté, should place him atop the others as the Beatle most connected to Canadian shores, but in fact it was Lennon who loomed largest as the Beatle to seek-out Canada as a place to deliver his message, ply his art and, generally, give back. Canada was also Lennon's test bed (pun intended) for a new maturity and future as a solo artist. We put his likeness and that of his wife on our money—the only time in its long history that the Royal Canadian Mint has put a rock star on legal Canadian tender.

Lennon was a gift to Canada. It's bittersweet and perhaps ironic that he would have the shortest time on earth among The Beatles yet have the most profound impact on Canadian society and Canada on him.

He visited Canada three times in eight months in 1969—covering three Canadian seasons—seemingly as a release valve from the constraints of being a Beatle and to set-out his own political and musical agenda with his new wife. Lennon's Canada was really three cities, Toronto, Montréal and Ottawa and photos of him buzzing around in snowmobiles during winter, visiting Niagara Falls or posing with a Canadiens hockey jersey are key and historic reminders of the joy he appropriated while here.

Lying in a Montréal bed, he spread a message of peace and proceeded to finish writing and record what would become a global plea to end war, "Give Peace a Chance"—a song saved from mediocrity by his co-producer and confidante André Perry, the Montréaler who guided the Beatle to releasing his first independent song outside of the band—replete with an overdubbed chorus of famous, un-credited French Canadian singers. It was in Canada that Lennon, the most psychologically complex of all the members of The Beatles, solidified a persona as a peace warrior and while so doing also revealed his delicate soul, contradictions and demons.

With all the negativity Ono has had to endure over the years, Perry went out of his way to state she was wonderful to him, and Lennon to her, when the three of them sat down to record "Remember Love" all those years ago. While in Canada, Lennon had Ono's back at every turn, nourishing and nurturing her art, creativity, opinions and collaborations instead of pushing her toward a gender-prescribed role, which was the societal default for too many women over a half-century ago. They seemed a co-dependent couple on an extended honeymoon. Tommy Schnurmacher made a similar observation after seeing the couple together for over a week in Montréal: "What John wanted to do was hang-out with Yoko. She was the one person he was interested in, and super attentive to, no matter what was happening or who was talking to him."[173] It is possible that Canada offered Lennon a place of penance—he did not treat women well in the past—where he began repairing his life, beginning with Ono.

During his Montréal Bed-In, Lennon felt genuine empathy for a 29-year-old Lillian Piché Shirt, a Cree protesting a lack of housing for Indigenous peoples in Alberta. He took the time to call an Edmonton radio station to locate her, get her on the telephone and learn about her cause. Just as Lennon offered to help Shirt, five years earlier he took journalist Janette Bertrand aside to better understand Québec's unique language and cultural status within Canada when his manager Epstein feared controversy. With all his fame, Lennon was open to other voices; he absorbed what mattered to him or what made him stronger as an artist. One wonders what stirred in Lennon's songwriting soul after hearing from these exceptional Canadian women.

Lennon was steadily gaining confidence as a live performer with musicians other than The Beatles and under late summer stars in 1969 he would follow his childhood rock 'n' roll idols on a concert stage at the University of Toronto.

While intellectually and creatively evolved at 29, the boy-man in Lennon was dramatically revealed in Toronto when, in a moment of naked vulnerability, he became sick and wept moments before he was to begin performing. As Lennon approached the stadium stage, looking out at tens of thousands without his Liverpool wingmen, Canadians bore first-hand witness to an open wound gaping deep beneath the surface that revealed an inner frailty. Despite this, a concert organizer still saw fit to describe Lennon as an apparition brighter than the sun when he stepped onto that Toronto stage.

That moment, that very human moment where the Beatle could no longer subvert his subconscious, gave rise to one of the most important events in rock history and set the stage for his divorce from The Beatles; Lennon crossed a psychological threshold, receiving a jolt a self-awareness that told him it was all right to be on his own. In Starr's view, what happened that September night stands as a permanent, groundbreaking part of The Beatles' history and it took place on Canadian soil.

A desire to assemble and play with new musicians and producers, to find another sound, another groove and absorb new inspiration is André Perry's theory on why The Beatles eventually parted ways. It's a theory shared by others and it cuts through the tiring media obsession with Ono, Allen Klein, McCartney's dominance and a myriad of soap operas that may or may not have cut short the band's career. By acting as Lennon's co-producer and confidante on "Give Peace a Chance", Perry is actually a key figure in his own theory—momentarily replacing George Martin's role on a Lennon recording. Is this enough to ascertain that Lennon's post-Beatles solo career took flight in Canada? Perhaps. What is certain is that Canada was a catalyst for Lennon and it set him free to do his own thing.

Canada even brought out her big guns as no fewer than five future Order of Canada recipients—Prime Minister Trudeau, musician Ronnie Hawkins, top media theorist Marshall McLuhan, future senator Hugh Segal, and the less-famous Heinz Lehmann—greeted him and Ono during their visits. How that must have irked Lennon's highest-profile adversary, President Richard Nixon, who viewed the Beatle with the intensity of an enemy combatant. It was on Nixon's watch that a half-million protesters sang "Give Peace a Chance" outside the oval office along Pennsylvania Avenue; a song that was created just north of the border in a land that thrice welcomed Lennon in 1969, including a sit-down with its prime minister. Could irritating the American president have been a part of Lennon's—or even Pierre Trudeau's—calculation all along? (Nixon didn't like Trudeau much either). Nearly two years to the day after a disgraced Nixon resigned in 1974 was Lennon finally granted permanent residency in the United States.

Lennon had an innate sense of his surroundings and saw Canada as a fair and compassionate place. It would be wonderful to believe that his peace meeting on Parliament Hill carried forward years later when, in Trudeau's final term as prime minister, the now elder statesman campaigned for peace through nuclear disarmament.

There are events in our history that change public consciousness. And while Lennon's peace offensive in Canada may have seemed to some a self-serving or even nutty endeavor at the time, its message was undeniable. Lennon and "Give Peace a Chance" played out on Canadian soil and may have given rise to Trudeau's humanity (and political instincts) and a nation's pacifism as tens of thousands of American draft dodgers found legal refuge in Canada and, under Trudeau's administration, an estimated 1,000 military deserters were given sanctuary during the Vietnam War.

(Decades later, Prime Minister Justin Trudeau led Canada's drive to accept 68,000 refugees from Syria to escape that tattered nation's civil war. Profoundly, two million Canadians have been personally involved in supporting the resettlement of those refugees).

In a biography of Pierre Trudeau entitled *Just Watch Me*, the author quotes the former prime minister: "I must say that give peace a chance has always seemed to me to be sensible advice."[174] Trudeau would be nominated for a Nobel Peace Prize in 1984. In an on-air conversation with Sean Lennon on the occasion of what would have been his father's 80th birthday in October 2020, Elton John told Sean that, had he lived, John Lennon would likely have been awarded the Nobel Peace Prize, a distinction never given to a rock star.

U2's Bono, who perhaps more than any other rocker of the modern era has picked up Lennon's mantle on the global peace front, once famously said the world needs more Canada, echoing Lennon's "a place like Canada looks like the only hope" many years earlier.

A curious (and, yes, historically quirky) coincidence emerged within the 35 years that followed Lennon's final visit in December 1969 visit as he and the three political leaders he met while in Canada all had airports named after them:

1. **Lester B. Pearson International Airport** (renamed in 1996 from the former Toronto International Airport and, previously, Malton Airport)

2. **John C. Munro Hamilton International Airport** (renamed in 1998 from Mount Hope Airport)

3. **Liverpool John Lennon Airport** (renamed in 2001 from Speke Airport and featuring a permanent display of several large-format Paul Saltzman Rishikesh photos in the departure hall)

4. **Pierre Elliott Trudeau International Airport** (renamed in 2004 from Montréal-Dorval International Airport)

Harrison had every reason to be sentimental about Canada but for someone who once considered moving here, his many appearances, interviews and book references lack mention of his Canadian nephew and niece and Canadian-raised cousins or the roots his uncle and sister laid down in Ontario and Québec. There is a glimmer of evidence, though, that he saw members of his Canadian family in 1964 during The Beatles' first Toronto concert. As the story goes, in the early afternoon of Monday, September 7, city mayor Philip Givens and his wife made their way to The Beatles' suite at the King Edward Hotel but were unceremoniously turned away by a handler telling his worship that "two of The Beatles were asleep and two others were with relatives."[175] Apart from a scant, unsubstantiated reference to McCartney having an aunt in Toronto, no other Beatle except Harrison had Canadian relatives which suggests his Toronto-area uncle Edmond French's family spent time with him at the King Eddy, and/or his sister Louise made her way up to Toronto from Illinois—her new home after living in northern Québec.

The key with Harrison lies in his subtly, beginning with the way he introduced the first Canadian connection to the music of The Beatles: Eric Clapton. And while we know that Clapton doesn't identify as Canadian, that's what part of him is by way of a Montréal-born father.

Consider for a moment how their relationship bore early fruit when Harrison invited his friend to record with The Beatles. Harrison broke an unspoken tradition and marched an outsider with a Canadian father into The Beatles' sacrosanct lair—*their* recording studio—to play a central part in "While My Guitar Gently Weeps". By all accounts, the other three relinquished their domain, and were even gracious, to their half-Canadian guest.

The goodwill resulted in one of the finest Beatles songs ever made. And that spur-of-the-moment manoeuvre by Harrison set in motion a Beatles precedent, opening the door for a guest appearance that would transform latter-day Beatles music—Billy Preston. The Texas-born keyboardist laid down an indelible stamp on nearly every track on the *Let it Be* album and two songs on *Abbey Road*.

Harrison's loyalty to Clapton denied Winnipeg's Randy Bachman a shot at gaining a foothold as a guitarist in Harrison's band yet another Canadian, Toronto-born Robbie Robertson, established a close friendship with the Beatle. That bond led Harrison to pick up the guitar again, something The Beatles' lead guitarist had, to a certain degree, abandoned for a couple of years while learning to play the sitar. Just as Lennon's time in Canada and working with Perry emboldened him to consider life without The Beatles, Harrison observed through Robertson a fresh, new song-writing ethic and another path.

The Band's Canadian musical groove—and predominantly American-themed songwriting—transported Harrison's creative spirit and lit his imagination enough to write "All Things Must Pass". But in trying to bring the song to life with The Beatles, he realized even the world's greatest band couldn't replicate the emotional, gospel rock depth he was hearing in his head—"other sounds," as he put it, and a new, achievable standard that was revealed by The Band.

Our tears had finally dried from losing Lennon when Harrison drew his last breath on November 29, 2001 at age 58. In the only North American tour of his career, he chose to launch in Vancouver in 1974. Harrison was a generous collaborator with the Canadians in his circle. He privately played his sitar for Paul Saltzman, gave John Rowlands a guitar lesson and, under the hilarious Italian pseudonym "*L'Angelo Misterioso*" (Mysterious Angel), wrote and recorded "Badge" with Clapton—the only time a Beatle shared a writing credit with anyone of Canadian blood—and permitted the blind Toronto rocker Jeff Healey not only to record "While My Guitar Gently Weeps" but played on the track too.

If The Band proved that Canadian musicians were capable of inspiring Beatles latter-day music, then the reverse—The Beatles inspiring Canadian musicians—is a foregone reality given the count-less bands that concede The Beatles provided the artistic stimulus for them to make music. But while many Canadian musicians—especially from Nova Scotia—simply surrendered to a greater power by recording Beatles covers, Klaatu's break-out 1976 album *3:57 EST* was so profoundly Beatles-esque the young men from Toronto who recorded it were, for a brief shining moment, confused with being The Beatles themselves!

Harrison broke ranks from his attempt at anonymity to speak to Dali Sanschagrin in one of his last ever television interviews. Also emerging from his time in Montréal, Harrison saw eye-to-eye with fellow visionary, Québec City's Guy Laliberté and, from that, *The Beatles LOVE* partnership with Cirque de Soleil helped the company become a cultural and economic jewel in the province of Québec and around the world (although in recent months the COVID-19 pandemic has hurt the entertainment giant).

McCartney's actions in Canada spoke louder than words. To give 10 local pipe and drum bands in six provinces the once-in-a-lifetime hometown thrill of playing on stage with him was probably enough to inform Canadians of his respect for the place in the least, or how he held a genuine connection to Canada at best. Two weeks after 47 people perished in the horrific 2013 train accident at Lac-Mégantic, Québec, he offered 1,000 free tickets to survivors and family of the deceased for his Québec City concert where, in French, he dedicated "Let it Be" to the victims. It was McCartney who told *CNN*: "In the international arena, Canada is known as a great country, a great people."

To borrow from Harrison's songwriting pseudonym, McCartney may well be a true angel on earth—*Un Vero Angelo*, who wraps himself in the Canadian flag when performing throughout the country, bringing joy to many. Seemingly touched by grace, he is a genius songwriter, legendary and gifted musician of multiple instruments, artist, poet, composer, humanitarian, and philanthropist and, well, the endless list of artistic accolades doesn't stop there. As a children's author he collaborated with Canadian Kathryn Durst not once but twice, giving the talented young illustrator a place in his remarkable history.

And what's more, McCartney and his mates put their social consciousness on display in Canada—a country he viewed in his youth as a stepping-stone to the big prize in show business: America. They used their platform as celebrities to aim the spotlight on issues that mattered here and to a broader audience. They were mega wealthy rock stars who raised awareness for marginalized and disadvantaged people and even took a stand on the rights of animals.

McCartney went out of his way to applaud the preservation of Mi'kmaq culture (through language) when applied so exquisitely to a young Canadian's version of his song "Blackbird" and align himself with the United Nations International Year of Indigenous Languages with a song that is itself was about racial inequality. That year's earlier Lennon took an active interest in the living conditions of Canada's First Nations people, offers a thread of moral continuity between John and Paul—something rooted in Canadian history, exposing a nation's dark underbelly with respect to the treatment of its founding people.

McCartney and Starr are big supporters of The David Lynch Foundation, which has far reaching social implications including here in Canada where a chapter in Toronto promotes education and peace through the study of Transcendental Meditation.

Starr's connections to Canada include time spent in country with his (and Lennon's) musician and party friend Harry Nilsson. In a sparsely documented series of visits during the 1970s, the two were in Toronto and Vancouver, with Starr preferring the latter city: "Toronto, man! I spent the coldest winter of my life there … long time ago in the 70s with Harry Nilsson. It was cold! … We would go and hang out in Vancouver because it was quite a rocking town," he told *CBC Radio's* Tom Powers in 2019. In fact Starr played at Vancouver's Queen Elizabeth Theatre on what would have been Lennon's 75th birthday in October 2015.

Starr returned to Ontario in 2008, 2010 and 2012 as a launching point for tours with his All-Starr band that assembled each time at Fallsview Casino Resort in Niagara Falls for weeklong rehearsal sessions. He had this to say about one of Canada's great natural wonders: "We see the falls out of our windows. It puts me in my place every morning. When you think you're such a big shot, you open the curtain and there's Niagara Falls. It right sizes me immediately, so the day starts out good."[176]

More than any other Beatle, Starr tapped into Canadian-born talent in pursuit of his solo career and recorded a live DVD at Ontario's Casino Rama Resort during the opening night of his 2003 summer tour. Starr also played with The Band, made up of mostly Canadian artists, at its farewell concert and to date is the only Beatle to perform Canadian-written tunes to live audiences. When you consider The Beatles began as a cover band over 60 years ago, it's sweet déjà vu that Starr would include Canadian compositions whilst returning to his performing roots.

When she was asked to sing with Starr, Ontario's Cindy Gomez's reaction was, "Oh my God, it's a Beatle"—in stark contrast to, say, Saskatchewan's Art Ellefson fifty years earlier who wanted the world to overlook his Beatles experience. It says a lot about how the passage of time and our cultural absorption of The Beatles has raised their prominence and relevance even in the youngest hearts and minds—just ask the Tennant kids and youngsters all over the world who download Beatles music and continue to sell out McCartney and Starr concerts.

With the advent of music streaming, re-releases, Beatles-loving grandparents and parents like the Tennants who by instilling Beatles music in their children helped shape them, and a zealous publicity machine at Apple Records that has worked so well at ensuring The Beatles have outlived, well, The Beatles, it's entirely possible that The Beatles are more popular today than ever before. No less than the likes of filmmaker extraordinaire Peter Jackson is directing *The Beatles: Get Back* motion picture coming in November 2021. Closer to home, Toronto's Ron Chapman has been pegged to direct a music documentary (for release in 2022) about Lennon's bold first foray on stage without The Beatles at Varsity Stadium in 1969.

Every generation seems to find something in music—whether a rhythm, a groove or something deeply human—that washes over it like a comforting light rain. Beatles music has forever appeal; it is transcendent and multigenerational. Look no further than Emma Stevens to understand just how far Canada and societies everywhere have come when young, aspiring performers are inspired by The Beatles and layers of future generations will no doubt continue to be so. The Beatles' music still matters and there are many wondrous links to Canada that have helped to make their songs timeless, making their Canadian legacy a story that's never quite done being told. Is there any other nation on earth whose elected, national leader stopped London traffic to imitate The Beatles' street crossing at Abbey Road? Not likely, and it's a beautiful thing.

Someone once said Beatles music will be playing for as long as the earth is spinning. There has never been a band as complete, life changing and genre busting since and after The Beatles. Shining a light on Canada through their lens and, in turn, their contributions to its society rank as a proud and notable footnote in Canadian history. That both ordinary and luminary Canadians alike, quite innocently at times, had an impact on their lives and music is also so very gratifying; it gives this author flight. Thank you for joining me on this journey.

Canada, Canadians and The Beatles. An undeniable love story. Connected for all of time. Long may they reign.

EPILOGUE

Johnny's Top Ten Canadian Bands and Their Beatles Connections

The following is the result of an utterly self-indulgent thought experiment wherein the author, lazing at a Caribbean swim-up bar, tries to explain the essence of Canadian music to another tourist. I skip the bits about our unique character, sports, diverse geography and liberal democratic traditions, and jump straight to our 10 greatest English-language musical assets. In many ways, The Beatles were the gateway sound that brought me closer to Canadian folk and rock.

My top ten are all part of the Canadian Music Hall of Fame (birthplace or band origin and induction year in parentheses) and all have varying degrees of Beatles connections; step into my dream ...

1. Rush (Toronto, Ontario, Canadian Music Hall of Fame induction in 1994)

Canada's blessed trinity Rush is my no-brainer first choice all-time greatest Canadian bands but their direct Beatles connections are thin apart, of course, for The Beatles' influence on the roots of their musicality. When discussing his reasons for taking up bass guitar, for instance, Geddy Lee had this to say about McCartney's playing: "Yet, there were others that were subconscious influences and I think we all have those when we listen to music. I mean ... people remember The Beatles for their tunefulness and for the great vocals. However, Paul

McCartney was quite an influential bass player. If you listen to 'Come Together' that's a bold bass part in that in song. If you listen to 'Tax Man', that's heavy metal before there was heavy metal."[177]

Rush's long-time producer Terry Brown also produced the debut Klaatu album *3:57* in 1976—the same record that started all The Beatles' reunion rumours. Moreover, Brown was behind the mixing board for Joe Cocker's version of "A Little Help from my Friends" and also recorded The Beatles' Rishikesh friend Donovan's "Mellow Yellow".

Coincidentally, when Rush drummer Neil Peart passed away on January 7, 2020, at age 67 it was Lennon's former publicist and current spokesperson for the Lennon estate, Elliott Mintz, who represented the Peart family and, along with the band's survivors, broke the news to the media.

2. Gordon Lightfoot (Orillia, Ontario, 1986)

Beatle connections to the timeless troubadour are a little hazy. Apart from the fact his birthplace Orillia hosted one of Canada's largest Beatles festivals from 2007 to 2015, most connections involve coincidental producers and musicians with whom he and members of The Beatles have recorded.

For instance, Russ Titelman co-produced Harrison's eighth solo album, the self-titled *George Harrison* in 1979 as well as Lightfoot's *Dream Street Rose* album a year later.

Jim Gordon, the troubled Los Angeles drummer, was featured on Harrison's triple album *All Things Must Pass*, Lennon's debut solo album *John Lennon/Plastic Ono Band*, plus his song "It's So Hard", and on Lightfoot's 1976 song "The House You Live In".

The late Hugh McCracken's guitar playing connections spanned three decades with members of The Beatles and Lightfoot including the latter's third album *Did She Mention My Name* in 1968, guitar and mandolin on several McCartney albums including *Ram* in 1971 and guitar on two Lennon albums including 1980's *Double Fantasy* and the posthumous *Milk and Honey* in 1984.

In a 2019 documentary film Lightfoot recounted how the rapid-fire release of Beatles music in the mid-1960s repressed sales of his own albums and very nearly derailed his career: "Every time I would have an album coming out, The Beatles would eat us alive with record sales."[178]

3. The Tragically Hip (Kingston, Ontario, 2005)

A Canadian cultural artifact, The Hip covered "Come Together"—a song whose composition Lennon initiated while in Canada—at a concert in Wisconsin in 2007. Quite randomly, the Abbey Road Studios website took notice of their late leader and singer/songwriter and quite accurately concluded: "To the group's fervent admirers, Mr. (Gord) Downie and his band were as closely linked to Canada as The Beatles are to England or the U2 singer Bono is to Ireland."[179]

4. The Guess Who (Winnipeg, Manitoba, 1987)

One-time band member Bruce Decker made his famous attempt to meet The Beatles on the runway apron at Winnipeg Airport in 1964. Randy Bachman and Burton Cummings recorded a version of The Beatles' "Happy Just to Dance with You" and both (separately) toured with Ringo Starr; Bachman is also a certifiable Beatlemaniac who not only applied for a job as a guitarist in Harrison's band 51 years ago during The Guess Who's *American Woman* album peak of 1970, but has also recorded an entire album of Harrison songs.

5. April Wine (Waverley, Nova Scotia, 2010)

April Wine covered The Beatles' "Tell Me Why" and paid dual homage to the British Invasion by using the guitar hooks in "Day Tripper" and "Satisfaction" on 1980's "I Wanna Rock", one of countless April Wine hits during the band's remarkable five decades of pounding out uniquely Canadian roadhouse rock 'n' roll.

6. The Band (from Ontario, Rick Danko, Norfolk Country, Garth Hudson, Windsor, Richard Manuel, Stratford and Robbie Robertson, Toronto, and Levon Helm of Elaine, Arkansas, 1989)

Arguably, the mostly Canadian musical collective possesses the biggest and most direct link with at least two Beatles: The Band invited Starr on stage as a guest drummer at their Last Waltz final concert and celebration, and its unique and soulful brand of musicianship deeply inspired Harrison and even kick-started his guitar playing and song-writing after the Beatle flew to New York to meet with them. Beatle contributor and collaborator Clapton was so turned on by The Band's *Music from Big Pink* that he wanted to join them. Band members were part of the earliest incarnations of Ringo's All-Starr band and Robbie Robertson had multiple studio and on-line collaborations with Starr, and in the late 1960s befriended Harrison.

7. Neil Young (Toronto, Ontario, 1982)

Young and McCartney have been friends for decades, nearly on par with famous Canadian-Beatle friendships like Harrison and Robertson, and Clapton and Harrison, although Harrison was on record as not being a Young fan.

It was Young who inducted McCartney in the Rock and Roll Hall of Fame and the two have performed together many times, including a blistering version of "A Day in the Life" in London's Hyde Park in 2009. The Lennon-McCartney classic that ends *Sgt. Pepper's Lonely Hearts Club Band* was a Young staple, playing it to empty auditoriums as a warm-up song during his 1978 *Rust Never Sleeps* tour.

In February 2012, at the Music Cares concert he performed a version of "I Saw Her Standing There" with his band Crazy Horse where he inserts the original, unrecorded Lennon/McCartney line of "well she was just seventeen, and she wasn't a beauty queen."

8. Alanis Morissette (Ottawa, Ontario, 2015)

One of the most melodic voices ever to emerge from these parts, Alanis's 1995 smash hit "Ironic" left grammarians puzzled by the song's, well, lack of irony; it didn't, however, stop her from expanding The Beatles' use of the contraction "isn't" as in "isn't it good, Norwegian Wood", when Morissette actually sang the words "is not it good, Norwegian Wood" during an otherwise superb live performance of the *Rubber Soul* tune in the San Francisco Bay area in 1997. In the studio, Morissette added vocals to Starr's 1998 *Vertical Man* album and on stage in 2001 sang a stirring, respectful version of "Dear Prudence" during a tribute event to Lennon.

9. Bryan Adams (Kingston, Ontario, 2006)

Like Bachman, this Canadian rocker wears his colours proudly as a true Beatlemaniac.

On March 17, 2020, a bespectacled Adams took to social media to sing John Lennon's "Isolation" as an ode to the act of self-quarantine in the early days of the COVID-19 pandemic. Jeff Lynne, who produced The Beatles' 1995 comebacks "Free As a Bird" and "Real Love" and is a long-time solo Beatles collaborator, also produced Adams' 2015 album *Get Up* and the two even co-wrote a song. (Lynne has famously produced Harrison and McCartney albums and, with Harrison, was a member of the Traveling Wilburys super group and has recorded and toured with Beatle scion Dhani Harrison, the only child to George and Olivia Harrison.)

In 2014, Adams performed a version of The Beatles "Any Time at All" in London, England; the song also appears on his *Tracks of My Years* album from the same year. A special 2007 *BBC Radio* anniversary re-recording of *Sgt. Pepper's Lonely Hearts Club Band* featured Adams on guitar and vocals for the title track. He also sang and played guitar alongside McCartney in a star-studded rendition of "I Saw Her Standing There" at the Prince's Trust All-Star Rock Concert on June 20, 1986, at London's Wembley Stadium.

10. Joni Mitchell (Fort MacLeod, Alberta, 1981)

The Alberta-born, Saskatchewan-raised songwriter and voice-of-the-ages Joni Mitchell sang harmonies with fellow Canadians Neil Young and Rick Danko to Bob Dylan's "I Shall Be Released" at The Band's Last Waltz while Ringo Starr and Levon Helm played drums.

Mitchell's career management falls under the care of Los Angeles-based Peter Asher Management, and there are Beatles tie-ins there. Peter and Gordon (Peter Asher and Gordon Waller) were a British recording duo who scored a number one hit in Canada in 1964 with the Lennon-McCartney composition "World Without Love". Later, Asher was the one who signed James Taylor to The Beatles' Apple Records label in 1968. His sister, actress Jane Asher, was once engaged to McCartney.

Mitchell very nearly recorded with Harrison. She and members of her touring band, L.A. Express, visited Harrison at his Friar Park estate while in England in 1974. While there the band recorded two songs with Harrison for his *Dark Horse* album but Mitchell decided not to join them and returned to London.

Her seminal 1971 album, *Blue*, borrowed the talents of the same steel pedal guitar player as did Lennon for his 1973 *Mind Games* album: Sneaky Pete Kleinow. Long-time and loyal Lennon and Harrison drummer Jim Keltner also played on Mitchell's 1994 song "Sunny Sunday".

She once told *Lava Magazine*: "*Rubber Soul* was the Beatle album I played over and over. I think they were discovering Dylan, and the songs often had an acoustic feel, I used to sing (Norwegian Wood) in my coffeehouse days in Detroit before I started writing for myself. The whole scenario has this whimsical, charmingly wry quality with a bit of a dark undertone. I'd sing it to put some levity in my set. I got a kick out of throwing it in there amongst all these tragic English folk ballads."[180]

AUTHOR INTERVIEWS

E-Mail exchange with Dr. Holly Tessler, May 12, 2021

E-Mail interview with Terry Draper, Mar. 4, 2021

E-Mail interview with Paul Saltzman, Feb. 23, 2021

Telephone and E-Mail interviews with Robert Decker, January 2021

Telephone interviews with Don Groom, Nov. 26 and Dec. 30, 2020

Telephone and E-Mail interviews with Tommy Schnurmacher, Nov. 11 and Dec. 8, 2020

E-mail interviews with Ocean Tennant, June and December, 2020

Facebook Messenger interview with Emma Stevens, Nov. 29, 2020

E-Mail exchange with Hugh Segal, Nov. 7, 2020

E-Mail interview with Camilla van der Kooij, Oct. 28, 2020

E-Mail exchange with Kathryn Durst, Oct. 8, 2020

Telephone and E-Mail interviews with John MacCallum, Summer 2020

Telephone and E-Mail interviews with Scott Balinson and Ben Jaeckle, Jul. 15, 2020

E-Mail exchange with Alexandre Reeves, Jun. 25, 2020

E-Mail interview with Cheryl Finn, Jun. 4, 2020

Telephone and E-Mail interviews with André Perry, May 30, 2020

E-Mail Interview with Buff Allen, May 14, 2020

Telephone and E-Mail interviews with Dali Sanschagrin, March, April, June 2020

END NOTES

For Main Narrative

1

Montréalgazette.com, "Canadian graduates in Beatles class", Randy Boswell, Jan. 25, 2011

2

theguardian.com, "Toppermost of the Poppermost", Michael Faber, Oct. 11, 2008

3

rollingstone.com, "Ten Best Beatles Books", Colin Fleming, Apr. 10, 2020

4

Boyhood, Richard Linklater, IFC Films/Universal Pictures, 2014

5/8/9/11

Tune In: The Beatles All These Years, Mark Lewisohn, Three Rivers Press, 2013, pp. 231, 282, 330, 331 and 678

6

lettersfrommum.com/

7
youtube.com, "The Frost Interview–Paul McCartney", Nov. 10, 2012

10
Howard Stern Show, SiriusXM Radio, Nov. 27, 2018

12/14
Eric Clapton: Life in 12 Bars, Lili Fini Zanuck, BBC, 2017

13
Love, Sex and War: Changing Values 1939-1945, John Costello, Pan Books, 1986, p. 277 (extrapolation of the statistic "one third of 5.3 million births in Britain during WWII were illegitimate")

15/18
The Beatles, Bob Spitz, Little, Brown and Company, 2005, pp. 56 and 58

16/17
Tune In: The Beatles All These Years, Mark Lewisohn, Three Rivers Press, 2013, pp. 123, 124 and 125

19/20
The Beatles Anthology, Chronicle Books, Apple Corps Ltd, 2000, pp. 23 and 31

21/26
Tune In: The Beatles All These Years, Mark Lewisohn, Three Rivers Press, 2013, pp. 428 and 665

22/23 Beatle, The Pete Best Story, Patrick Doncaster and Pete Best, Plexus Publishing, 1985, pp. 98 and 99

24
The Beatles in Canada: The Origins of Beatlemania!, Piers Hemmingsen, Wise Publications, 2016

25

Magical Mystery Tours: My Life with The Beatles, Tony Bramwell and Rosemary Kingsland, St. Martin's Griffin, 2006, p. 34

27

forbes.com, "Five Common Myths About The Beatles' … ", John Covach, Feb. 7, 2014

28

theglobeandmail.com, "Paul White the man who introduced … ", Nicholas Jennings, Mar. 23, 2018

29

Ottawacitizen.com/entertainment/canada/9409013/story.html

30

The Beatles Anthology, Chronicle Books, Apple Corps Ltd, 2000, p. 107

31

businessmanagement.news, "Top 20 Best Beatles Songs … ", May 24, 2017

32

Montréalgazette.com, "Canadian graduates in Beatles class", Randy Boswell, Jan. 25, 2011

33/34

My Way: An Autobiography, Paul Anka and David Dalton, St. Martin's Publishing Group, 2013, pp. 132 and 134

35

Manitobamusicmuseum.com, "The Decker Dash … "

36

archeion.ca/bruce-decker-fonds, Archives Association of Ontario

37

cbc.ca/news, " ... The Beatles Played Vancouver ... ", Lee Rosevere, Aug. 22, 2014

38

Eight Days a Week: The Touring Years. Ron Howard. Apple Corps Limited and Imagine Entertainment, 2016

39

Maclean's magazine, David Lewis Stein, Jul. 4, 1964, p. 48

40

pressreader.com/canada/vancouver-sun/20120225/

41

youtube.com, "Beatles Interview in Toronto, Canada, 1964"

42

desertsun.com, "Beatles British journalist ... ", Bruce Fessier, Feb. 27, 2015

43

terryott.blogspot.com/2004/07

44

nationalpost.com, "When The Beatles Rocked ... ", Chris Selby, Jun. 22, 2016

45

journaldemontréal.com, "Marquant pour plusieurs vedettes", Élizabeth Ménard, Sept. 7, 2014

46

beatlesinterviews.org "Beatles Press Conference: Montréal 9/8/1964"

47/51/53

The Beatles Anthology, Chronicle Books, Apple Corps Ltd, 2000, pp. 153, 241 and 208

48

theglobeandmail.com, Brad Wheeler, Feb. 4, 2014

49

Torontolife.com, "Seven Rare Vintage Photos ... ", Luke Fox, Jul. 19, 2016

50

Torontoplaques.com/Pages/Beatles.html

52

Serious Jibber Jabber with Conan O'Brien, Team Coco, Jun. 4, 2016

54

ajournalofmusicalthings.com, "Exclusive: The Real Sgt. Pepper was Canadian ... ", Thomas Shaw, May 31, 2017

55

Tony Aspler's Cellar Book, Tony Aspler, Random House Canada, 2009

56

theguardian.com, "Road Trips, Yogo and LSD ... ", Craig Brown, Mar. 28, 2020

57/61

The Gospel According to The Beatles, Steven Turner, Westminster John Knox Press, 2006, pp. 117 and 116

58

Lennon: The Definitive Biography, Ray Coleman, Harper Perennial, 1986, p. 335

59

The Beatles Anthology, Chronicle Books, Apple Corps Ltd, 2000, p. 194

60

rollingstone.com, "Beatles Acid Test … ", Mikal Gilmore, Aug. 25, 2016

62

telegraph.co.uk, "More than Love", Oct. 14, 2009

63

guitarworld.com, "September 6, 1968 Eric Clapton records his While My Guitar … "

64/69/71

vulture.com, "Beatles songs ranked … ", Bill Wyman, Jun. 7, 2017

65

therecord.com, "Randy Bachman's Beatle Connections … ", Joel Rubinoff, Mar. 2, 2018

66/72

The Beatles Recording Sessions, Mark Lewisohn, Harmony Books, 1988, pp. 161 and 142

67

The Beatles 50th Anniversary White Album accompanying booklet, 2018, Calderstone Productions/Apple Corps

68

instagram.com, "todayinthebeatleshistory", Oct. 1, 2020

70

The Beatles Anthology, Chronicle Books, Apple Corps Ltd, 2000. p. 306

73

theguardian.com, obituaries, Peter Vacher, Jun. 13, 2006

74

While My Guitar Gently Weeps: The Music of George Harrison, Simon Leng, Firefly Publishing, 2006, p. 47

75/76
The Beatles in India, Paul Saltzman, Insight Editions, 2018, pp. 15 and 18

77
beatlesstory.com, "Interview with Paul Saltzman ... ", Jun. 29, 2017

78
rollingstone.com, "The Beatles in India: 16 Things ... ", David Chiu, Feb. 14, 2021

79
Tune In: The Beatles All These Years, Mark Lewisohn, Three Rivers Press, 2013, p. 228

80
John, Cynthia Lennon, Crown Publishers, 2005, p. 92

81
Facebook: The Beatles' Wives and Girls

82
The Beatles Anthology, Chronicle Books, Apple Corps Ltd, 2000, p. 157

83
CBS Interview, Dec. 18, 2010

84
cbc.ca/news, "RCMP spied on Lennon, Ono ... ", Jul. 23, 2007.

85
beatlesbible.com, "John and Yoko's First Bed-In ... ", May 25, 1969

86
rollingstone.com, "John and Yoko in Canada ... ", Jun. 28, 1969

87
beatles.ncf.ca, The Globe and Mail, Linda Bohen, May 26, 1969

88

beatles.ncf.ca, "Lennon and Ono bring message … ", The Globe and Mail, Ritchie Yorke, May 27, 1969

89/90

I Met the Walrus, Jerry Levitan, HarperCollins Publishers, 2009, p. 97

91

Ringo: With A Little Help, Michael Seth Starr, Backbeat, Michael, Chapter Eight

92

nationalpost.com, "The Beatle and the separatist … ", Tristin Hopper, Feb. 18, 2004

93

Vancouversun.com, John Mackie, Feb. 18, 2014

94

The Canadian Press, "Security guard from Lennon's Montréal bed-in shares … ", Matthew Kruk, 2008

95

The John Lennon Letters, Hunter Davies, Little, Brown and Company, 2012, p. 149

96/98

Montréalgazette.com, "From the archive: All we are saying … ", Dave Bist, May 26, 2014

97

youtube.com, "John Lennon, Yoko Ono, Allan Rock, A Concession … "

99

Mojo Magazine, Special "Lennon" Edition, Winter 2000, p. 114

100/104
The Beatles Anthology, Chronicle Books, Apple Corps Ltd, 2000, p. 334

101
Gimme Some Truth boxed set booklet, Capitol Records, Aug. 25, 2020

102
vulture.com, "Beatles songs ranked … ", Bill Wyman, Jun. 7, 2017

103
Ottawa Journal, "The Beatle is Coming", Jun. 3 1969, p. 5

105
cbc.ca/news, "Give peace a chance lyrics sell … ", Tom Parry, Jul. 10, 2008

106
npr.org, "After 40 Years, The Bed-in Reawakens", Margot Adler, Aug. 25, 2009

107
cbc.ca/news, "Yoko Ono Returns to Montréal … ", Mar. 31, 2009

108
Canada News Wire, "Fairmont The Queen Elizabeth Celebrates … ", May 1, 2019

109
mint.ca, "Royal Canadian Mint Silver Coin Celebrates 50th Anniversary … "

110
vice.com (originally on Noisey Canada), "The Domino Effect … ", Juliette Jagger, Apr. 14, 2015

111/117
The Beatles Anthology, Chronicle Books, Apple Corps Ltd, 2000, p. 347

112/116
And in the End, Ken McNab, Thomas Dunne Books, 2019, pp. 219 and 220

113/114
cavehollywood.com, Harvey Kubernik, Oct. 31, 2013

115
everythingzoomer.com, "Remembering John Lennon ...", Mike Crisolago, Sept. 13, 2019

118
The Sunday Times Magazine, The Lost Interviews, Ray Connolly, Jun. 9, 2009

119
youtube.com, "John Lennon & Yoko Ono with Marshall McLuhan ... "

120
instagram.com/johnlennon, A Bag of Laughs, Feb. 28, 2020

121
Ottawalife.com, Michael Moriarty, Oct. 17, 2012

122
Memories of John Lennon, HarperCollins Publishers, 2009, p. 273

123
cbc.ca, digital archives, "Lennon, Ono and Pierre Trudeau ... "

124
Ottawa Citizen, "Drugs: John pledges help", Tracey Morey, Dec. 24, 1969

125
everythingzoomer.com, "Fifty Years Ago, John Lennon ... ", Robert Morrison, Dec. 24, 2019

126
Vancouversun.com/news, Apr. 3, 2012

127
John & Yoko: Above Us Only Sky, Michael Epstein, 2018, Eagle Rock Entertainment Ltd

128
vanityfair.com, "The Birth of Bond", David Kamp, Sept. 18, 2012

129
Inside the Songs of the Sixties, Brian L. Forsythe, 2013

130
Kiss Bang! Bang!: The Unofficial James Bond Film Companion, Alan and Marcu Hearn, Batsford Books, 1997, pp. 110 and 111

131
theguardian.com, "The name's Saltzman, Harry Saltzman", John Patterson, Sept. 28, 2012

132
George Harrison Behind the Locked Door, Graeme Thomson, Omnibus Press, 2015, p. 258

133
songfacts.com, "Basketball Jones by Cheech & Chong"

134
beatlesnews.com, "John Loved Anny Murray's ... "

135
David Foster: Off The Record, @10940160 Canada Inc., Melbar Entertainment Group, 2020

136
Slowhand, Philip Norman, Little, Brown and Company, 2018, p. 288

137
intelligencer.ca, "Cultivating Creativity: Special docfest screening … ", Nov. 22, 2019

138
The Band: The Authorized Video Biography, Rearview Mirror Music, Hallway, Inc. 1995

139
George Harrison Behind the Locked Door, Graeme Thomson, Omnibus Press, 2015, p. 159

140/141
Facebook: Pop Goes the 60s, "All Things Must Pass Was Not Rejected … ", Oct. 24, 2020

142
The Music of George Harrison: While My Guitar Gently Weeps, Simon Leng, Firefly Publishing, 2003, p. 310

143
The Beatles Anthology, Chronicle Books, Apple Corps Ltd, 2000, p. 316

144
goldminemag.com, "Being compared to The Beatles … ", Conrad Stinnett, Dec. 8, 2013

145
wikipedia.org/wiki, "Ringo Starr All Starr Band"

146
victorbaissait.fr, "All Starr Band 1992 General Information"

147

jeffhealey.com, "Essential Jeff Healey ... ", Rog, Apr. 1, 2013

148

rollingstone.com, "Beatles producer George Martin ... ", Joe Rosenthal, Oct. 23, 1998

149

All The Songs, Black Dog and Leventhal Publishers, p. 8

150

rockhall.com/inductees, "Paul McCartney"

151

rollingstone.com, "Rolling Stone readers pick the top ten ... ", Mar. 15, 2011

152

newsweek.com, "Mrs. George Harrison on the new Beatles show", Jun. 22, 2006

153

youtube.com, "George Harrison, Montréal 2000"

154

Profile 2019: Economic Report on the Screen Based Media Production Industry in Canada, CMPA, p. 10

155

Newfoundland and Labrador News Releases "Premier Invites Sir Paul ... ", Mar. 1, 2006

156

transcripts.cnn.com, transcript 0603/03/lkl.01, Mar. 3, 2006

157

underwatertimes.com, "Did Canadian Seal Hunt Protest Lead to ... ", Oct. 18, 2006

158
macleans.ca, "Cindy Gomez Cinderella Story", Anne Kingston, Sept. 24, 2009

159
nationalpost.com, "Separatists decry McCartney ... ", Graeme Hamilton, Jul. 16, 2008

160
wikipedia.org/wiki/Frisson

161
bigissue.com, "Making Mull of Kintyre", Malcolm Jack, Dec. 18, 2018

162
cbc.ca, "Winnipeg pipe band recalls McCartney's 1993 show"

163/165/167
youtube.com, "Paul McCartney–Halifax Commons ... "
youtube.com, "Paul McCartney invites fans up on stage ... "
youtube.com, "Paul McCartney's Vancouver shout-out ... "

164
setlist.fm, "Paul McCartney 2016 FirstOntario ... "

166
thebrightagency.com, Behind the Book: Hey Grandude!, Sept. 25, 2019

168
warmuseum.ca, Chronology of Military History, The Royal Canadian Air Force 1939-45 and Going Home 1945-46

169
archives.gov.on.ca, "Eaton's Goes to War"

170

huffingtonpost.ca, "Ronnie Hawkins recalls getting stoned ... ", Oct. 4, 2013

171

commentarymagazine.com, "Pop Goes the Island", May 1965

172

theguardian.com, "The name's Saltzman, Harry Saltzman", John Patterson, Sept. 28, 2012

173

Author Interviews with Tommy Schnurmacher, Nov. 11, 2020 & Dec. 8, 2020

174

Just Watch Me: The Life of Pierre Elliott Trudeau, John English, Vintage Canada, 1968-2000

175

beatlesbible.com, "Live Maple Leaf Gardens ... "

176

CBC Radio, Q with Tom Powers, Nov. 8, 2019

177

cosmicmagazine.com, Riley Fitzgerald, Nov. 22, 2019

178

Gordon Lightfoot: If You Could Read My Mind, Greenwich Entertainment, Apr. 27, 2019

179

shop.abbeyroad.com, "Day for night ... "

180

lavarocks.org, December 2009

END NOTES

For Sidebar Stories

1

scotbeat.wordpress.com, "Anti Lothian Beatlemania", Jan. 3, 2018 and youtube.com, "Andi Lothian Remembers … " Oct. 6, 2013

2

beatles.ncf.ca, John Whelan, Mar. 17, 2000

3

mountainx.com, "Reviews: How I Won the War", Ken Hanke, Feb. 10, 2015

4

polle.no "Tommy Reilly MBE …"

5

youtube.com, "John Lennon's Last BBC Interview", Dec. 6, 1980

6

beatlesbible.com, "Plastic Ono Band Perform Toronto … ", Sept. 13, 1969

7

thecoast.ca, "How Halifax's Concert Scandal … ", Tim Bousquet, Dec. 5, 2001

8

vocal.media, "Beat: History of the lighter at concerts", Will Vasquez

9

beatlesinterviews.org, "Playboy interview with John Lennon … ", Playboy Press, David Sheff, September 1980

10

theglobeandmail.com, "An Epochal Concert at … ", Ritchie Yorke, Sept. 11, 2009

11

loudersound.com, "Why I Love George … ", Michael Hann, Aug. 21, 2019

12

ualberta.ca/arts, "Was John Lennon's Imagine Inspired by … ", Geoff McMaster, Dec. 10, 2018

AUTHOR'S NOTE

By His Daughter Terra-Ann Arnone

The author, John Robert Arnone. Photo by Justin Tang.

John Robert Arnone was born on the kind of freeze-your-unmentionables frigid February day all southwestern Ontarians know well. If you ask his mother Ida Maria, those temperatures account for my father's premature arrival several weeks ahead of anticipation. These days, he prefers to spend Februaries in the south of Spain, but by spring, summer and autumn you'll find my dad on the shores of beautiful Georgian Bay, where he and mom Tamara have a little home they like to call paradise. Dad bid adieu a 35-year career in journalism and corporate communications, with mandates to find or create news across Canada's vast spaces, when he retired in 2018. Dad has been talking-up The Beatles for as long as I can remember, teaching me the words to "If I Fell" in a bathtub when I was two. But it was my father who quite figuratively was bathed in The Beatles' music all of his life; that his first book should be about his heroes from Liverpool is a surprise "For No One"!

DEDICATION

By the Author

Us and Them is dedicated to Mario Arnone. A proud immigrant who raised a large family solely on his earnings as a barber, my dad loved music and tolerated my brothers Pat, Rob, Frank and I playing The Beatles on the family turntable. Dad also read a lot of newspapers. Each summer and on some weekends in the 1960s and 1970s, my brothers and I took turns shining shoes for dad's clientele at his barbershop. We grew up in that place. It was there, in between cuts and shoe shines, he would tell me stories including one about *Toronto Telegram* journalist Scott Young's adolescent son, Neil, and his hopeless long-haired existence of busking guitar. Dad might have missed the mark on Neil Young, but he was right about most things. I miss him so much.

ACKNOWLEDGEMENTS

Us and Them has been my one and truest love in the time of pandemic. One of my first interviews was with Dali Sanschagrin who recalled with crystal clarity her chance encounter with George Harrison. The brilliant recollections of Bed-In alumni André Perry and Tommy Schnurmacher inspired an entire chapter, and Don Groom's unfailing memory brought a unique P.E.I. story to life, fulfilling an objective to connect The Beatles, or the people in their immediate orbit, to all of Canada's 10 provinces.

The talented musicians whose souls are invested in the Fab Four, Scott Balinson, Ben Jaeckle, Emma Stevens, Carter Chiasson, Terry Draper, John MacCallum, Jody Tennant and Camilla van der kooij were very helpful.

Susan Perez shared her late father Joe Black's artful photography in an act of kindness I won't soon forget, same goes for Jason Ransom and Mitch Francis; to super fans like Ocean Tennant, and to the family members of those departed who were part of The Beatles' Canadian history like Cheryl Finn, Michael McLuhan and especially Robert Decker—thank you, thank you, thank you.

There are too many sources to recognize but if not for Mark Lewisohn, Bob Spitz, Piers Hemmingsen, Paul Saltzman, *Montréal Gazette*, *The Guardian*, *Wikipedia*, *YouTube*, *Instagram*, *Facebook*, *Rolling Stone*, *Ottawa Beatles Site*, *The Beatles Anthology*, *The Beatles Bible*, *CBC*, *Maclean's*, *The Globe and Mail*, *The Beatles Story in Liverpool*, Bill Wyman, Buff Allen, Corinne George, Elliott Mintz,

Pete Best and the late Ritchie Yorke this project would never have blossomed.

Araba Dodd did a superb job designing the cover and Greg Oliver helped to steer the good ship *Us and Them* toward calmer seas, thank you to both. Big, out-stretched hugs go to my family, including wife Tamara, daughter Terra-Ann and mom Ida Maria. Thank you to nephew Richard Arnone and cousin Michael Santi for helping to create my circus poster, and cousin Eric Noce for designing the dancing Beatles for the chapter title pages.

ABOUT THE AUTHOR

John Robert Arnone is a lifelong Beatles fan. After graduating with a BA in Journalism from Ryerson University, Arnone worked as a reporter and editor in Saskatchewan and Ontario and was awarded the prestigious AJAC Journalist of the Year Award. In 1988, he launched a 30-year career as a communicator in the automotive and aviation industries in Canada and The United States, appearing in many high-profile media stories.

Well travelled, Arnone spends winters in southern Europe. He enjoys languages, guitar, paddle boarding and hockey. Home base is shared between Oakville and Victoria Harbour, Ontario.